The Eucharist

At the Center
of Pope John Paul II's
Pastoral Plan for
the New Millennium

The Eucharist

At the Center of Pope John Paul II's Pastoral Plan for the New Millennium

**Written and Compiled by
Fr. Bill McCarthy, MSA**

Queenship

PUBLISHING COMPANY
P.O. Box 220 • Goleta, CA 93116
(800) 647-9882 • (805) 692-0043 • Fax: (805) 967-5133
www.queenship.org

Library of Congress Number # 2003099657

Published by:
    Queenship Publishing
    P.O. Box 220
    Goleta, CA 93116
    (800) 647-9882 • (805) 692-0043 • Fax: (805) 967-5133
    www.queenship.org

Printed in the United States of America

ISBN: 1-57918-239-9

This book is dedicated to Ferdinand and Barbara Roccanti, lay evangelists and great apostles of the Eucharist

and

To Sister Bernadette Sheldon and the Community of *My Father's House,* whose devotion to Mass and Eucharistic Adoration is so exemplary.

Most special thanks to Mary Chalupsky who typed and edited every word.

Table of Contents

Introduction

The Holy Father's Pastoral Plan

Pope John Paul II, on the very day that he closed the Holy Year Door, January 6, 2001, issued a brand new document entitled *Tertio Millennio Ineunte* — "As We Enter the Third Millennium". In this magnificent apostolic letter, the Holy Father gave his pastoral plan for the whole Church in the new millennium and emphasized seven pastoral priorities for each and every Catholic. It was the first time in recorded history that any Holy Father has done such. He calls it his program.

Not a New Program

He states: "It is not, therefore, a matter of inventing a 'new program'. The program already exists. It is a plan found in the gospel and, in the living tradition, it is the same as ever. Ultimately, it has its center in Christ Himself, who is to be known, loved and imitated so that in Him we may live the life of the Trinity, and with Him transform history until its fulfillment in the heavenly Jerusalem. This is a program which does not change with shifts of time and cultures, even though it takes account of time and culture for the sake of true dialogue and effective communication. This program for all times is our program for the third Millennium. But it must be translated into *pastoral initiatives adapted to the circumstances of each community.*"

His seven pastoral priorities are:
1. Holiness
2. Prayer as a reciprocal conversation with God
3. The centrality of the Eucharist in Catholic belief and practice
4. Frequent confession
5. To live by grace and by the Spirit
6. Frequent meditation on the Scriptures and the New Catechism
7. The new evangelization

The Eighth

Then on the 16th of October, 2002, he issued another apostolic letter on the rosary. In this, he added an eighth pastoral priority, namely the frequent recitation of the rosary.

Eucharist Is Central

Subsequently, on Holy Thursday, April 7, 2003, he issued his 14th encyclical on the Eucharist summing up everything he encouraged in the Eucharist. In fact, he poignantly begins the very first sentence of *Ecclesia De Eucharistia* (The Church from the Eucharist) with the words, "The Church draws her very life from the Eucharist." He went on to say, "The Eucharist recapitulates the heart of the Church and is the deepest fulfillment of Our Lord's promise, 'Behold, I am with you always'." He further states, "The Holy Eucharist contains the Church's entire spiritual wealth. It is the summit of Catholic devotion."

The Incarnate Presence of Christ in the Church

He encourages all of us to gaze constantly toward the Lord present in the sacrament of the altar to discover the full manifestation of His boundless wisdom, love and power. He sums up the essence of His new vision in Section 6 where he states,

"I would like to rekindle this Eucharistic 'amazement' by the present Encyclical Letter, in continuity with the Jubilee heritage which I have left to the Church in the Apostolic Letter *Novo Millennio Ineunte* and its Marian crowning, *Rosarium Virginis Mariae*. To contemplate the face of Christ, and to contemplate it with Mary, is the "program" which I have set before the Church at the dawn of the third millennium, summoning her to put out into the deep on the sea of history with the enthusiasm of the new evangelization. To contemplate Christ involves being able to recognize Him where He manifests Himself, in His many forms of presence, but above all in the living sacrament of His Body and His Blood. The Church draws her life from Christ in the Eucharist; by Him she is fed and by Him she is enlightened. The Eucharist is both a mystery of faith and a 'mystery of light'. Whenever the Church celebrates the Eucharist, the faithful can in some way relive the experience of the two disciples on the road to Emmaus: 'Their eyes were opened and they recognized Him'." (*Lk* 24:31).

To See Thee More Clearly

The Holy Father has stated that he wants to open up all our eyes to that amazement at those things that eyes have not seen nor have ears heard nor has it entered into the minds of men the glories and happiness that God has revealed in the Eucharist and in the Church. And that which we behold with our eyes we will learn to love.

To Love Thee More Dearly

The Holy Father is asking the whole Church to renew the liturgy of the Mass to make it more present, operative, personal, and powerful in the lives of the faithful so that they will be filled with the very love of Christ for the Father and for each other. He reminds us that the Eucharistic Christ is a man for others. Therefore, we who receive Him become men and women for others...for God, the Church and especially the poor.

To Follow Thee More Nearly

Thus filled with the Eucharistic presence of God's wisdom, love and power, we become lights to a dark and broken world. We become another Jesus capable of continuing across our time and space the redemptive, healing, evangelizing work of Jesus. We become His hands, His eyes, His lips, His feet, His very body. We become apostles of truth, of love and of action. Accordingly, we become participants in the Pope's new evangelization to bring Christ to every person and every strata of human endeavor...into our courts, our offices, our working environments, our art, our sport, our homes, and our world. We become proclaimers in word and in deed that Christ is risen, lives and reigns through us.

The Church's Greatest Doctor

This present pope will go down in history as the Church's greatest doctor. From September 5, 1979 to November 28, 1984, he gave an extended catechesis on marriage, the family, celibacy, the theology of the body and human love in the divine plan. He also wrote an apostolic exhortation, *Familiaris Consortio* (November 22, 1981) on marriage and the family and wrote a Letter to Families on February 2, 1994.

God the Father

Pope John Paul wrote an encyclical on God the Father, *Dives in Misericordia*, (Nov. 30, 1980). From January 16, 1985 to June 25, 1986, he gave an extended catechesis on God the Father including four on the fullness of the Father's revelation, 13 on revelation and faith, 12 on the existence and nature of God, 11 on the Trinity, nine on God as Creator, and nine on the Father's divine providence. And then during the Year of the Father, 1999, he gave another 28 teachings in his catechesis on God the Father. The greatest official doctor of God the Father that the Catholic Church has thus far produced is John Paul II.

The Angels

He followed this catechesis with a short catechesis on angels from July 9, 1986 to August 20, 1986.

God the Son

John Paul's first encyclical, *Redemptor Hominis*, (Redeemer of Man, 1979) was on God the Son. From August 27, 1986 to April 19, 1989, he gave an extended catechesis on sin and our Redeemer, Christ. He added another 28 discourses during the Year of Christ, 1997, in preparation for the Jubilee Year. In every encyclical, allocution, letter, and homily, he centers us on Christ. The greatest *Christological* doctor that the Catholic Church has thus far produced, is, of course, John Paul II.

God the Holy Spirit

John Paul II wrote an entire encyclical on the Holy Spirit, *The Lord and Giver of Life* issued on Pentecost, May 18, 1986 – the Pope's birthday-followed shortly by seven reflections on the gifts of the Spirit in 1989. He also presented an extended 80-part catechesis on the Holy Spirit from April 26, 1989 to July 3, 1991. He provided continuous teachings during the Year of the Spirit, 1998, in preparation for the new millennium; and presented additional Pentecost discourses on the Holy Spirit that culminated on Pentecost 1998 with a magnificent talk to a half million charismatics in St. Peter's Square in which he stated:

"Whenever the Spirit intervenes, He leaves people astonished. He brings about events of amazing newness; He radically changes persons and history. This was the unforgettable experience of the Second Vatican Ecumenical Council during which, under the guidance of the same Spirit, the Church rediscovered the charismatic dimension as one of her constitutive elements: 'it is not only through the sacraments and the ministrations of the Church that the Holy Spirit makes holy the people, leads them and enriches them with His virtues. Allotting His gifts as He wills (cf. *1 Cor* 12:11), He also distributes special graces among the faithful of every rank ... He makes them fit and ready to undertake various tasks and offices for the renewal and building up of the Church'." (*Lumen Gentium*, n 12).

All of these discourses on the Holy Spirit I have included in my book, *The Holy Spirit in the Writings of Pope John Paul II*. He is the most Charismatic of popes, and, thus far, the greatest official doctor of *Pneumatology*.

The Church

The Holy Father also gave an extended catechesis on the Church. It contains the series of his catecheses on the article: "I believe in one, holy, catholic and apostolic Church." The series contains 137 catecheses given between July 10, 1991, and August

30, 1995. Included in these talks were 37 homilies on the nature and mystery of the Church in the plan of God, including one on April 8, 1992 on the Eucharist as the source of the Church's life. He gave eight talks on the theology of bishops, 11 on the theology of the papacy, 18 on the theology of priests, three on the theology of deacons, 27 on the theology of the lay apostolate, 19 on the theology of consecrated life, 16 on the missionary activity of the Church and ecumenism. He is the greatest modern doctor on *Ecclesiology*.

Mary

Pope John Paul II is the greatest modern Marian pope. His entire pontificate is devoted to Mary and his coat of arms is *Totus Tuus* (Totally Yours). He wrote an encyclical on March 25, 1987, the Feast of the Annunciation, entitled Mother of the Redeemer (*Redemptoris Mater*). He then gave a 70-part catechesis on Mary from September 6, 1995 to November 12, 1997 emphasizing that Mary, in addition to being our mother, mediatrix, and messenger is also a perfect realization of the Church's holiness and its model. He stressed her unique role in salvation history as mother of us all. He ends every apostolic letter, homily, constitution or encyclical by reflecting on Mary. All of these I have included in my book, *Mary in the Church Today*.

The Trinity

During the Jubilee Year 2000, he presented an entire series of talks on the Trinity. This occurred after completing three years of preparation by giving an entire series of talks in 1997 on the Son, in 1998 on the Spirit and in 1999 on the Father. He sees the Trinity as the familiar model for the Church. Since God is above all family, what God is above all doing on earth is creating family His way. Since God is holy and one, he is creating one, holy family. And since God loves everyone, he is creating one, holy, catholic, apostolic family for all nations. He stresses that all life, all holiness comes from the Father through the Son by the working of the Holy Spirit.

The Eucharist

He followed these talks with nine talks on the Eucharist that are reprinted in their entirety in this book, stressing the centrality of the Eucharist in salvation history and God's work in transforming us into other Christs so that we, with unveiled faces, can reflect like mirrors the brightness of the Son of God who is our glory. The more we receive Him, the more we will become like Him. The more we worship Him, the more He fills us with His Spirit. He stresses that the greatest way to worship the Father in spirit and in truth is in and through the Holy Sacrifice of the Mass.

Prayers of the Liturgy

He is now giving an extensive catechesis on the prayers, psalms and canticles of the Liturgy of the Office stressing the importance of prayer in his life and in our lives and in the life of the Church.

To Priests

In addition to his 18 talks in his catechesis to priests contained within the catechesis on the Church, he wrote a special letter to his priests on Holy Thursday and has issued an apostolic exhortation *Pastores Dabo Vobis* (I Will Give You Shepherds) on March 25, 1992.

Encyclicals

This encyclical on the Eucharist is his 14th. He wrote one on the *Father* (1980); one on the *Son* (1979); one on the *Spirit* (1986); three on social issues—on *Work* (1981), on *Solicitude for Social Concerns* (1987) and one on the *100th Anniversary* of the first social encyclical of Leo XIII (1991); one on *Mary* (1987); two on moral issues—the *Gospel of Life* (1995) and the *Splendor of the Truth* (1993); one on the *Mission of the Redeemer* (1990); one on *Ecumenism* (1995); one on *Faith and Reason* (1998); and one on *The Apostles of the Slavic People* (1985).

To Set Out Into the Deep

Now the Holy Father is issuing a new call to set out into the deep, which is his rallying cry taken from the words of Jesus to His own apostles: "to cast out into the deep" (*Duc in Altum*). Father Frank Anderson from Australia has written a song that captures the feeling of this great pope:

> "*So I leave my boats behind, leave them on familiar shores, set my heart upon the deep, follow you again, my Lord.*" This is the battle cry for the new millennium – to be more deeply involved with the Father's plan, to be more deeply immersed in Eucharistic awareness, to be more deeply committed to the missionary activity of the Church, to be more deeply imbued with the Spirit of Christ.

Towards that end, the Holy Father has given his seven powerful but practical priorities centering them all upon the Eucharist. He is asking for Eucharistic adoration in every church throughout the world for he has comprehended a tremendous spiritual principle, namely that the more you sow unto the heavens, the more God will sow unto the earth. That is, the more you worship and praise God, the more you will come into His glory, His divine presence. The more you enter His presence, the stronger will be the anointing of the Spirit upon you. And the stronger the anointing, the more wisdom, love and power you will have to transform the world in the image and likeness of Christ, until that eschatological day when every knee will bend before Jesus and proclaim to the Father that Jesus Christ is Lord.

Part I

Pope John Paul II and the Eucharist

The Greatest of All the Sacraments
The Summit of Christian Life
The Fulfillment of the Passover
The Incarnate Presence of Christ in His Church
The Source from which the Church Draws Her Very Life

Including

His Nine Discourses in the Jubilee Year on the Eucharist
The Encyclical, *Ecclesia De Eucharistia*
Apostolic Letter, *Dies Domini*
And His Other Eucharistic Writings

Preface

No one in the history of the church has written more consistently, eloquently or devotionally on the Eucharist than our present reigning Pope John Paul II. He has been called and truly is an apostle of the Eucharist. He has included the theme of Eucharistic devotion and adoration in every one of his major addresses and encyclicals. In fact, the signature that he has placed on all his writings are two themes: devotion to the Eucharist and devotion to Mary, our mother, who is the mother of the Eucharist. The following is compiled from the Pope's writings on the Eucharist.

I. The Eucharist, the Core of Christian Life

From the Eucharist, we all receive the *grace* and strength for everyday life, for living a truly Christian existence, in the *joy* of knowing that God loves us, that Christ has died for us and that the Holy Spirit lives in us.

Full Participation in the Eucharist

Our full participation in the Eucharist is the true source of that Christian spirit we should like to see in our own lives and in every aspect of society. Wherever we work – in politics, in the economy, in culture, in the social or scientific fields – it does not matter what our job may be – the Eucharist is a challenge to our daily lives.

There must always be consistency between what we believe and what we do. We cannot live on the glories of our Christian past. Our union with Christ in the Eucharist must be manifest in the truth of our lives today: in our actions, in our sense of values, in our life-style and in our relationships with others.

Summoned To Live as True Followers of Christ

For each of us, the Eucharist is a summons to make an ever greater effort to live as true followers of Christ: truthful in what we say, generous in what we do, caring for and respectful of the dignity and rights of all, whatever their class or their income may be. We are true followers of Christ if we are ready to make personal sacrifices, are loyal and just, generous, prudent, compassionate and self-disciplined; aiming toward the good of our families, of our young people, of our country, of Europe, and of the world. The truth of our union with Christ in the Eucharist is attested by whether or not we truly love our neighbors, whoever they may be, and by the way we treat other people, especially our own families: husbands and wives, children and parents, brothers and sisters. It is attested by the effort we really make to be reconciled with our enemies, to forgive those who wrong us or offend us.

Given the agnostic society in which we live – a sadly hedonistic and permissive one – it is essential to deepen our teaching on the august mystery of the Eucharist, in such a way as to acquire and maintain absolute certainty over the nature and purpose of the Sacrament which is rightly called the core of the Christian message and of the life of the Church. The Eucharist is the mystery of mysteries; so its acceptance means totally accepting the nexus "Christ-and-the-Church", from the preambles of the Faith to the doctrine of the Redemption, to the concept of sacrifice and of consecrated priesthood, to the dogma of "transubstantiation", to the importance of legislation in liturgical matters.

Restore the Eucharist and Priesthood

Today, this certainty is necessary before all else, in order to restore the Eucharist and priesthood to their absolutely central position, to have a proper sense of the importance of Holy Mass and Holy Communion, to return to eucharistic pedagogy, this being the source of priestly and religious vocations and inner strength for practicing the Christian virtues.

Today is a time for reflection, for meditation and for prayer for Christians to recover their sense of worship, their fervor. Only from the Eucharist profoundly known, loved and lived can we hope for that unity in truth and charity which is willed by Christ and urged on all by the Second Vatican Council.

Sacrament of His Body and Blood

The Eucharist is the sacrament of His Body and Blood, which He Himself has offered once and for all (cf. *Heb* 9:26-28), to set us free from sin and death, and which He has entrusted to His Church for her to make the same offering under the species of bread and wine and so to feed His faithful people forever – that is, us who stand about His altar. The Eucharist is thus the sacrifice par excellence, that of Christ on the Cross, by means of which we receive Christ Himself, Christ entire, God and man.

The Son's sacrifice is unique and unrepeatable. It was made one single time in human history. And this unique and unrepeatable sacrifice 'endures'. The happening on Golgotha belongs to the past. The reality of the Trinity constitutes a divine "today" forever. Thus, it is that all humanity shares in this "today" of the Son's sacrifice. The Eucharist is the sacrament of this unfathomable "today". The Eucharist is the sacrament – the greatest one the Church has – by which the divine "today" of the Redemption of the world meets our human "today" in a manner ever human.

Sunday Eucharist

We must once again emphasize how important it is, in obedience to the precept of the Church, to take part in the celebration of the Sunday Eucharist. For everyone, this is the highest act of worship in the exercise of the universal priesthood, just as the sacramental offering of the Mass is the highest act of worship, for priests, in the exercise of the priestly ministry. Participation in the eucharistic banquet is a vital condition for everyone for union with Christ, as He Himself has said: "In all truth I tell you, if you do not eat the Flesh of the Son of Man and drink His Blood, you will have not life in you" (*Jn* 6:53).

Participation of the Laity

The Catechism of the Catholic Church reminds all the faithful about the significance of participating in the Sunday Eucharist (cf. *nn. 2181-2182*). Here I wish to conclude with those famous words in the First Letter of Peter, which portray the laity participating in the Eucharist-Church mystery: "You too must become living stones making a spiritual house as a holy priesthood, to offer the spiritual sacrifices made acceptable to God through Jesus Christ" (*1 Pt* 2:5).

For every faithful Catholic, participation at Holy mass on Sunday is at once a duty and a privilege: a sweet obligation to respond to God's love for us, so that we can then bear witness to this love in our daily lives. The fulfilling of the dominical precept ought, for every Christian family, to be a fundamental source of joy and unity. Every Sunday, all and everyone of you have an appointment with God's love. Don't fail to keep it!

II. The Two Tables of the Lord
And the Common Possession of the Church

The Table of the Word of God

We are well aware that from the earliest times, the celebration of the Eucharist has been linked not only with prayer but also with the reading of Sacred Scripture and with singing by the whole assembly. As a result, it has long been possible to apply to the Mass the comparison, made by the Fathers, with the two tables, at which the Church prepares for her children the word of God and the Eucharist, that is, the bread of the Lord. We must therefore go back to the first part of the sacred mystery, the part that at present is most often called the *Liturgy of the Word*, and devote some attention to it.

The reading of the passages of Sacred Scripture chosen for each day has been subjected by the Council to new criteria and requirements. As a result of these norms of the Council a new collection of readings has been made, in which there has been applied, to some extent, the principle of continuity of texts and the principle of making all the sacred books accessible. The insertion of the Psalms with responses into the liturgy makes the participants familiar with the great wealth of Old Testament prayer and poetry. The fact that these texts are read and sung in the vernacular enables everyone to participate with fuller understanding.

Eucharistic Mystery

Nevertheless, there are also those people who, having been educated on the basis of the old liturgy in Latin, experience the lack of this "one language," which in all the world was an expression of the unity of the Church and through its dignified character elicited a profound sense of the Eucharistic Mystery. It is therefore necessary to show not only understanding but also full respect towards these sentiments and desires. As far as possible, these sentiments and desires are to be accommodated, as is moreover provided for in the new dispositions. The Roman Church has special obligations towards Latin, the splendid language of ancient

Rome, and she must manifest them whenever the occasion presents itself.

Witnesses and Sharers in the Celebration

The possibilities that the post-conciliar renewal has introduced in this respect are indeed often utilized so as to make us witnesses of and sharers in the authentic celebration of the Word of God. There is also an increase in the number of people taking an active part in this celebration. Groups of readers and cantors, and still more often choirs of men or women, are being set up and are devoting themselves with great enthusiasm to this aspect. The Word of God, Sacred Scripture, is beginning to take on new life in many Christian communities. The faithful gathered for the liturgy prepare with song for listening to the Gospel, which is proclaimed with the devotion and love due to it.

All this is noted with great esteem and gratitude, but it must not be forgotten that complete renewal makes yet other demands. These demands consist in a new sense of responsibility towards the Word of God transmitted through the liturgy in various languages, something that is certainly in keeping with the universality of the gospel and its purposes. The same sense of responsibility also involves the performance of the corresponding liturgical actions (reading or singing), which must accord with the principles of art. To preserve these actions from all artificiality, they should express such capacity, simplicity and dignity as to highlight the special character of the sacred text, even by the very manner of reading or singing.

Word of God in the Liturgy

Accordingly, these demands, which spring from a new responsibility for the Word of God in the liturgy, go yet deeper and *concern the inner attitude* with which the ministers of the Word perform their function in the liturgical assembly. This responsibility also concerns the choice of texts. The choice has already been made by the competent ecclesiastical authority, which has also made provision for the cases in which readings more suited to a particular situation may be chosen. Furthermore, it must always be remembered that only the Word of God can be used for Mass readings. The reading of Scripture cannot be replaced by the reading of other texts, however much they may be endowed with undoubted religious and moral values. On the other hand, such texts can be used very profitably in the homily.

Indeed, the homily is supremely suitable for the use of such texts, provided that their content corresponds to the required conditions, since it is one of the tasks that belong to the nature of the homily to show the points of convergence between revealed divine wisdom and noble human thought seeking the truth by various paths.

The Table of the Bread of the Lord

The other table of the Eucharistic Mystery, that of the Bread of the Lord, also requires reflection from the viewpoint of the present-day liturgical renewal. This is a question of the greatest importance, since it concerns a special act of living faith and, indeed, as has been attested since the earliest centuries, is a manifestation of worship of Christ, who in Eucharistic communion entrusts Himself to each one of us, to our hearts, our consciences, our lips and our mouths, in the form of food. Therefore, there is special need, with regard to this question, for the watchfulness spoken of by the Gospel, on the part of the pastors who have charge of eucharistic worship and on the part of the People of God, whose "sense of the faith" must be very alert and acute particularly in this area.

Care By Episcopate for Entrusted Churches

I therefore wish to entrust this question to the heart of each one of you, venerable and dear brothers in the episcopate. You must, above all, make it part of your care for all the churches entrusted to you. I ask this of you in the name of the unity that we have received from the Apostles as our heritage, collegial unity. This unity came to birth, in a sense, at the table of the Bread of the Lord on Holy Thursday. With the help of your brothers in the priesthood, do all you can to safeguard the sacred dignity of the eucharistic ministry and that deep spirit of Eucharistic Communion which belongs in a special way to the Church as the People of God, and which is also a particular heritage transmitted to us from the

Apostles, by various liturgical traditions, and by unnumbered generations of the faithful, who were often heroic witnesses to Christ, educated in "the school of the cross" (Redemption) and of the Eucharist.

Continuous Invitation

It must be remembered that the Eucharist as the table of the Bread of the Lord is a continuous invitation. This is shown in the liturgy when the celebrant says, "This is the Lamb of God. Happy are those who are called to His supper." It is also shown by the familiar Gospel parable of the guests invited to the marriage banquet. Let us remember that in this parable there are many who excuse themselves from accepting the invitation for various reasons.

Sin vs. Conscience

Moreover, our Catholic communities certainly do not lack people who could participate in Eucharistic Communion and do not, even though they have no serious sin on their conscience as an obstacle. To tell the truth, this attitude, which in some people is linked with an exaggerated severity, has changed in the present century, though it is still to be found here and there. In fact, what one finds most often is not so much a feeling of unworthiness as a certain lack of interior willingness, if one may use this expression, a lack of Eucharistic "hunger" and "thirst," which is also a sign of lack of adequate sensitivity towards the great sacrament of love and a lack of understanding of its nature.

Role of the Sacrament of Penance

However, we also find in recent years another phenomenon. Sometimes, indeed quite frequently, everybody participating in the eucharistic assembly goes to Communion; and on some such occasions, as experienced pastors confirm, there has not been due care to approach the sacrament of Penance so as to purify one's conscience. This can of course mean that those approaching the Lord's table find nothing on their conscience, according to the objective law of God, to keep them from this sublime and joyful act of being sacramentally united with Christ.   But there can also be, at least at times, another idea behind this: the idea of the Mass as only a banquet in which one shares by receiving the Body of Christ in order to manifest, above all else, fraternal communion. It is not hard to add to these reasons a certain human respect and mere "conformity."

Christian Conscience

This phenomenon demands from us watchful attention and a theological and pastoral analysis guided by a sense of great responsibility.   We cannot allow the life of our communion to lose the good quality of sensitiveness of Christian conscience, guided solely by respect for Christ, who, when He is received in the Eucharist, should find in the heart of each of us a worthy abode.   This question is closely linked not only with the practice of the sacrament of Penance but also with a correct sense of responsibility for the whole deposit of moral teaching and for the precise distinction between good and evil.   This distinction then becomes for each person sharing in the Eucharist the basis for a correct judgment of self to be made in the depths of the personal conscience.   St. Paul's words, "Let a man examine himself," are well known. This judgment is an indispensable condition for a personal decision whether to approach Eucharistic Communion or to abstain.

Eucharistic Table

Celebration of the Eucharist places before us many other requirements regarding the ministry of the eucharistic table.   Some of these requirements concern only priests and deacons, others concern all who participate in the Eucharistic Liturgy.   Priests and deacons must remember that the service of the table of the Bread of the Lord imposes on them special obligations which refer in the first place to Christ Himself present in the Eucharist and secondly to all who actually participate in the Eucharist or who might do so. With regard to the first, perhaps it will not be superfluous to recall the words of the Pontificale which, on the day of ordination, the bishop addresses to the new priest as he hands to him on the paten and in the chalice the bread and wine offered by the faithful and prepared by the deacon: *"Accipe oblationem plebis sanctae Deo offerendam. Agnosce quod agis, imitare quod tractabis, et vitam tuam mysterio dominicae crucis conforma."* ("Accept the oblation of your holy people offered to God. Mark well what you do. Imitate what you touch. Conform your life to the mystery of the Lord's cross.") This last admonition made to him by the bishop should remain as one of the most precious norms of his eucharistic ministry.

Examine Handling of Body And Blood

It is from this admonition that the priest's attitude in handling the bread and wine which have become the Body and Blood of the Redeemer should draw its inspiration. Thus, it is necessary for all of us who are ministers of the Eucharist to examine carefully our actions at the altar, in particular the way in which we handle that food and drink which are the Body and Blood of the Lord our God in our hands: the way in which we distribute Holy Communion; the way in which we perform the purification.

All these actions have a meaning of their own. Naturally, scrupulosity must be avoided, but God preserve us from behaving in ways that lack respect, from undue hurry or from an impatience that causes scandal. Over and above our commitment to the evangelical mission, our greatest commitment consists in exercising this mysterious power over the Body of the Redeemer, and all that is within us should be decisively ordered to this. We should always remember that, to this ministerial power we have been sacramentally consecrated, having been chosen from among men "for the good of men." We especially, the priests of the Latin Church, whose ordination rite added in the course of the centuries the custom of anointing the priest's hands, should think about this.

Receiving in the Hand or on the Tongue

In some countries the practice of receiving Communion in the hand has been introduced. This practice has been requested by individual episcopal conferences and has received approval from the Apostolic See. However, cases of a deplorable lack of respect towards the eucharistic species have been reported, cases which are imputable not only to the individuals guilty of such behavior but also to the pastors of the church who have not been vigilant enough regarding the attitude of the faithful towards the Eucharist. It also happens, on occasion, that the free choice of those who prefer to continue the practice of receiving the Eucharist on the tongue is not taken into account in those places where the distribution of Communion in the hand has been authorized. It is therefore difficult in the context of this present letter not to mention the sad phenomena previously referred to. This is in no way meant to refer to those who, receiving the Lord Jesus in the hand, do so with profound reverence and devotion, in those countries where this practice has been authorized.

The Hands of the Priest

But one must not forget the primary office of priests, who have been consecrated by their ordination to represent Christ, the Priest: for this reason their hands, like their words and their will, have become the direct instruments of Christ. Through this fact, that is, as ministers of the Holy Eucharist, they have a primary responsibility for the sacred species, because it is a total responsibility: they offer the bread and wine, they consecrate it, and then distribute the sacred species to the participants in the assembly who wish to receive them. Deacons can only bring to the altar the offerings of the faithful and, once they have been consecrated by the priest, distribute them. How eloquent therefore, even if not of ancient custom, is the rite of the anointing of the hands in our Latin ordination, as though precisely for these hands a special grace and power of the Holy Spirit is necessary!

Privilege of the Ordained

To touch the sacred species and to distribute them with their own hands is a privilege of the ordained, one which indicates an active participation in the ministry of the Eucharist. It is obvious that the Church can grant this faculty to those who are neither priests nor deacons, as is the case with acolytes in the exercise of their ministry, especially if they are destined for future ordination, or with other lay people who are chosen for this to meet a just need, but always after an adequate preparation.

The Eucharist

The Greatest of All the Sacraments
The Summit of the Christian Life
The Fulfillment of the Passover
The Incarnate Presence of Christ in His Church

The Greatest Of All The Sacraments

The greatest of all the sacraments is the Eucharist. It is the summit of the Christian life. The greatest way to worship the Father in spirit and truth is to celebrate Mass and to receive His precious Body, Blood, Soul and Divinity. At the Mass, we offer the highest praise to the Father. At this sacred liturgy, we join all the angels and saints in their continuous act of worship to the Father, with the Son, in the power of the Spirit.

The New Passover

The Mass is the Passover fulfilled and renewed. The Paschal lamb has been replaced by Jesus, who is the Lamb of God; for by His shed Blood, we pass over from death to life. The bitter herbs have been replaced by the bitter agony of Christ's death on the cross. At the Last Supper, Jesus said, "I have desired to eat this Passover with you." Then He took the bread, gave thanks, blessed it and said, "This is My Body, do this in remembrance of Me." Likewise, after He supped, He took the chalice of wine, blessed it and said, "Take this and drink all of you, this is the chalice of My Blood, the new and everlasting covenant. This shall be shed for you and for all so that sins might be forgiven. Do this in memory of Me." In and through the Mass, Jesus has offered to us an everlasting sharing in the Paschal mystery; that is, His death and resurrection. We share His death to selfishness and sin and His resurrection to new life and hope.

Food For The Journey

The Eucharist is the food or sustenance of Christian life. Every time we receive the Holy Eucharist, we come into the deepest communion with Christ. This is why the Holy Eucharist is called Holy Communion. With Jesus eucharistically present in the depths of our hearts, we listen as He speaks to us through the thoughts that He puts into our minds and the desires that He inflames in our hearts. We speak to Him – worshipping Him, praising and thanking Him for all that He is and has done and is doing for us. Like Mary, our mother, we too can say, "He lives in me." *We have become a tabernacle – a dwelling place for our Savior.* This indwelling presence of our Eucharistic Lord transforms us. Our minds are enlightened with the insights that He gives to us. Our hearts are aflame with the desires He now pours into them. Our spirits are enlivened with a new strength and power to do the works of God and to resist the temptations of the flesh towards laziness, worldliness, lust, control, and selfishness.

A Great Mystery

Nonetheless, the Eucharist remains a great mystery. Its full significance and presence are just too much for our feeble human minds to grasp. The mysterious union of Father and Son in the Holy Spirit is re-presented in us. We have become what we have received – bone of His bone, flesh of His flesh, humility of His humility, holiness of His holiness. We can truthfully say with St. Paul, "I live now, not I but Christ lives within me."

A Foretaste Of Heaven

One of the things that St. Paul refers to when he says, "Eye has not seen nor ear heard, nor has it entered into the mind of man the glories that God has prepared for those who love Him, these things have been revealed to us" (*1 Cor* 2:9), is the Eucharist. *The Eucharist is a foretaste of heaven and a pledge of everlasting life.* It is a foretaste of heaven because each time we receive the Eucharist, we are transcending the human to participate in the divine. We pierce the heavenlies and enter into the very manifest presence of God – Father, Son and Holy Spirit. We are surrounded by the celestial choir of angels and saints singing, *Holy Holy Holy Lord God of hosts.* Into their eternal celestial liturgy of worship and praise we have now entered. The Eucharist is also a pledge of eternal glory because Christ has promised this when He said, "He who eats My Flesh and drinks My Blood I will raise him up on the last day" (*Jn* 6:54).

A Reenactment Of The Mysteries Of Christ's Life
The Eucharist is a reenactment of Christ's life, death and resurrection. The incarnation is present because Jesus is enfleshed now in the Eucharist. His hidden life at Nazareth is present because He now lies hidden under the appearance of bread and wine. His public ministry is present because from the altar now He proclaims His gospel and ratifies the covenant in the liturgy of the word. His presentation is present in the offertory, His full gift of self to the Father. His death is present in the separation of the bread (His Body) and the wine (His Blood). The Last Supper is present because Jesus, once again, offers Himself to the Father, consecrates the bread and wine, and gives His Body and Blood in communion to us, His apostles.

The Eucharist, Food from Two Tables
At the Mass, we are fed food from two tables. At the table of the pulpit during the liturgy of the word, we are fed with the gospels and epistles of Paul, John, Jude, Peter, and James. This wisdom is food and sustenance for our minds. Herein, we put on the mind of Christ. We partake of His wisdom. We are inspired to think loving, holy, pure, kind, generous, zealous and forgiving thoughts. We are inspired with the very teachings of Jesus and the apostles. The beatitudes become our mental attitudes. Our minds are enlightened by spiritual insights, understandings and promises.

At the liturgy of the Eucharist, we receive from the altar of sacrifice the very Body and Blood of Christ. *We are transformed* from glory into glory into Him whom we have received.

A Pivotal Chapter – John 6
The magnificent 6th Chapter of John's gospel is the key text for understanding the Eucharist. It begins by saying that the Jewish feast of the Passover is near (*v* 4). Most likely, this Passover took place one year before the Last Supper. In any event, it is the

Eucharist that was promised. The first thing that Jesus does is miraculously feed the 5,000, thereby showing His miraculous power over bread that can be eaten as sustenance. The next day, the crowds followed Him to Capernaum. There, in the synagogue, He promises them living bread come down from heaven, not like the manna their forefathers ate in the desert. "Whoever eats this bread will live forever." "Lord give us always this bread," is their response.

My Own Flesh For The Life Of The World

Then Jesus startles them by saying, "The bread that I will give is My own Flesh for the life of the world." Their response is one of unbelief. "How can this man give us His own flesh to eat?" Jesus' answer is most powerful. He says,

> "With all of the earnestness I possess I tell you this, unless you eat of the Flesh of the Son of Man and drink His Blood you have no life in you. Whoever eats My Flesh and drinks My Blood has eternal life, and I will raise him up on the last day. For My Flesh is real food and My Blood is real drink. Whoever eats My Flesh and drinks My Blood abides in Me and I in him. Just as the living Father sent Me and I have life because of the Father, so also the one who feeds on Me will have life because of Me. This is the bread come down from heaven. Unlike your ancestors who ate and still died, whoever eats this bread will live forever" (*Jn* 6:53-60).

Plain And Clear Words

These words are so clear, so simple, so direct, and so plain. Jesus, in His Eucharistic promise, is declaring that He will make a way for us to receive His Body and Blood so we may live out of Him in the same way He lives out of the Father. He is the new Passover lamb. And just as the unblemished male Paschal lamb had to be eaten in its entirety, so also the new Passover lamb has to be eaten and digested. We become what we have received.

The Disciples Mixed Reaction

These words that so centralize the Christian life are met with mixed response right from the beginning. Many of His disciples said, "This is a hard saying. Who can accept it?" They returned to their former way of life and no longer accompanied Him" (*v* 66). Turning to the twelve, Jesus asked, "Do you also want to leave?" Notice here that Jesus does not take back any of the realism or sting of His words. He does not try to explain them away as merely symbolic. It is so obvious that He is so willing, if necessary, to let them all walk away.

Thank God For Peter

But Peter, His first pope, says with great faith, "Lord, to whom shall we go. You have the words of eternal life." Yes Peter, that is exactly what Jesus has – words of eternal life. The Eucharist is about Christ's eternal life within us.

The Church's Understanding

Jesus left behind Him the Church that would be one, true, universal and apostolic as the pillar and the standard of truth; and as the official interpreter of the scriptures. The Church has always understood these words literally. St. Paul, for example, some 30 years later, said,

> "For I receive from the Lord what I also passed on to you; the Lord Jesus, on the night He was betrayed, took bread, and when He had given thanks, He broke it and said, 'This is My Body, which is for you; do this in remembrance of Me'. In the same way, after supper, He took the cup saying, 'This cup is the new covenant in My Blood; do this whenever you drink it in remembrance of Me'. Whenever you eat this Bread and drink this Blood, you proclaim the Lord's death until He comes. Therefore, whoever eats the Bread or drinks the cup of the Lord in an unworthy manner will be guilty of sinning against the Body and Blood of the Lord. A man ought to examine himself before he eats of the Bread and drinks of the cup, for anyone who eats or

drinks without recognizing the Body and Blood of the Lord eats and drinks judgment on himself. That is why many of you are weak and sick and a number of you have died" (1 *Cor* 11:23-30). It's so obvious that Paul believed in the presence of Jesus without equivocation.

The Fathers Of the Church

The references of St. Ignatius of Antioch (d 107) to the Eucharist, in the seven authentic letters he wrote while on his way to Rome to suffer martyrdom, are sufficient to indicate that the mystery of the Lord's Body and Blood was a most significant aspect in his thought and in his own spiritual life. In his letter to the Christians of Tralles, for example, he apparently compares the virtues of faith and love to the Eucharistic Mystery when he writes: "Therefore, arming yourselves with gentleness, renew yourselves in faith, which is the Flesh of the Lord, and in charity, which is the Blood of Jesus Christ. Hold nothing against your neighbor."

His letter to the Romans is almost mystical in its Eucharistic allusions. He compares his own coming tortures to the process that the wheat must undergo. In facing death, Ignatius states that his only remaining desire is to encounter Him who has made Himself the food and drink of Christians:

> "I am God's grain, and I am being ground by the teeth of wild beasts in order that I may be found (to be) pure bread for Christ. My (earthly) love has been crucified, and there is in me no fire of material love, but rather a living water, speaking in me and saying within me, 'Come to the Father.' I take no pleasure in corruptible food or in the delights of this life. I want the Bread of God, which is the Flesh of Jesus Christ, who is of the seed of David; and as drink I want His Blood, which is incorruptible."

St. Thomas Aquinas

From Thomas Aquinas in his Selected Writings is found this reverence for the Eucharist. "Let no one, therefore, approach this wondrous Table without reverent devotion and fervent love, without true penitence or without remembering His redemption. For it is the pure Lamb that is eaten in the unleavened Bread . . . Approach the Lord's Supper, the table of wholeness and holiness, child of faith, in such a way that at the end you may enter into the wedding feast of the Lamb . . . There we shall be filled with the abundance of God's house; then we shall behold the King of Glory and the Lord of Hosts in His beauty, and shall taste the Bread of our Father's kingdom; our host shall be our Lord Jesus Christ, whose power and reign are without end. Amen."

Decree On The Ministry And Life Of Priests, The Documents Of Vatican II

"The other sacraments, as well as every ministry of the Church and every work of the apostolate, are linked with the Holy Eucharist and are directed toward it. For the most blessed Eucharist contains the Church's entire spiritual wealth, that is, Christ Himself, our Passover and living bread. Through His very Flesh, made vital and vitalizing by the Holy Spirit, He offers life to men. They are, thereby, invited and led to offer themselves, their labors, and all created things together with Him. Hence the Eucharist shows itself to be the source and the apex of the whole work of preaching the gospel. Those under instruction are introduced by stages to a sharing in the Eucharist. The faithful, already marked with the sacred seal of baptism and confirmation, are through the reception of the Eucharist fully joined to the Body of Christ" (No. 5).

The Catechism Of The Catholic Church

"The mode of Christ's presence under the Eucharistic species is unique. It raises the Eucharist above all the sacraments as 'the perfection of the spiritual life and the end to which all the sacraments tend' (St. Thomas Aquinas). In the most Blessed Sacrament of the Eucharist, "the Body and Blood, together with the Soul and Divinity of our Lord Jesus Christ and, *therefore, the whole Christ is truly, really and substantially* contained (Council of Trent)." We call this presence "real" not in an exclusive way, as if His other modes of being present were not real, but because it is a presence par excellence, since it is substantial, in the sense that Christ, whole and entire God and Man, becomes present (No. 1374).

The Council of Trent - Transubstantiation

The Council of Trent summarizes the Catholic faith by declaring: "Because Christ our Redeemer said that it was truly His Body that He was offering under the species of bread, it has always been the conviction of the Church, and this Holy Council declares it again that, by the consecration of the bread and wine, there takes place a change of the whole substance of the bread into the substance of the Body of Christ our Lord and of the whole substance of the wine into the substance of His Blood. The Catholic Church fittingly and properly called this change 'transubstantiation'." (ref. No. 1376).

Pope John Paul II

Pope John Paul II has spoken repeatedly on the Eucharist and its impact on our lives. He said, "The mysterious reality of the Eucharist introduces us into the plan of God, Creator and Redeemer. God wanted His only Son to be incarnate and ever-present among us as our traveling companion on the arduous journey toward eternity."

Message to the Eucharistic Congress at Lourdes, July 21, 1981: "The sacrifice of the cross is so decisive for the future of man that Christ did not carry it out and did not return to the Father until He had left us the means to take part in it as if we had been present. Christ's offering on the Cross – which is the real Bread of Life broken – is the first value that must be communicated and shared. The Mass and the Cross are but one and the same sacrifice. Nevertheless, the Eucharistic breaking of bread has an essential function, that of putting at our disposal the original offering of the Cross. It makes it actual today for our generation. By making the Body and Blood of Christ really present under the species of bread and wine, it makes—simultaneously—the Sacrifice of the Cross actual and accessible to our generation, this Sacrifice which remains in its uniqueness, the turning point of the history of salvation, the essential link between time and eternity."

Fulfillment Of The Law And Prophets

Jesus comes to bring the old covenant to fulfillment (cf. *Mt* 5:17). "I have not come to destroy the law but to bring it into fulfillment." In the Old Testament, salvation "came from the Jews." In the New Testament, it comes from the Cross of Christ reenacted in the Mass. The Mass perpetuates the sacrifice of Calvary. There is no greater participation in the fruits of Calvary than the Mass. The Mass is, in fact, a reenactment of the passion and death of Christ now in an unbloodied manner. Christ, in His passion, death, and resurrection, is fully present.

The Real Presence of Jesus Christ in the Eucharist, Cardinal Gaetano De Lai. Two sacrifices of the Old Law were, before all others, representative of the Sacrifice of the Divine Redeemer. The first is that of Abraham, who, in obedience to God's command, offers his son Isaac as a holocaust; but God accepts his goodwill and spares the life of Isaac. The second very celebrated example, also in the time of Abraham, and more nearly figurative of the Eucharist, is the sacrifice of Melchizedek, king of Salem (Jerusalem).

Melchizedek Offering Bread And Wine

Abraham was returning victorious, and bearing the spoils of his victory over the five kings of Upper Asia. He meets the king of Salem, who, in thanksgiving for the victory, offers bread and wine as a holocaust, exclaiming: "Blessed be Abraham ... and blessed be the Most High God, by Whose protection thy enemies are in thy hands" (*Gen 14:19-20*).

The prophet David, St. Paul the apostle, the synagogue, and all Christian tradition agree that the Messiah, the Divine Redeemer, Christ Jesus, was prefigured in Melchizedek, "a priest forever according to the order of Melchizedek." There is then no doubt (the Fathers of the Church and Christian sentiment are in agreement) that the Holy Christian Sacrifice of our altars was foretold and represented 2000 years beforehand in the sacrifice of bread and wine offered to God by Melchizedek. And, therefore, as the clean oblation foretold by Malachy foreshadows the Eucharist, so does the sacrifice of bread and wine that was offered by Melchizedek, foreshadow the same sacrament.

The Way Of Divine Love

Words of Our Lord to Sr. Josefa Menendez, *The Way of Divine Love.*

"The Blessed Sacrament is the invention of Love. It is life and fortitude for souls, a remedy for every fault, and a viaticum for the last passage from time to eternity. In it sinners recover life for their souls; tepid souls, true warmth; fervent souls, tranquillity and the satisfaction of every longing . . . saintly souls, wings to fly towards perfection . . . pure souls, sweet honey and rarest sustenance. Consecrated souls find in it a dwelling, their love and their life. In it they will seek and find the perfect exemplar of those sacred and hallowed bonds that unite them inseparably to their heavenly Bridegroom.

"Indeed, O consecrated souls, you will find a perfect symbol of your vow of Poverty in the small, round, light and smooth host; for so must the soul that professes poverty be: no angles, that is to say, no petty natural affections, either for things used nor for her employments, or for family or country . . . but she (Lady Poverty) must ever be ready to leave, or give up, or change . . . Her heart must be free, with no attachments whatever . . .

"This by no means signifies insensibility of heart; no, for the more it loves, the more it will preserve the integrity of the vow of Poverty. What is essential for religious souls is first that they should possess nothing without the permission and approbation of Superiors, and secondly, that they should possess and love nothing that they are not ready to give up at the first sign."

The Story of Therese Neumann

The secret of Therese Neumann's abundant life, despite her complete abstinence from all earthly food, is revealed in her statement that she is sustained by a heavenly food, the Body of her

Eucharistic Lord.

On Palm Sunday evening in 1930, the third year of her absolute fast, Father Hartl asked her if she was hungry. "You know very well that I do not eat," she answered. The curate of the village church then asked, "Do you wish to be greater than the Savior? He ate when He was on earth." Therese smiled and said, "The Savior can do all things. Or do you not think He is all-powerful?" Turning to the other priest present, Father Helmut Fahsel of Berlin, she declared with great earnestness, "The Savior sustains me. He said, 'My body is food indeed,' so why shouldn't it be actually true for once, if He wills it?"

The Eucharist And Healing, John Bertolucci

Did you know that every Sunday, at all the Masses in all the Catholic churches in the world, millions of people join in prayers for healing? The fact that most people are surprised by that statement merely shows our lack of attention to the words we pray. For every Catholic immediately recognizes the prayer I am talking about, which the priest and congregation recite together just before Communion: "Lord, I am not worthy to receive You. But only say the word, and *I shall be healed.*"

As even that one prayer indicates, the Eucharist is truly a sacrament of healing. The Eucharist celebrates our covenant with God—the covenant that frees us from sin and from all the effects of sin, including affliction and death. Through the Eucharist, we take part in Jesus' sacrifice of His very life, the sacrifice that has become life and healing for us.

The Eucharist brings us into the most intimate possible contact with Jesus Himself. His Blood flows through our veins; His Body becomes one with ours. His mind touches our mind; His very being touches our being. When we enter this moment with real awareness of what is happening and with genuine faith in the Lord's presence, how can it help but be a moment of healing? "With faith in your love and mercy I eat your Body and drink your Blood. Let it not bring me condemnation, but *health in mind and body.*"

A Powerful Witness

Miracles Do Happen, **Sister Briege McKenna, OSC**, tells this story in her book, *Miracles Do Happen.* "A young priest phoned me, very anxious and afraid. He had just found out he had cancer of the vocal chords and he had to have his voice box removed in three weeks. He was telling me he was desperate. He had been ordained only about six years. As I prayed with him, I felt the Lord wanted me to tell him about the Eucharist. I said, 'Father, I can pray with you now on the phone, and I will. But this morning, didn't you meet Jesus? Don't you meet Him every day?'

"What I didn't know was that this priest didn't celebrate Mass daily. I told him, 'Father, every single day when you go to Mass, when you take that sacred Host, when you eat it, you meet Jesus. The woman only touched the hem of Jesus' cloak. But you touch Jesus and receive Him into your body. You have Him as food. Do you realize that Jesus is actually going down through your throat? There is no better one to go to than to Jesus. You ask Jesus to heal you.'

"I heard him crying over the phone. He kept saying to me, 'Oh, Sister, thank you. Thank you.' Three weeks later, he went in for his surgery. He phoned me later to tell me that he didn't have the surgery. The doctors discovered the cancer was gone and he had brand new vocal chords."

The Fruits Of Holy Communion

According to the New Catechism, the Eucharist augments our union with Christ (1391), separates us from sins (1393), wipes away venial sins (1394), preserves us from future mortal sins (1395), increases the unity of the mystical body (1396), commits us to the poor (1397), and leads to the unity of Christians (1398). That is why the Catechism clearly teaches, "It is in keeping with the very meaning of the Eucharist that the faithful, if they have the required dispositions, *receive communion each time* they participate in the Mass (1388)."

Eucharistic Overtones of the Easter Sunday Appearances of Jesus

According to St. Luke, Jesus made five post-resurrection appearances to His disciples on Easter Sunday. He now had to prepare His disciples for the time when He would ascend, as He said "to My Father and your Father." But He would still send the Holy Spirit to be with us, even to the end of time.

The first of these post-resurrection appearances is related in Luke 24. It was preceded by the angel's words to Mary Magdalene, Joanna, Mary the mother of James, and the others with them who told the apostles what the angel had said: "Why do you look for the living among the dead. He is not here. He has risen. Remember how He told you while He was still with you in Galilee: the Son of Man must be delivered into the hands of sinful men, be crucified, and on the third day be raised again." Then they remembered His words. When they came back from the tomb, they told all these things to the eleven and to all the others. But they did not believe the women because the words seemed to them like nonsense. Peter and John, however, got up and ran to the tomb.

1. Jesus Reveals Himself to Mary Magdalene

We now pick up the story in *John 20:20*,10ff. When Peter and John went back to their homes (v 10), Mary Magdalene stood outside the tomb weeping and as she wept she bent over to look into the tomb and saw two angels in white seated where Jesus' Body had been. The angel asked her, "Woman, why are you weeping?" She answered, "They have taken my Lord away and I do not know where they have put Him." At this, she turned around and saw Jesus standing there, but she did not realize that it was Jesus. "Woman," He said, "Why are you weeping? Who is it that you are looking for?" Thinking He was the gardener, she said, "Sir, if you have carried Him away, tell me where you have put Him and I will get Him." Jesus said to her, "Mary." She turned toward Him and cried out in Aramaic, "Teacher." Jesus said, "Do not cling to Me for I have not yet returned to the Father. Go instead to My brothers and tell them I'm returning to My Father and your Father, to My God and your God." Mary Magdalene went to the disciples with the news, "I have seen the Lord;" and she told them that He had said these things to her.

Spiritual Implications

First - Mary stayed and wept. Whenever anyone of us lingers long with the Lord, we usually open up ourselves to His ongoing revelations. Especially after communion, if we stay and linger with Him allowing Him to fill us with His presence and to speak to us through our minds and hearts, we will receive more personal ongoing revelation. That is why the Church recommends quiet time alone with Jesus, especially in Eucharistic Adoration. We have to be willing to let everything and everyone go so that we can linger alone with Jesus.

Second - Mary Wept.

The longing in her heart had reached a fever-pitch point. It so deeply touched her heart that she wept. And, as we know, whenever anyone reaches that point, whether that person is David weeping for his son or the widow who has just lost her son, or the family of Jairus who just lost their daughter, Jesus comes running. Just like a father, he cannot stand any of His children to weep. And so if we want Jesus to come running, try tears.

Third - Jesus Comes Unrecognized

So in the Eucharist, we do not physically see the Lord but only the appearance of bread and wine. And in most all of these post-resurrection appearances, Jesus comes unrecognized for He is preparing us for His new presence not only in the Eucharist but in His Mystical Body. Without faith, we would not recognize Him.

Fourth - Jesus Calls Her By Her Name

One of the ways that God deals with us is individually and personally. He calls us each by name. He gives us a personal, here-and-now, existential, concrete revelation of Himself. Nobody else has the same faith walk as you do. Nobody else has the same personality, problems, worries, fears, or relationship with Jesus that you do. To the Church in general, Jesus speaks *logos,* a general word for everyone. But to you and me, He speaks *rheyma*, a personal word. He calls us by name. Every time we receive the Eucharist, He comes to us personally.

Fifth - He Gives Us Detailed Instructions

"Do not cling to Me. Go to the brothers." In much the same way, whenever we linger with the Lord, especially in Eucharistic Adoration, He gives us detailed instructions on what His will is for our life. We all know that we are called, above all, to do the will of God. But we cannot do God's will unless He reveals it to us. And He cannot reveal it to us unless we linger with Him and say, "Speak Lord, your servant is listening." There is a balance here between the contemplative and the active life. At times, Jesus says, "Come apart and cling only to Me; talk to Me heart to heart. Allow Me to speak to you, heal you, love you, and fill you with My Spirit." But there is also a time when He tells us to go to the brothers, His Mystical Body, to reach out to them, to evangelize them, to forgive, help and support them.

2. Jesus Appears to His Disciples on the Road to Emmaus, Luke 24

"Now that same day two of them were going to a village called Emmaus, about seven miles from Jerusalem. They were talking with each other about everything that had happened. As they talked and discussed these things with each other, Jesus Himself came up and walked along with them; but they were kept from recognizing Him.

He asked them, "What are you discussing together as

you walk along?"

They stood still, their faces downcast. One of them, named Cleopas, asked him, "Are you the only resident in Jerusalem and do not know the things that have happened there these past three days?"

"What things?" he asked.

"About Jesus of Nazareth," they replied. "He was a prophet, powerful in word and deed before God and all the people. The chief priest and our rulers handed Him over to be sentenced to death, and they crucified Him; but we had hoped that He was the one who was going to re- deem Israel. And what is more, it is the third day since all this took place. In addition, some of our women amazed us. They went to the tomb early this morning but didn't find His Body. They came and told us that they had seen a vision of angels, who said He was alive. Then some of our companions went to the tomb and found it just as the women had said, but they did not see Him."

He said to them, "How foolish you are, and how slow of heart to believe all that the prophets have spoken! Did not the Christ have to suffer these things and then enter His glory?" And beginning with Moses and all the Proph- ets, He explained to them what was said in all the Scrip- tures concerning Himself.

As they approached the village to which they were go- ing, Jesus acted as if He were going farther. But they urged Him strongly, "Stay with us, for it is nearly evening; the day is almost over." So He went in to stay with them.

When He was at the table with them, He took bread, gave thanks, broke it and began to give it to them. Then their eyes were opened and they recognized Him, and He disappeared from their sight. They asked each other, "Were not our hearts burning within us while He talked with us on the road and opened the Scriptures to us?"

They got up and returned at once to Jerusalem. There they found the Eleven and those with them, assembled to- gether and saying, "It is true! The Lord has risen and has

appeared to Simon." Then the two told what had happened on the way, and how Jesus was recognized by them
when He broke the bread.

Spiritual Implications
One - letting oneself be helped.

This very moving story presents us with another appearance of
Jesus on the very afternoon of His resurrection. Two disciples are
making their way to the village of Emmaus, having lost all hope
because Christ, in whom they had placed the whole meaning of
their lives, was dead. Our Lord catches up with them, as if He, too,
was just another traveler on the road, and walks with them without
being recognized. They engage in broken conversation, as happens when people talk as they are going along. They speak about
their preoccupation: what has happened in Jerusalem on the Friday
evening – the death of Jesus of Nazareth. The Crucifixion of Our
Lord had been a very severe test for the hopes of all those who
considered themselves to be His disciples and who to some extent
or another had placed their trust in Him. Things had all taken place
very quickly and they still hadn't got over all they had seen with
their very eyes.

These men who are returning to their home village after having
celebrated the Paschal feast in Jerusalem show by the tone of their
conversation their great sadness and how discouraged and discon-
certed they are: *We had hoped that He was the one to redeem Israel.*
But now they speak of Jesus as a reality belonging to the past: *Concerning Jesus of Nazareth, who was a prophet mighty indeed …
Notice the contrast. They say 'who was!' … And He is there by
their side. He is walking with them, in their company, trying to
uncover the reason, the most intimate roots of their sadness!*

'Who was!', they say. We too, if only we would examine ourselves sincerely, with an attentive examination of our sadness, our
discouragement, our being a little tired of life, would find a clear
link with this Gospel passage. We would discover how we spontaneously remark, 'Jesus was', 'Jesus said', because we forget that,
just as on the road to Emmaus, Jesus is alive and by our side at this
very moment. This is a discovery which enlivens our faith and

revives our hope, a finding that points to Jesus as a joy that is ever present: Jesus is, Jesus prefers, Jesus says, Jesus commands now at this very moment. *Jesus lives!*

Two - Hope

These men did know about Christ's promise of rising on the third day. They had heard that morning the message of the women who had seen the empty tomb and the angels. Things had been sufficiently clear for them to have nourished their faith and their hope; but instead, they speak of Christ as belonging to the past, as a lost opportunity. They are a living picture of discouragement. Their minds are in darkness and their hearts are numbed.

Christ Himself – whom they did not at first recognize but whose company and conversation they accept – interprets those events for them in the light of the Scriptures. Patiently He restores in them their faith and their hope. And the two of them recover also their joy and their love: *Did not our hearts burn within us*, they say later, *while He talked to us on the road, while He opened to us the Scriptures?*

It is possible that we too may sometimes meet with discouragement and lack of hope because of defects that we cannot manage to root out, or of difficulties in the apostolate or in our work that seem to be insurmountable.... On these occasions, provided we allow ourselves to be helped, Jesus will not allow us to be parted from Him. Perhaps it will be in spiritual direction, once we open our souls in all sincerity, that we will come to see Our Lord again. And with Him, there will always come joy and the desire to begin again as soon as possible: *And they rose that same hour and returned to Jerusalem.* But it is essential that we allow ourselves to be helped, and that we be ready to be docile to the advice that we receive.

Three - The Same Day

Jesus always comes to us in the now. And it is always one of His Easter Sunday appearances, for He is now the resurrected Christ, gloriously reigning, never to suffer or die again. Our encounter with Him in the Eucharist is always fresh, always new. He always gives us our daily bread. He is not the God who says, "I was." Nor the God who says, "I will be." But rather the God who says, "I am." "I am the bread of life for you today. Come receive Me now this day."

Four - Two of Them

This is not surprising since He sends out his disciples two by two (cf. *Lk 10:1*). Apparently, two of them are still together and we know that wherever there are two of them in His name, Jesus comes and walks with them in their midst. This is happening even now to you in the Church. He comes to us personally, but only so that we can walk side by side with others in our mission of bringing His spirit to a dark and broken world.

Five - Jesus Walks With Us

Jesus accompanies us on our faith journey. He not only walks with us, He walks within us enlightening our minds with ongoing insights and inflaming our hearts with ever new desires to do His will.

Six - We Do Not Recognize Him With
The Eyes Of The Flesh

Just like the two disciples, ours is a faith walk. He is truly with us, but we see Him under the appearance of bread and wine and recognize Him only by faith.

Seven - Jesus Constantly Asks Us Questions

Jesus always asks the disciples questions, "What about you?" "Who do you say that I am?" "Do you want to see?" "Do you want to be healed?" "Do you love Me?" These penetrating, personal questions call for a response. He knows the answers, but He wants to engage our minds and hearts. He doesn't want to be a God way up there, but a God whom we recognize as being with us. He is not simply a God way back there who used to speak and used to heal, but a God in the now who wants to speak to us and heal us.

Eight - Jesus Changes Our Vision And Hopes Into His
Like these two disciples, we often get discouraged and lose
hope, precisely because our plans are not coming to fruition. Just
like them, He brings us to the end of ourselves so that we will be
open to His will.

Nine - He Opens The Scriptures For Us
As we listen to the word proclaimed at Mass and as we meditate upon it, our hearts begin to burn inside us as He opens our
minds to the real meaning of that personal *rheyma* that is meant
just for us in the moment.

Ten - We Recognize Him In The Breaking Of The Bread
Jesus has left us the Eucharist. But unlike the disciples, when
we recognize Him, He does not depart but rather stays with us.

3. Jesus Appears To His Priests

*On the evening of that first day of the week, when the
disciples were together, with the doors locked for fear of
the Jews, Jesus came and stood among them and said,
"Peace be with you! After He said this, He showed them
His hands and side. The disciples were overjoyed when
they saw the Lord.*
*Again Jesus said, "Peace be with you! As the Father
has sent Me, I am sending you." And with that He breathed
on them and said, "Receive the Holy Spirit. If you forgive
anyone his sins, they are forgiven; if you do not forgive
them, they are not forgiven" (Jn 20:19-20).*

Spiritual Implications
One - Jesus gives to His apostles the power to forgive sins.
St. Paul tells us in *1 Cor.* 27-30, "Whoever eats the bread or drinks
the cup of the Lord in an unworthy manner will be guilty of sin-
ning against the Body and Blood of the Lord. A person ought to
examine his conscience before he eats of the Bread and drinks of
the cup. For anyone who eats and drinks without recognizing the

Body of the Lord, eats and drinks judgment on himself. That is why many among you are weak and sick and a number of you have fallen asleep."

We see here the intimate connection between the Sacraments of Confession and the Eucharist that the Church has always proclaimed. It is not surprising, therefore, that after appearing to His disciples on the road to Emmaus and teaching them to eat from the two tables of the Mass—the liturgy of the Word and the liturgy of the Eucharist—He would now appear to His apostles and give to them who already have been given on Holy Thursday the power to celebrate the Eucharist, a new power to forgive sins so that men and women could receive the Eucharist worthily.

Two - First Pubic Act of Jesus With His Priests

This is the first public appearance of Jesus with His priests after His resurrection. On the cross on Good Friday, He won the right to forgive all men their sins by His shed Blood. Now, He allows that Blood to be poured over the mercy seat of the confessional with the instrumentality of the absolution of His priests. This is the way it was in the tabernacle of old when the high priest on the feast of Yom Kippur took the blood of the lamb into the holy of holies and poured it over the holy seat that was never occupied by anyone until Jesus now occupies it.

Three - Three Miracles of Grace

Every time a person goes to confession, he experiences three miracles of grace. First, every bit of sin and guilt is washed clean through the Blood of the Lamb administered by the priest. Second, all bitterness, hatred and unforgiveness are released. Third, we are given the awesome power to totally forgive ourselves, to stand in His righteousness and get on with our lives.

Four - No Other Way

The implication of this public act of Jesus is astounding, for there is no other way that a persons' sins can be forgiven except by the Blood of the Lamb administered by His priests. Jesus says, "As the father has sent Me, I now send you." Therefore, there is no psychological way that a person's sins can be forgiven. In fact, no psychologist has ever discovered a way to relieve people's souls of guilt and sin. What psychologists *do* tell us is that most people repress guilt, deny guilt, rationalize guilt or project guilt – all with harmful effects. But they don't get rid of it until they confess it and receive forgiveness at the hands of a priest.

Epilogue

Turning back to Luke's account of the Easter Sunday appearances, it says, "While they were still talking about this, Jesus Himself stood among them and said 'peace be to you'." And then He said, "This is what I told you while I was still among you. Everything must be fulfilled that was written about Me in the law of Moses, the prophets and the psalms. Then He opened their minds so that they could understand the Scriptures. You are witnesses of these things. I'm going to send you what My Father has promised (the Holy Spirit). But stay in the city until you have been clothed from on high."

These beautiful Easter Sunday appearances of Christ are powerful. From Mary Magdalene we learn that we must linger with Him so that He can come and call us by name. From the two disciples, we learn that as we attend Mass our hearts will burn as He opens the Scriptures to us and we come to recognize Him in the breaking of the bread. And from the apostles we learn that our hearts are to be cleansed in preparation by frequent reception of the Sacrament of Reconciliation.

ECCLESIA DE EUCHARISTIA

Holy See's Summary of "Ecclesia de Eucharistia" Encyclical of Pope John Paul II
April 17, 2003

Following is a summary of John Paul II's encyclical published April 17, 2003 issued by the Vatican press office:

The fourteenth Encyclical Letter of Pope John Paul II is intended to offer a deeper reflection on the mystery of the Eucharist in its relationship with the Church. The document is relatively brief, but significant for its theological, disciplinary and pastoral aspects. It will be signed on Holy Thursday, during the Mass of the Lord's Supper, within the liturgical setting of the beginning of the Paschal Triduum.

The Eucharistic Sacrifice, "the source and summit of the Christian life", contains the Church's entire spiritual wealth: Jesus Christ, who offers himself to the Father for the redemption of the world. In celebrating this "mystery of faith", the Church makes the Paschal Triduum become "contemporaneous" with men and women in every age.

The first chapter, "The Mystery of Faith", explains the sacrificial nature of the Eucharist which, through the ministry of the priest, makes sacramentally present at each Mass the Body "given up" and the Blood "poured out" by Christ for the world's salvation. The celebration of the Eucharist is not a repetition of Christ's Passover, or its multiplication in time and in space; it is the one sacrifice of the Cross, which is re-presented until the end of time. It is, in the words of Saint Ignatius of Antioch, "a medicine of immortality, an antidote to death". As a pledge of the future Kingdom, the Eucharist also reminds believers of their responsibility for the present earth, in which the weak, the most powerless and the poorest await help from those who, by their solidarity, can give them reason for hope.

"The Eucharist Builds the Church" is the title of the second chapter. When the faithful approach the sacred banquet, not only do they receive Christ, but they in turn are received by Him. The consecrated Bread and Wine are the force which generates the Church's unity. The Church is united to her Lord who, veiled by the Eucharistic species, dwells within her and builds her up. She worships Him not only at Holy Mass itself, but at all other times, cherishing Him as her most precious "treasure".

The third chapter is a reflection on "The Apostolicity of the Eucharist and of the Church". Just as the full reality of Church does not exist without apostolic succession, so there is no true Eucharist without the Bishop. The priest who celebrates the Eucharist acts in the person of Christ the Head; he does not possess the Eucharist as its master, but as its servant for the benefit of the community of the saved. It follows that the Christian community does not "possess" the Eucharist, but receives it as a gift.

These reflections are developed in the fourth chapter, "The Eucharist and Ecclesial Communion". The Church, as the minister of Christ's Body and Blood for the salvation of the world, abides by all that Christ Himself established. Faithful to the teaching of the Apostles, united in the discipline of the sacraments, she must also manifest in a visible manner her invisible unity. The Eucharist cannot be "used" as a means of communion; rather it presupposes communion as already existing and strengthens it. In this context emphasis needs to be given to the commitment to ecumenism which must mark all the Lord's followers: the Eucharist creates communion and builds communion, when it is celebrated truthfully. It cannot be subject to the whim of individual or of particular communities.

"The Dignity of the Eucharistic Celebration" is the subject of the fifth chapter. The celebration of the "Mass" is marked by outward signs aimed at emphasizing the joy which assembles the community around the incomparable gift of the Eucharist. Architecture, sculpture, painting, music, literature and, more generally, every form of art demonstrate how the Church, down the centuries, has feared no extravagance in her witness to the love which unites her to her divine Spouse. A recovery of the sense of beauty is also needed in today's celebrations.

The sixth chapter, "At the School of Mary, 'Woman of the Eucharist'", is a timely and original reflection on the surprising analogy between the Mother of God, who by bearing the Body of Jesus in her womb became the first "tabernacle", and the Church who in her heart preserves and offers to the world Christ's Body and Blood. The Eucharist is given to believers so that their life may become a continuous Magnificat in honor of the Most Holy Trinity.

The Conclusion is demanding: those who wish to pursue the path of holiness need no new "programs". The program already exists: it is Christ Himself who calls out to be known, loved, imitated and proclaimed. The implementation of this process passes through the Eucharist. This is seen from the witness of the Saints, who at every moment of their lives slaked their thirst at the inexhaustible source of this mystery and drew from it the spiritual power needed to live fully their baptismal calling.

The Eucharist

Encyclical Letter
Ecclesia De Eucharista
of
His Holiness Pope John Paul ll
to
the Bishops Priests and Deacons
Men and Women in the consecrated life and
all the lay faithful on the Eucharist in its
relationship to the Church

INTRODUCTION

The Very Life of the Church

1. The Church draws her life from the Eucharist. This truth does not simply express a daily experience of faith, but recapitulates the *heart of the mystery of the Church*. In a variety of ways she joyfully experiences the constant fulfillment of the promise: "Lo, I am with you always, to the close of the age" (Mt 28:20), but in the Holy Eucharist, through the changing of bread and wine into the Body and Blood of the Lord, she rejoices in this presence with unique intensity. Ever since Pentecost, when the Church, the People of the New Covenant, began her pilgrim journey towards her heavenly homeland, the Divine Sacrament has continued to mark the passing of her days, filling them with confident hope.

The Second Vatican Council rightly proclaimed that the Eucharistic sacrifice is "the source and summit of the Christian life".[1] "For the most holy Eucharist contains the Church's entire spiritual wealth: Christ Himself, our passover and living bread. Through His own Flesh, now made living and life-giving by the Holy Spirit, He offers life to men".[2] Consequently the gaze of the Church is constantly turned to her Lord, present in the Sacrament of the Altar, in which she discovers the full manifestation of His boundless love.

The Upper Room

2. During the Great Jubilee of the Year 2000 I had an opportunity to celebrate the Eucharist in the Cenacle of Jerusalem where, according to tradition, it was first celebrated by Jesus Himself. *The Upper Room was where this most holy Sacrament was instituted.* It is there that Christ took bread, broke it and gave it to His disciples, saying: "Take this, all of you, and eat it: this is My Body which will be given up for you" (cf. *Mk* 26:26; *Lk* 22:19; *1 Cor* 11:24). Then he took the cup of wine and said to them: "Take this, all of you and drink from it: this is the cup of My Blood, the Blood of the new and everlasting covenant. It will be shed for you and for all, so that sins may be forgiven" (cf. *Mt* 14:24; *Lk* 22:20; *1 Cor* 11:25). I am grateful to the Lord Jesus for allowing me to repeat in that same place, in obedience to his command: "Do this in memory of Me" (*Lk* 22:19), the words which He spoke two thousand years ago.

Did the Apostles who took part in the Last Supper understand the meaning of the words spoken by Christ? Perhaps not. Those words would only be fully clear at the end of the *Triduum sacrum*, the time from Thursday evening to Sunday morning. Those days embrace the *mysterium paschale*; they also embrace the *mysterium eucharisticum*.

The Breaking of the Bread

3. The Church was born of the paschal mystery. For this very reason the Eucharist, which is, in an outstanding way, the sacrament of the paschal mystery, *stands at the center of the Church's life*. This is already clear from the earliest images of the Church found in the Acts of the Apostles: "They devoted themselves to the Apostles' teaching and fellowship, to the breaking of bread and the prayers" (2:42). The "breaking of the bread" refers to the Eucharist. Two thousand years later, we continue to relive that primordial image of the Church. At every celebration of the Eucharist, we are spiritually brought back to the paschal Triduum: to the events of the evening of Holy Thursday, to the Last Supper and to what followed it. The institution of the Eucharist sacramentally anticipated the events which were about to take place, beginning with the agony in Gethsemane.

Once again we see Jesus as He leaves the Upper Room, descends with His disciples to the Kidron valley and goes to the Garden of Olives. Even today that Garden shelters some very ancient olive trees. Perhaps they witnessed what happened beneath their shade that evening, when Christ in prayer was filled with anguish "and His sweat became like drops of Blood falling down upon the ground" (cf. *Lk* 22:44). The Blood which shortly before He had given to the Church as the drink of salvation in the sacrament of the Eucharist, *began to be shed*; its outpouring would then be completed on Golgotha to become the means of our redemption: "Christ... as high priest of the good things to come..., entered once for all into the Holy Place, taking not the blood of goats and calves but His own Blood, thus securing an eternal redemption" (*Heb* 9:11-12).

The Hour

4.   *The hour of our redemption*. Although deeply troubled, Jesus does not flee before His "hour". "And what shall I say? 'Father, save Me from this hour?' No, for this purpose I have come to this hour" (*Jn* 12:27). He wanted His disciples to keep Him company, yet He had to experience loneliness and abandonment: "So, could you not watch with Me one hour? Watch and pray that you may not enter into temptation" (*Mt* 26:40-41). Only John would remain at the foot of the Cross, at the side of Mary and the faithful women.

The agony in Gethsemane was the introduction to the agony of the Cross on Good Friday. *The holy hour*, the hour of the redemption of the world. Whenever the Eucharist is celebrated at the tomb of Jesus in Jerusalem, there is an almost tangible return to His "hour", the hour of His Cross and glorification. Every priest who celebrates Holy Mass, together with the Christian community which takes part in it, is led back in spirit to that place and that hour.

"He was crucified, He suffered death and was buried; He descended to the dead; on the third day He rose again". The words of the profession of faith are echoed by the words of contemplation and proclamation: *"This is the wood of the Cross, on which hung the Savior of the world. Come, let us worship"*. This is the

invitation which the Church extends to all in the afternoon hours of Good Friday. She then takes up her song during the Easter season in order to proclaim: *"The Lord is risen from the tomb; for our sake He hung on the Cross, Alleluia"*.

A Church Is Born

5. *"Mysterium fidei!* - The Mystery of Faith!*"*. When the priest recites or chants these words, all present acclaim: "We announce Your death, O Lord, and we proclaim Your resurrection, until You come in glory".

In these or similar words the Church, while pointing to Christ in the mystery of His passion, *also reveals her own mystery: Ecclesia de Eucharistia.* By the gift of the Holy Spirit at Pentecost the Church was born and set out upon the pathways of the world, yet a decisive moment in her taking shape was certainly the institution of the Eucharist in the Upper Room. Her foundation and wellspring is the whole *Triduum paschale*, but this is as it were gathered up, foreshadowed and "concentrated' for ever in the gift of the Eucharist. In this gift Jesus Christ entrusted to His Church the perennial making present of the paschal mystery. With it He brought about a mysterious "oneness in time" between that Triduum and the passage of the centuries.

The thought of this leads us to profound amazement and gratitude. In the paschal event and the Eucharist which makes it present throughout the centuries, there is a truly enormous "capacity" which embraces all of history as the recipient of the grace of the redemption. This amazement should always fill the Church assembled for the celebration of the Eucharist. But in a special way it should fill the minister of the Eucharist. For it is he who, by the authority given him in the sacrament of priestly ordination, effects the consecration. It is he who says with the power coming to him from Christ in the Upper Room: "This is My Body which will be given up for you. This is the cup of My Blood, poured out for you...". The priest says these words, or rather *he puts his voice at the disposal of the One who spoke these words in the Upper Room* and who desires that they should be repeated in every generation by all those who in the Church ministerially share in His priesthood.

To Rekindle Eucharistic Amazement

6.   I would like to rekindle this Eucharistic "amazement" by the present Encyclical Letter, in continuity with the Jubilee heritage which I have left to the Church in the Apostolic Letter *Novo Millennio Ineunte* and its Marian crowning, *Rosarium Virginis Mariae*. To contemplate the face of Christ, and to contemplate it with Mary, is the "program" which I have set before the Church at the dawn of the third millennium, summoning her to put out into the deep on the sea of history with the enthusiasm of the new evangelization. To contemplate Christ involves being able to recognize Him wherever He manifests Himself, in His many forms of presence, but above all in the living sacrament of His Body and His Blood. *The Church draws her life from Christ in the Eucharist*; by him she is fed and by Him she is enlightened. The Eucharist is both a mystery of faith and a "mystery of light".[3] Whenever the Church celebrates the Eucharist, the faithful can in some way relive the experience of the two disciples on the road to Emmaus: "their eyes were opened and they recognized Him" (*Lk* 24:31).

Holy Thursday Letters to Priests

7.   From the time I began my ministry as the Successor of Peter, I have always marked Holy Thursday, the day of the Eucharist and of the priesthood, by sending a letter to all the priests of the world. This year, the twenty-fifth of my Pontificate, I wish to involve the whole Church more fully in this Eucharistic reflection, also as a way of thanking the Lord for the gift of the Eucharist and the priesthood: "Gift and Mystery".[4] By proclaiming the Year of the Rosary, I wish to put this, my twenty-fifth anniversary, *under the aegis of the contemplation of Christ at the school of Mary.* Consequently, I cannot let this Holy Thursday 2003 pass without halting before the "Eucharistic face" of Christ and pointing out with new force to the Church the centrality of the Eucharist.

From it the Church draws her life. From this "living bread" she draws her nourishment. How could I not feel the need to urge everyone to experience it ever anew?

Recalling the Masses I Have Celebrated

8.   When I think of the Eucharist, and look at my life as a priest, as a Bishop and as the Successor of Peter, I naturally recall the many times and places in which I was able to celebrate it. I remember the parish church of Niegowiæ, where I had my first pastoral assignment, the collegiate church of Saint Florian in Krakow, Wawel Cathedral, Saint Peter's Basilica and so many basilicas and churches in Rome and throughout the world. I have been able to celebrate Holy Mass in chapels built along mountain paths, on lakeshores and seacoasts; I have celebrated it on altars built in stadiums and in city squares... This varied scenario of celebrations of the Eucharist has given me a powerful experience of its universal and, so to speak, cosmic character. Yes, cosmic! Because even when it is celebrated on the humble altar of a country church, the Eucharist is always in some way celebrated *on the altar of the world*. It unites heaven and earth. It embraces and permeates all creation. The Son of God became man in order to restore all creation, in one supreme act of praise, to the One who made it from nothing. He, the Eternal High Priest who by the Blood of His Cross entered the eternal sanctuary, thus gives back to the Creator and Father all creation redeemed. He does so through the priestly ministry of the Church, to the glory of the Most Holy Trinity. Truly this is the *mysterium fidei* which is accomplished in the Eucharist: the world which came forth from the hands of God the Creator now returns to Him redeemed by Christ.

Spirit for Food

9.   The Eucharist, as Christ's saving presence in the community of the faithful and its spiritual food, is the most precious possession which the Church can have in her journey through history. This explains the *lively concern* which she has always shown for the Eucharistic mystery, a concern which finds authoritative expression in the work of the Councils and the Popes. How can we not admire the doctrinal expositions of the Decrees on the Most Holy Eucharist and on the Holy Sacrifice of the Mass promulgated by the Council of Trent? For centuries those Decrees guided theology and catechesis, and they are still a dogmatic reference-point

for the continual renewal and growth of God's People in faith and in love for the Eucharist. In times closer to our own, three Encyclical Letters should be mentioned: the Encyclical *Mirae Caritatis* of Leo XIII (28 May 1902),[5] the Encyclical *Mediator Dei* of Pius XII (20 November 1947)[6] and the Encyclical *Mysterium Fidei* of Paul VI (3 September 1965).[7]

The Second Vatican Council, while not issuing a specific document on the Eucharistic mystery, considered its various aspects throughout its documents, especially the Dogmatic Constitution on the Church *Lumen Gentium* and the Constitution on the Sacred Liturgy *Sacrosanctum Concilium.*

I myself, in the first years of my apostolic ministry in the Chair of Peter, wrote the Apostolic Letter *Dominicae Cenae* (24 February 1980),[8] in which I discussed some aspects of the Eucharistic mystery and its importance for the life of those who are its ministers. Today I take up anew the thread of that argument, with even greater emotion and gratitude in my heart, echoing as it were the word of the Psalmist: "What shall I render to the Lord for all His bounty to me? I will lift up the cup of salvation and call on the name of the Lord" (*Ps* 116:12-13*).*

Source of Growth for Community

10. The Magisterium's commitment to proclaiming the Eucharistic mystery has been matched by interior growth within the Christian community. Certainly *the liturgical reform inaugurated by the Council* has greatly contributed to a more conscious, active and fruitful participation in the Holy Sacrifice of the Altar on the part of the faithful. In many places, *adoration of the Blessed Sacrament* is also an important daily practice and becomes an inexhaustible source of holiness. The devout participation of the faithful in the Eucharistic procession on the Solemnity of the Body and Blood of Christ is a grace from the Lord which yearly brings joy to those who take part in it. Other positive signs of Eucharistic faith and love might also be mentioned.

Unfortunately, alongside these lights, *there are also shadows.* In some places the practice of Eucharistic adoration has been almost completely abandoned. In various parts of the Church abuses have occurred, leading to confusion with regard to sound faith and Catholic doctrine concerning this wonderful sacrament. At times one encounters an extremely reductive understanding of the Eucharistic mystery. Stripped of its sacrificial meaning, it is celebrated as if it were simply a fraternal banquet. Furthermore, the necessity of the ministerial priesthood, grounded in apostolic succession, is at times obscured and the sacramental nature of the Eucharist is reduced to its mere effectiveness as a form of proclamation. This has led here and there to ecumenical initiatives which, albeit well-intentioned, indulge in Eucharistic practices contrary to the discipline by which the Church expresses her faith. How can we not express profound grief at all this? The Eucharist is too great a gift to tolerate ambiguity and depreciation.

It is my hope that the present Encyclical Letter will effectively help to banish the dark clouds of unacceptable doctrine and practice, so that the Eucharist will continue to shine forth in all its radiant mystery.

CHAPTER ONE

The Mystery of Faith

The Central Event of Salvation

11. "The Lord Jesus on the night He was betrayed" (*1 Cor* 11:23) instituted the Eucharistic Sacrifice of His Body and His Blood. The words of the Apostle Paul bring us back to the dramatic setting in which the Eucharist was born. The Eucharist is indelibly marked by the event of the Lord's passion and death, of which it is not only a reminder but the sacramental re-presentation. It is the sacrifice of the Cross perpetuated down the ages.[9] This truth is well expressed by the words with which the assembly in the Latin rite responds to the priest's proclamation of the "Mystery of Faith": "We announce Your death, O Lord".

The Church has received the Eucharist from Christ her Lord not as one gift – however precious – among so many others, but as *the gift par excellence*, for it is the gift of Himself, of His person in His sacred humanity, as well as the gift of His saving work. Nor does it remain confined to the past, since "all that Christ is – all that He did and suffered for all men – participates in the divine eternity, and so transends all times".[10]

When the Church celebrates the Eucharist, the memorial of her Lord's death and resurrection, this central event of salvation becomes really present and "the work of our redemption is carried out".[11] This sacrifice is so decisive for the salvation of the human race that Jesus Christ offered it and returned to the Father only *after He had left us a means of sharing in it* as if we had been present there. Each member of the faithful can thus take part in it and inexhaustibly gain its fruits. This is the faith from which generations of Christians down the ages have lived. The Church's Magisterium has constantly reaffirmed this faith with joyful gratitude for its inestimable gift.[12] I wish once more to recall this truth and to join you, my dear brothers and sisters, in adoration before this mystery: a great mystery, a mystery of mercy. What more could Jesus have done for us? Truly, in the Eucharist, He shows us a love which goes "to the end" (cf. Jn 13:1), a love which knows no measure.

A Sacrifice of the New Covenant

12.   This aspect of the universal charity of the Eucharistic Sacrifice is based on the words of the Savior Himself. In instituting it, He did not merely say: "This is My Body", "this is My Blood", but went on to add: "which is given for you", "which is poured out for you" (*Lk* 22:19-20). Jesus did not simply state that what He was giving them to eat and drink was His Body and His Blood; He also expressed *its sacrificial meaning* and made sacramentally present His sacrifice which would soon be offered on the Cross for the salvation of all. "The Mass is at the same time, and inseparably, the sacrificial memorial in which the sacrifice of the Cross is perpetuated and the sacred banquet of communion with the Lord's Body and Blood".[13]

The Church constantly draws her life from the redeeming sacrifice; she approaches it not only through faith-filled remembrance, but also through a real contact, since *this sacrifice is made present ever anew*, sacramentally perpetuated, in every community which offers it at the hands of the consecrated minister. The Eucharist thus applies to men and women today the reconciliation won once for all by Christ for mankind in every age. "The sacrifice of Christ and the sacrifice of the Eucharist are *one single sacrifice*".[14] Saint John Chrysostom put it well: "We always offer the same Lamb, not one today and another tomorrow, but always the same one. For this reason the sacrifice is always only one.... Even now we offer that victim who was once offered and who will never be consumed".[15]

The Mass makes present the sacrifice of the Cross; it does not add to that sacrifice nor does it multiply it.[16] What is repeated is its *memorial* celebration, its "commemorative representation" (*memorialis demonstratio*),[17] which makes Christ's one, definitive redemptive sacrifice always present in time. The sacrificial nature of the Eucharistic mystery cannot therefore be understood as something separate, independent of the Cross or only indirectly referring to the sacrifice of Calvary.

A Sacrifice Related to Calvary

13.   By virtue of its close relationship to the sacrifice of Golgotha, the Eucharist is *a sacrifice in the strict sense*, and not only in a general way, as if it were simply a matter of Christ's offering Himself to the faithful as their spiritual food. The gift of His love and obedience to the point of giving His life (cf. *Jn* 10:17-18) is in the first place a gift to His Father. Certainly it is a gift given for our sake, and indeed that of all humanity (cf. *Mt* 26:28; *Mk* 14:24; *Lk* 22:20; *Jn* 10:15), yet it is *first and foremost a gift to the Father*: "a sacrifice that the Father accepted, giving, in return for this total self-giving by His Son, who 'became obedient unto death' (*Phil* 2:8), His own paternal gift, that is to say the grant of new immortal life in the resurrection".[18]

In giving His sacrifice to the Church, Christ has also made His own the spiritual sacrifice of the Church, which is called to offer herself in union with the sacrifice of Christ. This is the teaching of the Second Vatican Council concerning all the faithful: "Taking part in the Eucharistic Sacrifice, which is the source and summit of the whole Christian life, they offer the divine victim to God, and offer themselves along with it".[19]

A Participation in His Resurrection

14.   Christ's Passover includes not only His passion and death, but also His resurrection. This is recalled by the assembly's acclamation following the consecration: "*We proclaim Your resurrection*". The Eucharistic Sacrifice makes present not only the mystery of the Savior's passion and death, but also the mystery of the resurrection which crowned His sacrifice. It is as the living and risen One that Christ can become in the Eucharist the "bread of life" (*Jn* 6:35, 48), the "living bread" (*Jn* 6:51). Saint Ambrose reminded the newly-initiated that the Eucharist applies the event of the resurrection to their lives: "Today Christ is yours, yet each day He rises again for you".[20] Saint Cyril of Alexandria also makes clear that sharing in the sacred mysteries "is a true confession and a remembrance that the Lord died and returned to life for us and on our behalf".[21]

A Real Presence Here and Now

15. The sacramental re-presentation of Christ's sacrifice, crowned by the resurrection, in the Mass involves a most special presence which – in the words of Paul VI – "is called 'real' not as a way of excluding all other types of presence as if they were 'not real', but because it is a presence in the fullest sense: a substantial presence whereby Christ, the God-Man, is wholly and entirely present".[22] This sets forth once more the perennially valid teaching of the Council of Trent: "the consecration of the bread and wine effects the change of the whole substance of the bread into the substance of the Body of Christ our Lord, and of the whole substance of the wine into the substance of His Blood. And the holy Catholic Church has fittingly and properly called this change transubstantiation".[23] Truly the Eucharist is a *mysterium fidei*, a mystery which surpasses our understanding and can only be received in faith, as is often brought out in the catechesis of the Church Fathers regarding this divine sacrament: "Do not see – Saint Cyril of Jerusalem exhorts – in the bread and wine merely natural elements, because the Lord has expressly said that they are His body and His Blood: faith assures you of this, though your senses suggest otherwise".[24]

Adoro te devote, latens Deitas, we shall continue to sing with the Angelic Doctor. Before this mystery of love, human reason fully experiences its limitations. One understands how, down the centuries, this truth has stimulated theology to strive to understand it ever more deeply.

These are praiseworthy efforts, which are all the more helpful and insightful to the extent that they are able to join critical thinking to the "living faith" of the Church, as grasped especially by the Magisterium's "sure charism of truth" and the "intimate sense of spiritual realities"[25] which is attained above all by the saints. There remains the boundary indicated by Paul VI: "Every theological explanation which seeks some understanding of this mystery, in order to be in accord with Catholic faith, must firmly maintain that in objective reality, independently of our mind, the bread and wine have ceased to exist after the consecration, so that the adorable Body and Blood of the Lord Jesus from that moment on are really before us under the sacramental species of bread and wine".[26]

A True Banquet

16. The saving efficacy of the sacrifice is fully realized when the Lord's Body and Blood are received in communion. The Eucharistic Sacrifice is intrinsically directed to the inward union of the faithful with Christ through communion; we receive the very One who offered Himself for us, we receive His Body which He gave up for us on the Cross and His blood which He "poured out for many for the forgiveness of sins" (*Mt* 26:28). We are reminded of His words: "As the living Father sent Me, and I live because of the Father, so he who eats Me will live because of Me" (*Jn* 6:57). Jesus Himself reassures us that union, which He compares to that of the life of the Trinity, is truly realized. *The Eucharist is a true banquet*, in which Christ offers Himself as our nourishment. When for the first time Jesus spoke of this food, His listeners were astonished and bewildered, which forced the Master to emphasize the objective truth of His words: "Truly, truly, I say to you, unless you eat the Flesh of the Son of Man and drink His Blood, you have no life within you" (*Jn* 6:53). This is no metaphorical food: "My Flesh is food indeed, and My Blood is drink indeed" (Jn 6:55).

A Powerful Source of the Spirit

17. Through our communion in His Body and Blood, Christ also grants us His Spirit. Saint Ephrem writes: "He called the bread His living Body and He filled it with Himself and His Spirit... He who eats it with faith, eats Fire and Spirit.... Take and eat this, all of you, and eat with it the Holy Spirit. For it is truly My Body and whoever eats it will have eternal life".[27] The Church implores this divine Gift, the source of every other gift, in the Eucharistic epiclesis. In the *Divine Liturgy* of Saint John Chrysostom, for example, we find the prayer: "We beseech, implore and beg You: send Your Holy Spirit upon us all and upon these gifts... that those who partake of them may be purified in soul, receive the forgiveness of their sins, and share in the Holy Spirit".[28] And in the *Roman Missal* the celebrant prays: "grant that we who are nourished by His Body and Blood may be filled with His Holy Spirit, and

become one body, one spirit in Christ".[29] Thus by the gift of His Body and Blood Christ increases within us the gift of His Spirit, already poured out in Baptism and bestowed as a "seal" in the sacrament of Confirmation.

With Eschatological Overtones

18. The acclamation of the assembly following the consecration appropriately ends by expressing the eschatological thrust which marks the celebration of the Eucharist (cf. *1 Cor* 11:26): *"until you come in glory"*. The Eucharist is a straining towards the goal, a foretaste of the fullness of joy promised by Christ (cf. *Jn* 15:11); it is in some way the anticipation of heaven, the "pledge of future glory".[30] In the Eucharist, everything speaks of confident waiting "in joyful hope for the coming of our savior, Jesus Christ".[31] Those who feed on Christ in the Eucharist need not wait until the hereafter to receive eternal life: *they already possess it on earth,* as the first-fruits of a future fullness which will embrace man in his totality. For in the Eucharist we also receive the pledge of our bodily resurrection at the end of the world: "He who eats My Flesh and drinks My Blood has eternal life, and I will raise him up at the last day" (*Jn* 6:54). This pledge of the future resurrection comes from the fact that the Flesh of the Son of Man, given as food, is His Body in its glorious state after the resurrection. With the Eucharist we digest, as it were, the "secret" of the resurrection. For this reason Saint Ignatius of Antioch rightly defined the Eucharistic Bread as "a medicine of immortality, an antidote to death".[32]

Our Communion With Heaven

19. The eschatological tension kindled by the Eucharist *expresses and reinforces our communion with the Church in heaven.* It is not by chance that the Eastern Anaphoras and the Latin Eucharistic Prayers honor Mary, the ever-Virgin Mother of Jesus Christ our Lord and God, the angels, the holy apostles, the glorious martyrs and all the saints. This is an aspect of the Eucharist which merits greater attention: in celebrating the sacrifice of the Lamb, we are united to the heavenly "liturgy" and become part of that great multitude which cries out: "Salvation belongs to our God

who sits upon the throne, and to the Lamb!" (*Rev* 7:10). The Eucharist is truly a glimpse of heaven appearing on earth. It is a glorious ray of the heavenly Jerusalem which pierces the clouds of our history and lights up our journey.

Offered For the World

20. A significant consequence of the eschatological tension inherent in the Eucharist is also the fact that it spurs us on our journey through history and plants a seed of living hope in our daily commitment to the work before us. Certainly the Christian vision leads to the expectation of "new heavens" and "a new earth" (*Rev* 21:1), but this increases, rather than lessens, our *sense of responsibility for the world today.* (33) I wish to reaffirm this forcefully at the beginning of the new millennium, so that Christians will feel more obliged than ever not to neglect their duties as citizens in this world. Theirs is the task of contributing with the light of the Gospel to the building of a more human world, a world fully in harmony with God's plan.

Many problems darken the horizon of our time. We need but think of the urgent need to work for peace, to base relationships between peoples on solid premises of justice and solidarity, and to defend human life from conception to its natural end. And what should we say of the thousand inconsistencies of a "globalized" world where the weakest, the most powerless and the poorest appear to have so little hope! It is in this world that Christian hope must shine forth! For this reason too, the Lord wished to remain with us in the Eucharist, making His presence in meal and sacrifice the promise of a humanity renewed by His love. Significantly, in their account of the Last Supper, the Synoptics recount the institution of the Eucharist, while the Gospel of John relates, as a way of bringing out its profound meaning, the account of the "washing of the feet", in which Jesus appears as the teacher of communion and of service (cf. *Jn* 13:1-20). The Apostle Paul, for his part, says that it is "unworthy" of a Christian community to partake of the Lord's Supper amid division and indifference towards the poor (cf. *1 Cor* 11:17-22, 27-34).(34)

Proclaiming the death of the Lord "until He comes" (*1 Cor*

11:26) entails that all who take part in the Eucharist be committed to changing their lives and making them in a certain way completely "Eucharistic". It is this fruit of a transfigured existence and a commitment to transforming the world in accordance with the Gospel which splendidly illustrates the eschatological tension inherent in the celebration of the Eucharist and in the Christian life as a whole: "Come, Lord Jesus!" (*Rev* 22:20).

CHAPTER TWO

The Eucharist Builds the Church

Forms the People of the New Covenant

21. The Second Vatican Council teaches that the celebration of the Eucharist is at the center of the process of the Church's growth. After stating that "the Church, as the Kingdom of Christ already present in mystery, grows visibly in the world through the power of God",[35] then, as if in answer to the question: "How does the Church grow?", the Council adds: "as often as the sacrifice of the Cross by which 'Christ our pasch is sacrificed' (*1 Cor* 5:7) is celebrated on the altar, the work of our redemption is carried out. At the same time in the sacrament of the Eucharistic bread, the unity of the faithful, who form one body in Christ (cf. *1 Cor* 10:17), is both expressed and brought about".[36]

A causal influence of the Eucharist is present at the Church's very origins. The Evangelists specify that it was the Twelve, the Apostles, who gathered with Jesus at the Last Supper (cf. *Mt* 26:20; *Mk* 14:17; *Lk* 22:14). This is a detail of notable importance, for the Apostles "were both the seeds of the new Israel and the beginning of the sacred hierarchy".[37] By offering them His Body and His Blood as food, Christ mysteriously involved them in the sacrifice which would be completed later on Calvary. By analogy with the Covenant of Mount Sinai, sealed by sacrifice and the sprinkling of blood,[38] the actions and words of Jesus at the Last Supper laid the foundations of the new messianic community, the People of the New Covenant.

The Apostles, by accepting in the Upper Room Jesus' invitation: "Take, eat", "Drink of it, all of you" (*Mt* 26:26-27), entered for the first time into sacramental communion with Him. From that time forward, until the end of the age, the Church is built up through sacramental communion with the Son of God who was sacrificed for our sake: "Do this in remembrance of Me... Do this, as often as you drink it, in remembrance of Me" (*1 Cor* 11:24-25; cf. *Lk* 22:19).

Perfects Our Baptism

22. Incorporation into Christ, which is brought about by Baptism, is constantly renewed and consolidated by sharing in the Eucharistic Sacrifice, especially by that full sharing which takes place in sacramental communion. We can say not only that *each of us receives Christ*, but also that *Christ receives each of us*. He enters into friendship with us: "You are My friends" (*Jn* 15:14). Indeed, it is because of Him that we have life: "He who eats Me will live because of Me" (*Jn* 6:57). Eucharistic communion brings about in a sublime way the mutual "abiding" of Christ and each of His followers: "Abide in Me, and I in you" (*Jn* 15:4).

By its union with Christ, the People of the New Covenant, far from closing in upon itself, becomes a "sacrament" for humanity,[39] a sign and instrument of the salvation achieved by Christ, the light of the world and the salt of the earth (cf. *Mt* 5:13-16), for the redemption of all.[40] The Church's mission stands in continuity with the mission of Christ: "As the Father has sent Me, even so I send you" (*Jn* 20:21). From the perpetuation of the sacrifice of the Cross and her communion with the Body and Blood of Christ in the Eucharist, the Church draws the spiritual power needed to carry out her mission. The Eucharist thus appears as both the source and the summit of all evangelization, since its goal is the communion of mankind with Christ and in Him with the Father and the Holy Spirit.[41]

Unites Us With Christ and Each Other

23. Eucharistic communion also confirms the Church in her unity as the Body of Christ. Saint Paul refers to this unifying power of participation in the banquet of the Eucharist when he writes to the Corinthians: "The bread which we break, is it not a communion in the body of Christ? Because there is one bread, we who are many are one Body, for we all partake of the one bread" (*1 Cor* 10:16-17). Saint John Chrysostom's commentary on these words is profound and perceptive: "For what is the bread? It is the Body of Christ. And what do those who receive it become? The Body of Christ – not many bodies but one body. For as bread is completely one, though made of up many grains of wheat, and these, albeit

unseen, remain nonetheless present, in such a way that their difference is not apparent since they have been made a perfect whole, so too are we mutually joined to one another and together united with Christ".[42] The argument is compelling: our union with Christ, which is a gift and grace for each of us, makes it possible for us, in Him, to share in the unity of His Body which is the Church. The Eucharist reinforces the incorporation into Christ which took place in Baptism though the gift of the Spirit (cf. *1 Cor* 12:13, 27).

The joint and inseparable activity of the Son and of the Holy Spirit, which is at the origin of the Church, of her consolidation and her continued life, is at work in the Eucharist. This was clearly evident to the author of the Liturgy of Saint James: in the epiclesis of the Anaphora, God the Father is asked to send the Holy Spirit upon the faithful and upon the offerings, so that the Body and Blood of Christ "may be a help to all those who partake of it ... for the sanctification of their souls and bodies".[43] The Church is fortified by the divine Paraclete through the sanctification of the faithful in the Eucharist.

Enhances Fraternity

24.   The gift of Christ and His Spirit which we receive in Eucharistic communion superabundantly fulfills the yearning for fraternal unity deeply rooted in the human heart; at the same time it elevates the experience of fraternity already present in our common sharing at the same Eucharistic table to a degree which far surpasses that of the simple human experience of sharing a meal. Through her communion with the Body of Christ the Church comes to be ever more profoundly "in Christ in the nature of a sacrament, that is, a sign and instrument of intimate unity with God and of the unity of the whole human race".[44]

The seeds of disunity, which daily experience shows to be so deeply rooted in humanity as a result of sin, are countered by the unifying power of the body of Christ. The Eucharist, precisely by building up the Church, creates human community.

Eucharistic Worship Outside of Mass

25.   *The worship of the Eucharist outside of the Mass* is of

inestimable value for the life of the Church. This worship is strictly linked to the celebration of the Eucharistic Sacrifice. The presence of Christ under the sacred species reserved after Mass – a presence which lasts as long as the species of bread and of wine remain [45] – derives from the celebration of the sacrifice and is directed towards communion, both sacramental and spiritual.[46] It is the responsibility of Pastors to encourage, also by their personal witness, the practice of Eucharistic adoration, and exposition of the Blessed Sacrament in particular, as well as prayer of adoration before Christ present under the Eucharistic species.[47]

It is pleasant to spend time with Him, to lie close to His breast like the Beloved Disciple (cf. *Jn* 13:25) and to feel the infinite love present in His heart. If in our time Christians must be distinguished above all by the "art of prayer",[48] how can we not feel a renewed need to spend time in spiritual converse, in silent adoration, in heartfelt love before Christ present in the Most Holy Sacrament? How often, dear brothers and sisters, have I experienced this, and drawn from it strength, consolation and support!

This practice, repeatedly praised and recommended by the Magisterium,[49] is supported by the example of many saints. Particularly outstanding in this regard was Saint Alphonsus Liguori, who wrote: "Of all devotions, that of adoring Jesus in the Blessed Sacrament is the greatest after the sacraments, the one dearest to God and the one most helpful to us".[50] The Eucharist is a priceless treasure: by not only celebrating it but also by praying before it outside of Mass, we are enabled to make contact with the very wellspring of grace. A Christian community desirous of contemplating the face of Christ in the spirit which I proposed in the Apostolic Letters, Novo *Millennio Ineunte* and *Rosarium Virginis Mariae* cannot fail also to develop this aspect of Eucharistic worship, which prolongs and increases the fruits of our communion in the Body and Blood of the Lord.

"In the course of the day the faithful should not omit visiting the Blessed Sacrament, which in accordance with liturgical law must be reserved in churches with great reverence in a prominent place. Such visits are a sign of gratitude, an expression of love and an acknowledgment of the Lord's presence": Paul VI, Encyclical Letter, *Mysterium Fidei* (3 September 1965): AAS 57 (1965), 771.

CHAPTER THREE

The Apostolicity of the Eucharist and of the Church

The Eucharist is One, Holy Catholic and Apostolic

26. If, as I have said, the Eucharist builds the Church and the Church makes the Eucharist, it follows that there is a profound relationship between the two, so much so that we can apply to the Eucharistic mystery the very words with which, in the Nicene-Constantinopolitan Creed, we profess the Church to be "one, holy, catholic and apostolic". The Eucharist too is one and catholic. It is also holy, indeed, the Most Holy Sacrament. But it is above all its apostolicity that we must now consider.

Founded Upon the Apostles

27. The Catechism of the Catholic Church, in explaining how the Church is apostolic – founded on the Apostles – sees three meanings in this expression. First, "she was and remains built on 'the foundation of the Apostles' (*Eph* 2:20), the witnesses chosen and sent on mission by Christ Himself".[51] The Eucharist too has its foundation in the Apostles, not in the sense that it did not originate in Christ Himself, but because it was entrusted by Jesus to the Apostles and has been handed down to us by them and by their successors. It is in continuity with the practice of the Apostles, in obedience to the Lord's command, that the Church has celebrated the Eucharist down the centuries.

The second sense in which the Church is apostolic, as the Catechism points out, is that "with the help of the Spirit dwelling in her, the Church keeps and hands on the teaching, the 'good deposit', the salutary words she has heard from the Apostles".[52] Here too the Eucharist is apostolic, for it is celebrated in conformity with the faith of the Apostles. At various times in the two-thousand-year history of the People of the New Covenant, the Church's Magisterium has more precisely defined her teaching on the Eucharist, including its proper terminology, precisely in order to safeguard the apostolic faith with regard to this sublime mystery. This faith remains unchanged and it is essential for the Church that it remain unchanged.

Apostles Continue to Guide the Church

28. Lastly, the Church is apostolic in the sense that she "continues to be taught, sanctified and guided by the Apostles until Christ's return, through their successors in pastoral office: the college of Bishops assisted by priests, in union with the Successor of Peter, the Church's supreme pastor".[53] Succession to the Apostles in the pastoral mission necessarily entails the sacrament of Holy Orders, that is, the uninterrupted sequence, from the very beginning, of valid episcopal ordinations.[54] This succession is essential for the Church to exist in a proper and full sense.

The Eucharist also expresses this sense of apostolicity. As the Second Vatican Council teaches, "the faithful join in the offering of the Eucharist by virtue of their royal priesthood",[55] yet it is the ordained priest who, "acting in the person of Christ, brings about the Eucharistic Sacrifice and offers it to God in the name of all the people".(56) For this reason, the Roman Missal prescribes that only the priest should recite the Eucharistic Prayer, while the people participate in faith and in silence.[57]

The Ministerial Priest

29. The expression repeatedly employed by the Second Vatican Council, according to which "the ministerial priest, acting in the person of Christ, brings about the Eucharistic Sacrifice",[58] was already firmly rooted in papal teaching.[59] As I have pointed out on other occasions, the phrase *in persona Christi* "means more than offering 'in the name of' or 'in the place of' Christ. In persona means in specific sacramental identification with the eternal High Priest who is the author and principal subject of this sacrifice of His, a sacrifice in which, in truth, nobody can take His place".[60] The ministry of priests who have received the sacrament of Holy Orders, in the economy of salvation chosen by Christ, makes clear that the Eucharist which they celebrate is *a gift which radically transcends the power of the assembly* and is in any event essential

for validly linking the Eucharistic consecration to the sacrifice of the Cross and to the Last Supper.

The assembly gathered together for the celebration of the Eucharist, if it is to be a truly Eucharistic assembly, absolutely requires the presence of an ordained priest as its president. On the other hand, the community is by itself incapable of providing an ordained minister. This minister is a gift which the assembly *receives through episcopal succession going back to the Apostles*. It is the Bishop who, through the Sacrament of Holy Orders, makes a new presbyter by conferring upon him the power to consecrate the Eucharist. Consequently, "the Eucharistic mystery cannot be celebrated in any community except by an ordained priest, as the Fourth Lateran Council expressly taught".[61]

A Source of Ecumenism

30.   The Catholic Church's teaching on the relationship between priestly ministry and the Eucharist and her teaching on the Eucharistic Sacrifice have both been the subject in recent decades of a fruitful dialogue *in the area of ecumenism*. We must give thanks to the Blessed Trinity for the significant progress and convergence achieved in this regard, which lead us to hope one day for a full sharing of faith. Nonetheless, the observations of the Council concerning the Ecclesial Communities which arose in the West from the sixteenth century onwards and are separated from the Catholic Church remain fully pertinent: "The Ecclesial Communities separated from us lack that fullness of unity with us which should flow from Baptism, and we believe that especially because of the lack of the sacrament of Orders they have not preserved the genuine and total reality of the Eucharistic mystery. Nevertheless, when they commemorate the Lord's death and resurrection in the Holy Supper, they profess that it signifies life in communion with Christ and they await His coming in glory".[62]

The Catholic faithful, therefore, while respecting the religious convictions of these separated brethren, must refrain from receiving the communion distributed in their celebrations, so as not to condone an ambiguity about the nature of the Eucharist and, consequently, to fail in their duty to bear clear witness to the truth.

This would result in slowing the progress being made towards full visible unity. Similarly, it is unthinkable to substitute for Sunday Mass ecumenical celebrations of the word or services of common prayer with Christians from the aforementioned Ecclesial Communities, or even participation in their own liturgical services. Such celebrations and services, however praiseworthy in certain situations, prepare for the goal of full communion, including Eucharistic communion, but they cannot replace it.

The fact that the power of consecrating the Eucharist has been entrusted only to Bishops and priests does not represent any kind of belittlement of the rest of the People of God, for in the communion of the one Body of Christ which is the Church this gift redounds to the benefit of all.

Center and Summit of Priestly Ministry

31.   If the Eucharist is the center and summit of the Church's life, it is likewise the center and summit of priestly ministry. For this reason, with a heart filled with gratitude to our Lord Jesus Christ, I repeat that the Eucharist "is the principal and central *raison d'être* of the sacrament of priesthood, which effectively came into being at the moment of the institution of the Eucharist".[63]

Priests are engaged in a wide variety of pastoral activities. If we also consider the social and cultural conditions of the modern world it is easy to understand how priests face the very real *risk of losing their focus* amid such a great number of different tasks. The Second Vatican Council saw in pastoral charity the bond which gives unity to the priest's life and work. This, the Council adds, "flows mainly from the Eucharistic Sacrifice, which is therefore the center and root of the whole priestly life".[64] We can understand, then, how important it is for the spiritual life of the priest, as well as for the good of the Church and the world, that priests follow the Council's recommendation to celebrate the Eucharist daily: "for even if the faithful are unable to be present, it is an act of Christ and the Church".[65] In this way priests will be able to counteract the daily tensions which lead to a lack of focus and they will find in the Eucharistic Sacrifice – the true center of their lives and ministry – the spiritual strength needed to deal with their different pastoral responsibilities. Their daily activity will thus become truly Eucharistic.

The centrality of the Eucharist in the life and ministry of priests is the basis of its centrality in the *pastoral promotion of priestly vocations*. It is in the Eucharist that prayer for vocations is most closely united to the prayer of Christ the Eternal High Priest. At the same time the diligence of priests in carrying out their Eucharistic ministry, together with the conscious, active and fruitful participation of the faithful in the Eucharist, provides young men with a powerful example and incentive for responding generously to God's call. Often it is the example of a priest's fervent pastoral charity which the Lord uses to sow and to bring to fruition in a young man's heart the seed of a priestly calling.

When a Priest is Lacking

32. All of this shows how distressing and irregular is the situation of a Christian community which, despite having sufficient numbers and variety of faithful to form a parish, does not have a priest to lead it. Parishes are communities of the baptized who express and affirm their identity above all through the celebration of the Eucharistic Sacrifice. But this requires the presence of a presbyter, who alone is qualified to offer the Eucharist *in persona Christi*. When a community lacks a priest, attempts are rightly made somehow to remedy the situation so that it can continue its Sunday celebrations, and those religious and laity who lead their brothers and sisters in prayer exercise in a praiseworthy way the common priesthood of all the faithful based on the grace of Baptism. But such solutions must be considered merely temporary, while the community awaits a priest.

The sacramental incompleteness of these celebrations should above all inspire the whole community to pray with greater fervor that the Lord will send laborers into his harvest (cf. Mt 9:38). It should also be an incentive to mobilize all the resources needed for an adequate pastoral promotion of vocations, without yielding to the temptation to seek solutions which lower the moral and formative standards demanded of candidates for the priesthood.

A Eucharistic Hunger Must be Kept Alive

33. When, due to the scarcity of priests, non-ordained members of the faithful are entrusted with a share in the pastoral care of a parish, they should bear in mind that – as the Second Vatican Council teaches – "no Christian community can be built up unless it has its basis and center in the celebration of the most Holy Eucharist".[66] They have a responsibility, therefore, to keep alive in the community a genuine "hunger" for the Eucharist, so that no opportunity for the celebration of Mass will ever be missed, also taking advantage of the occasional presence of a priest who is not impeded by Church law from celebrating Mass.

CHAPTER FOUR

The Eucharist and Ecclesial Communion

An Ecclesiology of Communion

34.   The Extraordinary Assembly of the Synod of Bishops in 1985 saw in the concept of an "ecclesiology of communion" the central and fundamental idea of the documents of the Second Vatican Council.[67] The Church is called during her earthly pilgrimage to maintain and promote communion with the Triune God and communion among the faithful. For this purpose she possesses the word and the sacraments, particularly the Eucharist, by which she "constantly lives and grows"[68] and in which she expresses her very nature. It is not by chance that the term *communion* has become one of the names given to this sublime sacrament.

The Eucharist thus appears as the culmination of all the sacraments in perfecting our communion with God the Father by identification with his only-begotten Son through the working of the Holy Spirit. With discerning faith a distinguished writer of the Byzantine tradition voiced this truth: in the Eucharist "unlike any other sacrament, the mystery [of communion] is so perfect that it brings us to the heights of every good thing: here is the ultimate goal of every human desire, because here we attain God and God joins Himself to us in the most perfect union".[69] Precisely for this reason it is good to *cultivate in our hearts a constant desire for the sacrament of the Eucharist.* This was the origin of the practice of "spiritual communion", which has happily been established in the Church for centuries and recommended by saints who were masters of the spiritual life. Saint Teresa of Jesus wrote: "When you do not receive communion and you do not attend Mass, you can make a spiritual communion, which is a most beneficial practice; by it the love of God will be greatly impressed on you".[70]

Both Invisible and Visible

35.   The celebration of the Eucharist, however, cannot be the

starting-point for communion; it presupposes that communion already exists, a communion which it seeks to consolidate and bring to perfection. The sacrament is an expression of this bond of communion both in its *invisible* dimension, which, in Christ and through the working of the Holy Spirit, unites us to the Father and among ourselves, and in its *visible* dimension, which entails communion in the teaching of the Apostles, in the sacraments and in the Church's hierarchical order. The profound relationship between the invisible and the visible elements of ecclesial communion is constitutive of the Church as the sacrament of salvation.[71] Only in this context can there be a legitimate celebration of the Eucharist and true participation in it. Consequently it is an intrinsic requirement of the Eucharist that it should be celebrated in communion, and specifically maintaining the various bonds of that communion intact.

Partakers in the Divine Nature

36. Invisible communion, though by its nature always growing, presupposes the life of grace, by which we become "partakers of the divine nature" (2 Pet 1:4), and the practice of the virtues of faith, hope and love. Only in this way do we have true communion with the Father, the Son and the Holy Spirit. Nor is faith sufficient; we must persevere in sanctifying grace and love, remaining within the Church "bodily" as well as "in our heart"; [72] what is required, in the words of Saint Paul, is "faith working through love" (Gal 5:6).

Keeping these invisible bonds intact is a specific moral duty incumbent upon Christians who wish to participate fully in the Eucharist by receiving the Body and Blood of Christ. The Apostle Paul appeals to this duty when he warns: "Let a man examine himself, and so eat of the bread and drink of the cup" (*1 Cor* 11:28). Saint John Chrysostom, with his stirring eloquence, exhorted the faithful: "I too raise my voice, I beseech, beg and implore that no one draw near to this sacred table with a sullied and corrupt conscience. Such an act, in fact, can never be called 'communion', not even were we to touch the Lord's Body a thousand times over, but 'condemnation', 'torment' and 'increase of punishment'".[73]

Along these same lines, the *Catechism of the Catholic Church* rightly stipulates that "anyone conscious of a grave sin must receive the sacrament of Reconciliation before coming to communion".[74] I therefore desire to reaffirm that in the Church there remains in force, now and in the future, the rule by which the Council of Trent gave concrete expression to the Apostle Paul's stern warning when it affirmed that, in order to receive the Eucharist in a worthy manner, "one must first confess one's sins, when one is aware of mortal sin".[75]

Eucharist and Penance

37.   The two sacraments of the Eucharist and Penance are very closely connected. Because the Eucharist makes present the redeeming sacrifice of the Cross, perpetuating it sacramentally, it naturally gives rise to a continuous need for conversion, for a personal response to the appeal made by Saint Paul to the Christians of Corinth: "We beseech you on behalf of Christ, be reconciled to God" (*2 Cor* 5:20). If a Christian's conscience is burdened by serious sin, then the path of penance through the sacrament of Reconciliation becomes necessary for full participation in the Eucharistic Sacrifice.

The judgment of one's state of grace obviously belongs only to the person involved, since it is a question of examining one's conscience. However, in cases of outward conduct which is seriously, clearly and steadfastly contrary to the moral norm, the Church, in her pastoral concern for the good order of the community and out of respect for the sacrament, cannot fail to feel directly involved. The *Code of Canon Law* refers to this situation of a manifest lack of proper moral disposition when it states that those who "obstinately persist in manifest grave sin" are not to be admitted to Eucharistic communion.[76]

Fully Incorporated

38.   Ecclesial communion, as I have said, is likewise *visible,* and finds expression in the series of "bonds" listed by the Council when it teaches: "They are fully incorporated into the society of the Church who, possessing the Spirit of Christ, accept her whole

structure and all the means of salvation established within her, and within her visible framework are united to Christ, who governs her through the Supreme Pontiff and the Bishops, by the bonds of profession of faith, the sacraments, ecclesiastical government and communion".[77]

The Eucharist, as the supreme sacramental manifestation of communion in the Church, demands to be celebrated *in a context where the outward bonds of communion are also intact.* In a special way, since the Eucharist is "as it were, the summit of the spiritual life and the goal of all the sacraments",[78] it requires that the bonds of communion in the sacraments, particularly in Baptism and in priestly Orders, be real. It is not possible to give communion to a person who is not baptized or to one who rejects the full truth of the faith regarding the Eucharistic mystery. Christ is the truth and He bears witness to the truth (cf. *Jn* 14:6; 18:37); the sacrament of His Body and Blood does not permit duplicity.

Open to the Whole Church

39. Furthermore, given the very nature of ecclesial communion and its relation to the sacrament of the Eucharist, it must be recalled that "the Eucharistic Sacrifice, while always offered in a particular community, is never a celebration of that community alone. In fact, the community, in receiving the Eucharistic presence of the Lord, receives the entire gift of salvation and shows, even in its lasting visible particular form, that it is the image and true presence of the one, holy, catholic and apostolic Church".[79] From this it follows that a truly Eucharistic community cannot be closed in upon itself, as though it were somehow self-sufficient; rather it must persevere in harmony with every other Catholic community.

The ecclesial communion of the Eucharistic assembly is a communion with its own *Bishop* and with the *Roman Pontiff*. The Bishop, in effect, is the *visible* principle and the foundation of unity within his particular Church.[80] It would therefore be a great contradiction if the sacrament *par excellence* of the Church's unity were celebrated without true communion with the Bishop. As Saint Ignatius of Antioch wrote: "That Eucharist which is celebrated under the Bishop, or under one to whom the Bishop has given this charge, may be considered certain".[81] Likewise, since "the Roman Pontiff, as the successor of Peter, is the perpetual and visible source and foundation of the unity of the Bishops and of the multitude of the faithful",[82] communion with him is intrinsically required for the celebration of the Eucharistic Sacrifice. Hence the great truth expressed which the Liturgy expresses in a variety of ways: "Every celebration of the Eucharist is performed in union not only with the proper Bishop, but also with the Pope, with the episcopal order, with all the clergy, and with the entire people. Every valid celebration of the Eucharist expresses this universal communion with Peter and with the whole Church, or objectively calls for it, as in the case of the Christian Churches separated from Rome".[83]

Creates and Fosters Communion

40. The Eucharist *creates communion* and *fosters communion*. Saint Paul wrote to the faithful of Corinth explaining how their divisions, reflected in their Eucharistic gatherings, contradicted what they were celebrating, the Lord's Supper. The Apostle then urged them to reflect on the true reality of the Eucharist in order to return to the spirit of fraternal communion (cf. *1 Cor* 11:17- 34). Saint Augustine effectively echoed this call when, in recalling the Apostle's words: "You are the Body of Christ and individually members of it" (*1 Cor* 12: 27), he went on to say: "If you are His Body and members of Him, then you will find set on the Lord's table your own mystery. Yes, you receive your own mystery".[84] And from this observation he concludes: "Christ the Lord... hallowed at His table the mystery of our peace and unity. Whoever receives the mystery of unity without preserving the bonds of peace receives not a mystery for his benefit but evidence against himself".[85]

The Day of the Lord

41. The Eucharist's particular effectiveness in promoting communion is one of the reasons for the importance of Sunday Mass. I have already dwelt on this and on the other reasons which make Sunday Mass fundamental for the life of the Church and of

individual believers in my Apostolic Letter on the sanctification of Sunday *Dies Domini.* [86] There I recalled that the faithful have the obligation to attend Mass, unless they are seriously impeded, and that Pastors have the corresponding duty to see that it is practical and possible for all to fulfill this precept.[87] More recently, in my Apostolic Letter *Novo Millennio Ineunte*, in setting forth the pastoral path which the Church must take at the beginning of the third millennium, I drew particular attention to the Sunday Eucharist, emphasizing its effectiveness for building communion. "It is" – I wrote – "the privileged place where communion is ceaselessly proclaimed and nurtured. Precisely through sharing in the Eucharist, *the Lord's Day* also becomes the *Day of the Church*, when she can effectively exercise her role as the sacrament of unity".[88]

Sacrament of the Church's Unity

42. The safeguarding and promotion of ecclesial communion is a task of each member of the faithful, who finds in the Eucharist, as the sacrament of the Church's unity, an area of special concern. More specifically, this task is the particular responsibility of the Church's Pastors, each according to his rank and ecclesiastical office. For this reason the Church has drawn up norms aimed both at fostering the frequent and fruitful access of the faithful to the Eucharistic table and at determining the objective conditions under which communion may not be given. The care shown in promoting the faithful observance of these norms becomes a practical means of showing love for the Eucharist and for the Church.

Relationship to Ecumenical Activity

43. In considering the Eucharist as the sacrament of ecclesial communion, there is one subject which, due to its importance, must not be overlooked: I am referring to the *relationship of the Eucharist to ecumenical activity*. We should all give thanks to the Blessed Trinity for the many members of the faithful throughout the world who in recent decades have felt an ardent desire for unity among all Christians. The Second Vatican Council, at the beginning of its Decree on Ecumenism, sees this as a special gift of God. [89] It was an efficacious grace which inspired us, the sons and daughters of

the Catholic Church and our brothers and sisters from other Churches and Ecclesial Communities, to set forth on the path of ecumenism. Our longing for the goal of unity prompts us to turn to the Eucharist, which is the supreme sacrament of the unity of the People of God, in as much as it is the apt expression and the unsurpassable source of that unity.[90] In the celebration of the Eucharistic Sacrifice the Church prays that God, the Father of mercies, will grant His children the fullness of the Holy Spirit so that they may become one body and one spirit in Christ.[91] In raising this prayer to the Father of lights, from whom comes every good endowment and every perfect gift (cf. *Jas* 1:17), the Church believes that she will be heard, for she prays in union with Christ her Head and Spouse, who takes up this plea of His Bride and joins it to that of His own redemptive sacrifice.

Ecumenical Guidelines

44. Precisely because the Church's unity, which the Eucharist brings about through the Lord's sacrifice and by communion in His Body and Blood, absolutely requires full communion in the bonds of the profession of faith, the sacraments and ecclesiastical governance, it is not possible to celebrate together the same Eucharistic liturgy until those bonds are fully re-established. Any such concelebration would not be a valid means, and might well prove instead to be *an obstacle, to the attainment of full communion*, by weakening the sense of how far we remain from this goal and by introducing or exacerbating ambiguities with regard to one or another truth of the faith. The path towards full unity can only be undertaken in truth. In this area, the prohibitions of Church law leave no room for uncertainty,[92] in fidelity to the moral norm laid down by the Second Vatican Council.[93]

I would like nonetheless to reaffirm what I said in my Encyclical Letter *Ut Unum Sint* after having acknowledged the impossibility of Eucharistic sharing: "And yet we do have a burning desire to join in celebrating the one Eucharist of the Lord, and this desire itself is already a common prayer of praise, a single supplication. Together we speak to the Father and increasingly we do so 'with one heart'".[94]

Intercommunion Not Yet

45. While it is never legitimate to concelebrate in the absence of full communion, the same is not true with respect to the administration of the Eucharist *under special circumstances, to individual persons* belonging to Churches or Ecclesial Communities not in full communion with the Catholic Church. In this case, in fact, the intention is to meet a grave spiritual need for the eternal salvation of an individual believer, not to bring about an intercommunion which remains impossible until the visible bonds of ecclesial communion are fully re-established.

This was the approach taken by the Second Vatican Council when it gave guidelines for responding to Eastern Christians separated in good faith from the Catholic Church, who spontaneously ask to receive the Eucharist from a Catholic minister and are properly disposed.[95] This approach was then ratified by both Codes, which also consider – with necessary modifications – the case of other non-Eastern Christians who are not in full communion with the Catholic Church.[96]

That They May Be One

46. In my Encyclical, *Ut Unum Sint* I expressed my own appreciation of these norms, which make it possible to provide for the salvation of souls with proper discernment: "It is a source of joy to note that Catholic ministers are able, in certain particular cases, to administer the sacraments of the Eucharist, Penance and Anointing of the Sick to Christians who are not in full communion with the Catholic Church but who greatly desire to receive these sacraments, freely request them and manifest the faith which the Catholic Church professes with regard to these sacraments. Conversely, in specific cases and in particular circumstances, Catholics too can request these same sacraments from ministers of Churches in which these sacraments are valid".[97]

These conditions, from which no dispensation can be given, must be carefully respected, even though they deal with specific individual cases, because the denial of one or more truths of the faith regarding these sacraments and, among these, the truth regarding the need of the ministerial priesthood for their validity, renders the person asking improperly disposed to legitimately receiving them. And the opposite is also true: Catholics may not receive communion in those communities which lack a valid sacrament of Orders.[98]

The faithful observance of the body of norms established in this area [99] is a manifestation and, at the same time, a guarantee of our love for Jesus Christ in the Blessed Sacrament, for our brothers and sisters of different Christian confessions – who have a right to our witness to the truth – and for the cause itself of the promotion of unity.

CHAPTER FIVE

The Dignity of the Eucharistic Celebration

Eucharistic Solemnity

47.   Reading the account of the institution of the Eucharist in the Synoptic Gospels, we are struck by the simplicity and the "solemnity" with which Jesus, on the evening of the Last Supper, instituted this great sacrament. There is an episode which in some way serves as its prelude: *the anointing at Bethany.* A woman, whom John identifies as Mary the sister of Lazarus, pours a flask of costly ointment over Jesus' head, which provokes from the disciples – and from Judas in particular (cf. *Mt* 26:8; *Mk* 14:4; Jn 12:4) – an indignant response, as if this act, in light of the needs of the poor, represented an intolerable "waste". But Jesus' own reaction is completely different. While in no way detracting from the duty of charity towards the needy, for whom the disciples must always show special care – "the poor you will always have with you" (*Mt* 26:11; *Mk* 14:7; cf. *Jn* 12:8) – he looks towards his imminent death and burial, and sees this act of anointing as an anticipation of the honor which His Body will continue to merit even after His death, indissolubly bound as it is to the mystery of His person.

The account continues, in the Synoptic Gospels, with Jesus' charge to the disciples to *prepare carefully the "large upper room"* needed for the Passover meal (cf. *Mk* 14:15; *Lk* 22:12) and with the narration of the institution of the Eucharist. Reflecting at least in part the Jewish rites of the Passover meal leading up to the singing of the Hallel (cf. *Mt* 26:30; *Mk* 14:26), the story presents with sobriety and solemnity, even in the variants of the different traditions, the words spoken by Christ over the bread and wine, which He made into concrete expressions of the handing over of His Body and the shedding of His Blood. All these details are recorded by the Evangelists in the light of a praxis of the "breaking of the bread" already well-established in the early Church. But certainly from the time of Jesus on, the event of Holy Thursday has shown visible traces of a liturgical "sensibility" shaped by Old Testament tradition and open to being reshaped in Christian celebrations in a way consonant with the new content of Easter.

Extravagance for the Unsurpassable Gift

48.   Like the woman who anointed Jesus in Bethany, *the Church has feared no "extravagance"*, devoting the best of her resources to expressing her wonder and adoration before the *unsurpassable gift of the Eucharist.* No less than the first disciples charged with preparing the "large upper room", she has felt the need, down the centuries and in her encounters with different cultures, to celebrate the Eucharist in a setting worthy of so great a mystery. In the wake of Jesus' own words and actions, and building upon the ritual heritage of Judaism, *the Christian liturgy was born.* Could there ever be an adequate means of expressing the acceptance of that self-gift which the divine Bridegroom continually makes to His Bride, the Church, by bringing the Sacrifice offered once and for all on the Cross to successive generations of believers and thus becoming nourishment for all the faithful? Though the idea of a "banquet" naturally suggests familiarity, the Church has never yielded to the temptation to trivialize this "intimacy" with her Spouse by forgetting that He is also her Lord and that the "banquet" always remains a sacrificial banquet marked by the Blood shed on Golgotha. *The Eucharistic Banquet is truly a "sacred" banquet*, in which the simplicity of the signs conceals the unfathomable holiness of God: *O sacrum convivium, in quo Christus sumitur!* The bread which is broken on our altars, offered to us as wayfarers along the paths of the world, is *panis angelorum*, the bread of angels, which cannot be approached except with the humility of the centurion in the Gospel: "Lord, I am not worthy to have You come under My roof " (*Mt* 8:8; *Lk* 7:6).

A Rich Artistic Heritage

49.   With this heightened sense of mystery, we understand how the faith of the Church in the mystery of the Eucharist has found historical expression not only in the demand for an interior disposition of devotion, but also in *outward forms* meant to evoke

and emphasize the grandeur of the event being celebrated. This led progressively to the development of *a particular form of regulating the Eucharistic liturgy,* with due respect for the various legitimately constituted ecclesial traditions. On this foundation *a rich artistic heritage* also developed. Architecture, sculpture, painting and music, moved by the Christian mystery, have found in the Eucharist, both directly and indirectly, a source of great inspiration.

Such was the case, for example, with architecture, which witnessed the transition, once the historical situation made it possible, from the first places of Eucharistic celebration in the *domus* or "homes" of Christian families to the solemn *basilicas* of the early centuries, to the imposing *cathedrals* of the Middle Ages, and to the churches, large and small, which gradually sprang up throughout the lands touched by Christianity. The designs of altars and tabernacles within Church interiors were often not simply motivated by artistic inspiration but also by a clear understanding of the mystery. The same could be said for *sacred music*, if we but think of the inspired Gregorian melodies and the many, often great, composers who sought to do justice to the liturgical texts of the Mass. Similarly, can we overlook the enormous quantity of *artistic production*, ranging from fine craftsmanship to authentic works of art, in the area of Church furnishings and vestments used for the celebration of the Eucharist?

It can be said that the Eucharist, while shaping the Church and her spirituality, has also powerfully affected "culture", and the arts in particular.

The Eucharist Church Breathes With Two Lungs: East and West

50. In this effort to adore the mystery grasped in its ritual and aesthetic dimensions, a certain "competition" has taken place between Christians of the West and the East. How could we not give particular thanks to the Lord for the contributions to Christian art made by the great architectural and artistic works of the Greco-Byzantine tradition and of the whole geographical area marked by Slav culture? In the East, sacred art has preserved a remarkably powerful sense of mystery, which leads artists to see their efforts at

creating beauty not simply as an expression of their own talents, but also as a genuine service to the faith. Passing well beyond mere technical skill, they have shown themselves docile and open to the inspiration of the Holy Spirit.

The architectural and mosaic splendors of the Christian East and West are a patrimony belonging to all believers; they contain a hope, and even a pledge, of the desired fullness of communion in faith and in celebration. This would presuppose and demand, as in Rublëv's famous depiction of the Trinity, *a profoundly Eucharistic Church* in which the presence of the mystery of Christ in the broken bread is, as it were, immersed in the ineffable unity of the three divine Persons, making of the Church herself an "icon" of the Trinity.

Within this context of an art aimed at expressing, in all its elements, the meaning of the Eucharist in accordance with the Church's teaching, attention needs to be given to the norms regulating *the construction and decor of sacred buildings.* As history shows and as I emphasized in my *Letter to Artists,*[100] the Church has always left ample room for the creativity of artists. But sacred art must be outstanding for its ability to express adequately the mystery grasped in the fullness of the Church's faith and in accordance with the pastoral guidelines appropriately laid down by competent Authority. This holds true both for the figurative arts and for sacred music.

Proper Inculturation

51. The development of sacred art and liturgical discipline which took place in lands of ancient Christian heritage is also taking place *on continents where Christianity is younger.* This was precisely the approach supported by the Second Vatican Council on the need for sound and proper "inculturation". In my numerous Pastoral visits, I have seen, throughout the world, the great vitality which the celebration of the Eucharist can have when marked by the forms, styles and sensibilities of different cultures. By adaptation to the changing conditions of time and place, the Eucharist offers sustenance not only to individuals but to entire peoples, and it shapes cultures inspired by Christianity.

It is necessary, however, that this important work of adaptation be carried out with a constant awareness of the ineffable mystery against which every generation is called to measure itself. The "treasure" is too important and precious to risk impoverishment or compromise through forms of experimentation or practices introduced without a careful review on the part of the competent ecclesiastical authorities. Furthermore, the centrality of the Eucharistic mystery demands that any such review must be undertaken in close association with the Holy See. As I wrote in my Post-Synodal Apostolic Exhortation *Eccleisa In Asia*, "such cooperation is essential because the Sacred Liturgy expresses and celebrates the one faith professed by all and, being the heritage of the whole Church, cannot be determined by local Churches in isolation from the universal Church".[(101)]

Warning Against Abuses

52.   All of this makes clear the great responsibility which belongs to priests in particular for the celebration of the Eucharist. It is their responsibility to preside at the Eucharist *in persona Christi* and to provide a witness to and a service of communion not only for the community directly taking part in the celebration, but also for the universal Church, which is a part of every Eucharist. It must be lamented that, especially in the years following the post-conciliar liturgical reform, as a result of a misguided sense of creativity and adaptation there have been a number of *abuses* which have been a source of suffering for many. A certain reaction against "formalism" has led some, especially in certain regions, to consider the "forms" chosen by the Church's great liturgical tradition and her Magisterium as non-binding and to introduce unauthorized innovations which are often completely inappropriate.

I consider it my duty, therefore to appeal urgently that the liturgical norms for the celebration of the Eucharist be observed with great fidelity. These norms are a concrete expression of the authentically ecclesial nature of the Eucharist; this is their deepest meaning. Liturgy is never anyone's private property, be it of the celebrant or of the community in which the mysteries are celebrated. The Apostle Paul had to address fiery words to the community of

Corinth because of grave shortcomings in their celebration of the Eucharist resulting in divisions (*schismata*) and the emergence of factions (*haireseis*) (cf. *1 Cor* 11:17-34). Our time, too, calls for a renewed awareness and appreciation of liturgical norms as a reflection of, and a witness to, the one universal Church made present in every celebration of the Eucharist. Priests who faithfully celebrate Mass according to the liturgical norms, and communities which conform to those norms, quietly but eloquently demonstrate their love for the Church. Precisely to bring out more clearly this deeper meaning of liturgical norms, I have asked the competent offices of the Roman Curia to prepare a more specific document, including prescriptions of a juridical nature, on this very important subject. No one is permitted to undervalue the mystery entrusted to our hands: it is too great for anyone to feel free to treat it lightly and with disregard for its sacredness and its universality.

CHAPTER SIX

At the School of Mary, "Woman of the Eucharist"

Mary Our Model

53. If we wish to rediscover in all its richness the profound relationship between the Church and the Eucharist, we cannot neglect Mary, Mother and model of the Church. In my Apostolic Letter *Rosarium Virginis Mariae*, I pointed to the Blessed Virgin Mary as our teacher in contemplating Christ's face, and among the mysteries of light I included *the institution of the Eucharist*.[102] Mary can guide us towards this most holy sacrament, because she herself has a profound relationship with it.

At first glance, the Gospel is silent on this subject. The account of the institution of the Eucharist on the night of Holy Thursday makes no mention of Mary. Yet we know that she was present among the Apostles who prayed "with one accord" (cf. *Acts* 1:14) *in the first community which gathered after the Ascension in expectation of Pentecost*. Certainly Mary must have been present at the Eucharistic celebrations of the first generation of Christians, who were devoted to "the breaking of bread" (*Acts* 2:42).

But in addition to her sharing in the Eucharistic banquet, an indirect picture of Mary's relationship with the Eucharist can be had, beginning with her interior disposition. *Mary is a "woman of the Eucharist" in her whole life*. The Church, which looks to Mary as a model, is also called to imitate her in her relationship with this most holy mystery.

Mary Our Guide

54. *Mysterium fidei!* If the Eucharist is a mystery of faith which so greatly transcends our understanding as to call for sheer abandonment to the word of God, then there can be no one like Mary to act as our support and guide in acquiring this disposition. In repeating what Christ did at the Last Supper in obedience to His command: "Do this in memory of Me!", we also accept Mary's

invitation to obey Him without hesitation: "Do whatever He tells you" (*Jn* 2:5). With the same maternal concern which she showed at the wedding feast of Cana, Mary seems to say to us: "Do not waver; trust in the words of my Son. If He was able to change water into wine, He can also turn bread and wine into His Body and Blood, and through this mystery bestow on believers the living memorial of His passover, thus becoming the 'bread of life'".

Mary's Eucharistic Faith

55. In a certain sense Mary lived her *Eucharistic faith* even before the institution of the Eucharist, by the very fact that *she offered her virginal womb for the Incarnation of God's Word.* The Eucharist, while commemorating the passion and resurrection, is also in continuity with the incarnation. At the Annunciation Mary conceived the Son of God in the physical reality of His Body and Blood, thus anticipating within herself what to some degree happens sacramentally in every believer who receives, under the signs of bread and wine, the Lord's Body and Blood.

As a result, there is a profound analogy between the *Fiat* which Mary said in reply to the angel, and the *Amen* which every believer says when receiving the Body of the Lord. Mary was asked to believe that the One whom she conceived "through the Holy Spirit" was "the Son of God" (*Lk* 1:30-35). In continuity with the Virgin's faith, in the Eucharistic mystery we are asked to believe that the same Jesus Christ, Son of God and Son of Mary, becomes present in His full humanity and divinity under the signs of bread and wine.

"Blessed is she who believed" (*Lk* 1:45). Mary also anticipated, in the mystery of the incarnation, the Church's Eucharistic faith. When, at the Visitation, she bore in her womb the Word made flesh, she became in some way a "tabernacle" – the first "tabernacle" in history – in which the Son of God, still invisible to our human gaze, allowed Himself to be adored by Elizabeth, radiating His light as it were through the eyes and the voice of Mary. And is not the enraptured gaze of Mary as she contemplated the face of the newborn Christ and cradled Him in her arms that unparalleled model of love which should inspire us every time we receive Eucharistic communion?

Mary's Role in the Eucharistic Sacrifice

56. Mary, throughout her life at Christ's side and not only on Calvary, made her own *the sacrificial dimension of the Eucharist.* When she brought the child Jesus to the Temple in Jerusalem "to present Him to the Lord" (*Lk* 2:22), she heard the aged Simeon announce that the child would be a "sign of contradiction" and that a sword would also pierce her own heart (cf. *Lk* 2:34-35). The tragedy of her Son's crucifixion was thus foretold, and in some sense Mary's *Stabat Mater* at the foot of the Cross was foreshadowed. In her daily preparation for Calvary, Mary experienced a kind of "anticipated Eucharist" – one might say a "spiritual communion" – of desire and of oblation, which would culminate in her union with her Son in His passion, and then find expression after Easter by her partaking in the Eucharist which the Apostles celebrated as the memorial of that passion.

What must Mary have felt as she heard from the mouth of Peter, John, James and the other Apostles the words spoken at the Last Supper: "This is My Body which is given for you" (*Lk* 22:19)? The Body given up for us and made present under sacramental signs was the same Body which she had conceived in her womb! For Mary, receiving the Eucharist must have somehow meant welcoming once more into her womb that heart which had beat in unison with hers and reliving what she had experienced at the foot of the Cross.

Mary, Mother of the Eucharist

57. "Do this in remembrance of Me" (*Lk* 22:19). In the "memorial" of Calvary all that Christ accomplished by His passion and His death is present. Consequently *all that Christ did with regard to His Mother* for our sake is also present. To her He gave the beloved disciple and, in him, each of us: "Behold, your Son!". To each of us He also says: "Behold your mother!" (cf. *Jn* 19: 26-27).

Experiencing the memorial of Christ's death in the Eucharist also means continually receiving this gift. It means accepting – like John – the one who is given to us anew as our Mother. It also means taking on a commitment to be conformed to Christ, putting ourselves at the school of His Mother and allowing her to accompany us. Mary is present, with the Church and as the Mother of the Church, at each of our celebrations of the Eucharist. If the Church and the Eucharist are inseparably united, the same ought to be said of Mary and the Eucharist. This is one reason why, since ancient times, the commemoration of Mary has always been part of the Eucharistic celebrations of the Churches of East and West.

Mary's Eucharistic Magnificat

58. In the Eucharist the Church is completely united to Christ and his sacrifice, and makes her own the spirit of Mary. This truth can be understood more deeply by *re-reading the Magnificat* in a Eucharistic key. The Eucharist, like the Canticle of Mary, is first and foremost praise and thanksgiving. When Mary exclaims: "My soul magnifies the Lord and my spirit rejoices in God my Savior", she already bears Jesus in her womb. She praises God "through" Jesus, but she also praises Him "in" Jesus and "with" Jesus. This is itself the true "Eucharistic attitude".

At the same time Mary recalls the wonders worked by God in salvation history in fulfillment of the promise once made to the fathers (*cf. Lk* 1:55), and proclaims the wonder that surpasses them all, the redemptive incarnation. Lastly, the *Magnificat* reflects the eschatological tension of the Eucharist. Every time the Son of God comes again to us in the "poverty" of the sacramental signs of bread and wine, the seeds of that new history wherein the mighty are "put down from their thrones" and "those of low degree are exalted" (*cf. Lk* 1:52), take root in the world. Mary sings of the "new heavens" and the "new earth" which find in the Eucharist their anticipation and in some sense their program and plan. The *Magnificat* expresses Mary's spirituality, and there is nothing greater than this spirituality for helping us to experience the mystery of the Eucharist. The Eucharist has been given to us so that our life, like that of Mary, may become completely a *Magnificat!*

CONCLUSION

My 25th Petrine Anniversary

59. *Ave, verum corpus natum de Maria Virgine!* Several years ago I celebrated the fiftieth anniversary of my priesthood. Today I have the grace of offering the Church this Encyclical on the Eucharist on the Holy Thursday which falls *during the twenty-fifth year of my Petrine ministry.* As I do so, my heart is filled with gratitude. For over a half century, every day, beginning on 2 November 1946, when I celebrated my first Mass in the Crypt of Saint Leonard in Wawel Cathedral in Krakow, my eyes have gazed in recollection upon the host and the chalice, where time and space in some way "merge" and the drama of Golgotha is re-presented in a living way, thus revealing its mysterious "contemporaneity". Each day my faith has been able to recognize in the consecrated bread and wine the divine Wayfarer who joined the two disciples on the road to Emmaus and opened their eyes to the light and their hearts to new hope (*cf. Lk* 24:13-35).

Allow me, dear brothers and sisters, to share with deep emotion, as a means of accompanying and strengthening your faith, my own testimony of faith in the Most Holy Eucharist. *Ave verum corpus natum de Maria Virgine, vere passum, immolatum, in cruce pro homine!* Here is the Church's treasure, the heart of the world, the pledge of the fulfilment for which each man and woman, even unconsciously, yearns. A great and transcendent mystery, indeed, and one that taxes our mind's ability to pass beyond appearances. Here our senses fail us: *visus, tactus, gustus in te fallitur*, in the words of the hymn *Adoro Te Devote*; yet faith alone, rooted in the word of Christ handed down to us by the Apostles, is sufficient for us. Allow me, like Peter at the end of the Eucharistic discourse in John's Gospel, to say once more to Christ, in the name of the whole Church and in the name of each of you: "Lord to whom shall we go? You have the words of eternal life" (*Jn* 6:68).

A New Program

60. At the dawn of this third millennium, we, the children of the Church, are called to undertake with renewed enthusiasm the

journey of Christian living. As I wrote in my Apostolic Letter, *Novo Millennio Ineunte*, "it is not a matter of inventing a 'new program'. The program already exists: it is the plan found in the Gospel and in the living Tradition; it is the same as ever. Ultimately, it has its center in Christ Himself, who is to be known, loved and imitated, so that in Him we may live the life of the Trinity, and with Him transform history until its fulfilment in the heavenly Jerusalem".[103] The implementation of this program of a renewed impetus in Christian living passes through the Eucharist.

Every commitment to holiness, every activity aimed at carrying out the Church's mission, every work of pastoral planning, must draw the strength it needs from the Eucharistic mystery and in turn be directed to that mystery as its culmination. In the Eucharist we have Jesus, we have His redemptive sacrifice, we have His resurrection, we have the gift of the Holy Spirit, we have adoration, obedience and love of the Father. Were we to disregard the Eucharist, how could we overcome our own deficiency?

Sacrifice, Presence, Banquet

61.   The mystery of the Eucharist – sacrifice, presence, banquet – *does not allow for reduction or exploitation;* it must be experienced and lived in its integrity, both in its celebration and in the intimate converse with Jesus which takes place after receiving communion or in a prayerful moment of Eucharistic adoration apart from Mass. These are times when the Church is firmly built up and it becomes clear what she truly is: one, holy, catholic and apostolic; the people, temple and family of God; the body and bride of Christ, enlivened by the Holy Spirit; the universal sacrament of salvation and a hierarchically structured communion.

The path taken by the Church in these first years of the third millennium is also a *path of renewed ecumenical commitment.* The final decades of the second millennium, culminating in the Great Jubilee, have spurred us along this path and called for all the baptized to respond to the prayer of Jesus *"ut unum sint"* (*Jn* 17:11). The path itself is long and strewn with obstacles greater than our human resources alone can overcome, yet we have the Eucharist, and in its presence we can hear in the depths of our hearts, as if they were addressed to us, the same words heard by the Prophet Elijah: "Arise and eat, else the journey will be too great for you" (*1 Kg* 19:7). The treasure of the Eucharist, which the Lord places before us, impels us towards the goal of full sharing with all our brothers and sisters to whom we are joined by our common Baptism. But if this treasure is not to be squandered, we need to respect the demands which derive from its being the sacrament of communion in faith and in apostolic succession.

By giving the Eucharist the prominence it deserves, and by being careful not to diminish any of its dimensions or demands, we show that we are truly conscious of the greatness of this gift. We are urged to do so by an uninterrupted tradition, which from the first centuries on has found the Christian community ever vigilant in guarding this "treasure". Inspired by love, the Church is anxious to hand on to future generations of Christians, without loss, her faith and teaching with regard to the mystery of the Eucharist. There can be no danger of excess in our care for this mystery, for "in this sacrament is recapitulated the whole mystery of our salvation".(104)

School of the Saints

62.   Let us take our place, dear brothers and sisters, *at the school of the saints*, who are the great interpreters of true Eucharistic piety. In them the theology of the Eucharist takes on all the splendor of a lived reality; it becomes "contagious" and, in a manner of speaking, it "warms our hearts". Above all, let us *listen to Mary Most Holy*, in whom the mystery of the Eucharist appears, more than in anyone else, as a *mystery of light*. Gazing upon Mary, we come to know *the transforming power present in the Eucharist*. In her we see the world renewed in love. Contemplating her, assumed body and soul into heaven, we see opening up before us those "new heavens" and that "new earth" which will appear at the second coming of Christ. Here below, the Eucharist represents their pledge, and in a certain way, their anticipation: "*Veni, Domine Iesu!*" (*Rev* 22:20).

In the humble signs of bread and wine, changed into His Body and Blood, Christ walks beside us as our strength and our food for the journey, and He enables us to become, for everyone, witnesses of hope. If, in the presence of this mystery, reason experiences its limits, the heart, enlightened by the grace of the Holy Spirit, clearly sees the response that is demanded, and bows low in adoration and unbounded love.

Let us make our own the words of Saint Thomas Aquinas, an eminent theologian and an impassioned poet of Christ in the Eucharist, and turn in hope to the contemplation of that goal to which our hearts aspire in their thirst for joy and peace:

Bone pastor, panis vere,
Iesu, nostri Miserere...

Come then, good Shepherd, bread divine,
Still show to us Thy mercy sign;
Oh, feed us, still keep us Thine;
So we may see Thy glories shine
in fields of immortality.

O Thou, the wisest, mightiest, best,
Our present food, our future rest,
Come, make us each Thy chosen guest,
Co-heirs of Thine, and comrades blest
With saints whose dwelling is with Thee.

Given in Rome, at Saint Peter's, on 17 April, Holy Thursday, in the year 2003, the Twenty-fifth of my Pontificate, the Year of the Rosary.

IOANNES PAULUS II

Notes

(1)   Second Vatican Ecumenical Council, Dogmatic Constitution on the Church *Lumen Gentium, 11.*

(2)   Second Vatican Ecumenical Council, Decree on the Ministry and Life of Priests   *Presbyterorum Ordinis,* 5.

(3)   Cf. John Paul II, Apostolic Letter *Rosarium Virginis Mariae* (16 October 2002), 21: AAS 95 (2003), 19.

(4)   This is the title which I gave to an autobiographical testimony issued for my fiftieth anniversary of priestly ordination.

(5)   Leonis XIII P.M. Acta, XXII (1903), 115-136.

(6)   AAS 39 (1947), 521-595.

(7)   AAS 57 (1965), 753-774.

(8)   AAS 72 (1980), 113-148.

(9)   Cf. Second Vatican Ecumenical Council, Constitution *Sacrosanctum Concilium,* 47: "... our Savior instituted the Eucharistic Sacrifice of His Body and Blood, in order to perpetuate the sacrifice of the Cross throughout time, until He should return".

(10)   Catechism of the Catholic Church, 1085.

(11)   Second Vatican Ecumenical Council, Dogmatic Constitution on the Church *Lumen Gentium,* 3.

(12)   Cf. Paul VI, Solemn Profession of Faith, 30 June 1968, 24: AAS 60 (1968), 442; John Paul II, Apostolic Letter *Dominicae Cenae* (24 February 1980), 12: AAS 72 (1980), 142.

(13)   Catechism of the Catholic Church, 1382.

(14)   Catechism of the Catholic Church, 1367.

(15)   *In Epistolam ad Hebraeos Homiliae, Hom.* 17,3: PG 63, 131.

(16)   Cf. Ecumenical Council of Trent, Session XXII, *Doctrina de ss. Missae Sacrificio,* Chapter 2: DS 1743: "It is one and the same victim here offering Himself by the ministry of His priests, who then offered Himself on the Cross; it is only the manner of offering that is different".

(17)   Pius XII, Encyclical Letter Mediator Dei (20 November 1947): AAS 39 (1947), 548.

(18)   John Paul II, Encyclical Letter *Redemptor Hominis* (15 March 1979), 20: AAS 71 (1979), 310.

(19)   Dogmatic Constitution on the Church *Lumen Gentium,* 11.

(20)   *De Sacramentis,* V, 4, 26: CSEL 73, 70.

(21)   *In Ioannis Evangelium,* XII, 20: PG 74, 726.

(22)   Encyclical Letter *Mysterium Fidei* (3 September 1965): AAS 57 (1965), 764.

(23)   Session XIII, *Decretum de ss. Eucharistia,* Chapter 4: DS 1642.

(24)   *Mystagogical Catecheses, IV, 6: SCh* 126, 138.

(25)   Second Vatican Ecumenical Council, Dogmatic Constitution on Divine Revelation   *Dei Verbum,* 8.

(26)   Solemn Profession of Faith, 30 June 1968, 25: AAS 60 (1968), 442-443.

(27)   *Sermo IV in Hebdomadam Sanctam*: CSCO 413/Syr. 182, 55.

(28)   Anaphora.

(29)   Eucharistic Prayer III.

(30)   Solemnity of the Body and Blood of Christ, Second Vespers, Antiphon to the Magnificat.

(31)   *Missale Romanum,* Embolism following the Lord's Prayer.

(32)   *Ad Ephesios*, 20: PG 5, 661.

(33)   Cf. Second Vatican Ecumenical Council, Pastoral Constitution on the Church in the Modern World *Gaudium et Spes*, 39.

(34)   "Do you wish to honor the Body of Christ? Do not ignore Him when He is naked. Do not pay Bim homage in the temple clad in silk, only then to neglect Him outside where He is cold and ill-clad. He who said: 'This is My Body' is the same who said: 'You saw Me hungry and you gave Me no food', and 'Whatever you did to the least of My brothers you did also to Me' ... What good is it if the Eucharistic table is overloaded with golden chalices when your brother is dying of hunger. Start by satisfying his hunger and then with what is left you may adorn the altar as well": Saint John Chrysostom, In *Evangelium S. Matthaei, hom.* 50:3-4: PG 58, 508-509; cf. John Paul II, Encyclical Letter *Sollicitudo Rei Socialis* (30 December 1987), 31: AAS 80 (1988), 553-556.

(35)   Dogmatic Constitution *Lumen Gentium*, 3.

(36)   11 Ibid.

(37)   Second Vatican Ecumenical Council, Decree on the Missionary Activity of the Church *Ad Gentes*, 5.

(38)   "Moses took the blood and threw it upon the people, and said: 'Behold the blood of the Covenant which the Lord has made with you in accordance with all these words'" (*Ex* 24:8).

(39)   Cf. Second Vatican Ecumenical Council, Dogmatic Constitution on the Church *Lumen Gentium,* 1.

(40)   1Cf. ibid., 9.

(41)   Cf. Second Vatican Ecumenical Council, Decree on the Life and Ministry of Priests *Presbyterorum Ordinis*, 5. The same Decree, in No. 6, says: "No Christian community can be built up which does not grow from and hinge on the celebration of the most holy Eucharist".

(42)   *In Epistolam I ad Corinthios Homiliae*, 24, 2: PG 61, 200; Cf. *Didache*, IX, 4: F.X. Funk, I, 22; Saint Cyprian, Ep. LXIII, 13: PL 4, 384.

(43)   PO 26, 206.

(44)   Second Vatican Ecumenical Council, Dogmatic Constitution on the Church *Lumen Gentium,* 1.

(45)   Cf. Ecumenical Council of Trent, Session XIII, *Decretum de ss. Eucharistia,* Canon 4: DS 1654.

(46)   Cf. *Rituale Romanum: De sacra communione et de cultu mysterii Eucharistici extra Missam*, 36 (No. 80).

(47)   Cf. ibid., 38-39 (Nos. 86-90).

(48)   John Paul II, Apostolic Letter *Novo Millennio Ineunte* (6 January 2001), 32: AAS 93 (2001), 288.

(49) "In the course of the day the faithful should not omit visiting the Blessed Sacrament, which in accordance with liturgical law must be reserved in churches with great reverence in a prominent place. Such visits are a sign of gratitude, an expression of love and an acknowledgment of the Lord's presence": Paul VI, Encyclical Letter *Mysterium Fidei* (3 September 1965): AAS 57 (1965), 771.

(50) *Visite al SS. Sacramento e a Maria Santissima, Introduction: Opere Ascetiche*, Avellino, 2000, 295.

(51) No. 857.

(52) Ibid.

(53) Ibid.

(54) Cf. Congregation for the Doctrine of the Faith, Letter *Sacerdotium Ministeriale* (6 August 1983), III.2: AAS 75 (1983), 1005.

(55) Second Vatican Ecumenical Council, Dogmatic Constitution on the Church *Lumen Gentium*, 10.

(56) Ibid.

(57) Cf. *Institutio Generalis: Editio typica tertia*, No. 147.

(58) Cf. Dogmatic Constitution on the Church *Lumen Gentium*, 10 and 28; Decree on the Ministry and Life of Priests *Presbyterorum Ordinis*, 2.

(59) "The minister of the altar acts in the person of Christ inasmuch as he is head, making an offering in the name of all the members": Pius XII, Encyclical Letter *Mediator Dei* (20 November 1947): AAS 39 (1947), 556; cf. Pius X, Apostolic Exhortation *Haerent Animo* (4 August 1908): Acta Pii X, IV, 16; Pius XI, Encyclical Letter *Ad Catholici Sacerdotii* (20 December 1935): AAS 28 (1936), 20.

(60) Apostolic Letter *Dominicae Cenae* (24 February 1980), 8: AAS 72 (1980), 128-129.

(61) Congregation for the Doctrine of the Faith, Letter *Sacerdotium Ministeriale* (6 August 1983), III.4: AAS 75 (1983), 1006; cf. Fourth Lateran Ecumenical Council, Chapter 1, Constitution on the Catholic Faith *Firmiter Credimus*: DS 802.

(62) Second Vatican Ecumenical Council, Decree on Ecumenism *Unitatis Redintegratio*, 22.

(63) Apostolic Letter *Dominicae Cenae* (24 February 1980), 2: AAS 72 (1980), 115.

(64) Decree on the Life and Ministry of Priests *Presbyterorum Ordinis*, 14.

(65) Ibid., 13; cf. Code of Canon Law, Canon 904; Code of Canons of the Eastern Churches, Canon 378.

(66) Decree on the Ministry and Life of Priests *Presbyterorum Ordinis*, 6.

(67) Cf. Final Report, II.C.1: *L'Osservatore Romano*, 10 December 1985, 7.

(68) Second Vatican Ecumenical Council, Dogmatic Constitution on the Church *Lumen Gentium*, 26.

(69) Nicolas Cabasilas, Life in Christ, IV, 10: SCh 355, 270.

(70) *Camino de Perfección,* Chapter 35.

(71) Cf. Congregation for the Doctrine of the Faith, Letter to the Bishops of

the Catholic Church on Some Aspects of the Church Understood as Communion *Communionis Notio* (28 May 1992), 4: AAS 85 (1993), 839-840.

(72)   Cf. Second Vatican Ecumenical Council, Dogmatic Constitution on the Church Lumen Gentium, 14.

(73)   *Homiliae in Isaiam*,6, 3: PG 56, 139.

(74)   No. 1385; cf. Code of Canon Law, Canon 916; Code of Canons of the Eastern Churches, Canon 711.

(75)   Address to the Members of the Sacred Apostolic Penitentiary and the Penitentiaries of the Patriarchal Basilicas of Rome (30 January 1981): AAS 73 (1981), 203. Cf. Ecumenical Council of Trent, Sess. XIII, *Decretum de ss. Eucharistia*, Chapter 7 and Canon 11: DS 1647, 1661.

(76)   Canon 915; Code of Canons of the Eastern Churches, Canon 712.

(77)   Dogmatic Constitution on the Church *Lumen Gentium*, 14.

(78)   Saint Thomas Aquinas, *Summa Theologiae*, III, q. 73, a. 3c.

(79)   Congregation for the Doctrine of the Faith, Letter to the Bishops of the Catholic Church on Some Aspects of the Church Understood as Communion *Communionis Notio* (28 May 1992), 11: AAS 85 (1993), 844.

(80)   Cf. Second Vatican Ecumenical Council, Dogmatic Constitution on the Church *Lumen Gentium*, 23.

(81)   *Ad Smyrnaeos*, 8: PG 5, 713.

(82)   Second Vatican Ecumenical Council, Dogmatic Constitution on the Church *Lumen Gentium*, 23.

(83)   Congregation for the Doctrine of the Faith, Letter to the Bishops of the Catholic Church on Some Aspects of the Church Understood as Communion *Communionis Notio* (28 May 1992), 14: AAS 85 (1993), 847.

(84)   Sermo272: PL 38, 1247.

(85)   Ibid., 1248.

(86)   Cf. Nos. 31-51: AAS 90 (1998), 731-746.

(87)   Cf. ibid., Nos. 48-49: AAS 90 (1998), 744.

(88)   No. 36: AAS 93 (2001), 291-292.

(89)   Cf. Decree on Ecumenism *Unitatis Redintegratio*, 1.

(90)   Cf. Dogmatic Constitution on the Church *Lumen Gentium*, 11.

(91)   "Join all of us, who share the one bread and the one cup, to one another in the communion of the one Holy Spirit": Anaphora of the Liturgy of Saint Basil.

(92)   Cf. Code of Canon Law, Canon 908; Code of Canons of the Eastern Churches, Canon 702; Pontifical Council for the Promotion of Christian Unity, Ecumenical Directory, 25 March 1993, 122-125, 129-131: AAS 85 (1993), 1086-1089; Congregation for the Doctrine of the Faith, Letter *Ad Exsequendam*, 18 May 2001: AAS 93 (2001), 786.

(93)   "Divine law forbids any common worship which would damage the unity of the Church, or involve formal acceptance of falsehood or the danger of deviation in the faith, of scandal, or of indifferentism": Decree on the Eastern Catholic Churches *Orientalium Ecclesiarum,* 26.

(94)   No. 45: AAS 87 (1995), 948.

(95)   Decree on the Eastern Catholic Churches *Orientalium Ecclesiarum*, 27.
(96)   Cf. Code of Canon Law, Canon 844 §§ 3-4; Code of Canons of the Eastern Churches, Canon 671 §§ 3-4.
(97)   No. 46: AAS 87 (1995), 948.
(98)   Cf. Second Vatican Ecumenical Council, Decree on Ecumenism *Unitatis Redintegratio*, 22.
(99)   Code of Canon Law, Canon 844; Code of Canons of the Eastern Churches, Canon 671.
(100) Cf. AAS 91 (1999), 1155-1172.
(101) No. 22: AAS 92 (2000), 485.
(102) Cf. No. 21: AAS 95 (2003), 20.
(103) No. 29: AAS 93 (2001), 285.
(104) Saint Thomas Aquinas, *Summa Theologiae*, III, q. 83, a. 4c.

The Pope's Catechesis on the Eucharist During the Jubilee Year 2000

1. The Eucharistic Celebration of Divine Glory

GENERAL AUDIENCE
Wednesday 27 September 2000

1. According to the program outlined in Tertio millennio adveniente, this Jubilee Year, the solemn celebration of the Incarnation, must be an "intensely Eucharistic" year (Tertio millennio adveniente, n.55). Therefore, after having fixed our gaze on the glory of the Trinity that shines on man's path, let us begin a catechesis on that great yet humble celebration of divine glory which is the Eucharist. Great, because it is the principal expression of Christ's presence among us "always, to the close of the age" (Mt 28:20); humble, because it is entrusted to the simple, everyday signs of bread and wine, the ordinary food and drink of Jesus' land and of many other regions. In this everyday nourishment, the Eucharist introduces not only the promise but the "pledge" of future glory: "futurae gloriae nobis pignus datur" (St Thomas Aquinas, Officium de festo Corporis Christi). To grasp the greatness of the Eucharistic mystery, let us reflect today on the theme of divine glory and of God's action in the world, now manifested in the great events of salvation, now hidden beneath humble signs which only the eye of faith can perceive.

2. In the Old Testament, the Hebrew word kabód indicates the revelation of divine glory and of God's presence in history and creation. The Lord's glory shines on the summit of Sinai, the place of revelation of the divine Word (cf. Ex 24:16). It is present in the

sacred tent and in the liturgy of the People of God on pilgrimage in the desert (cf. Lev 9:23). It dominates in the temple, the place - as the Psalmist says - "where your glory dwells" (Ps 26:8). It surrounds all the chosen people as if in a mantle of light (cf. Is 60:1): Paul himself knows that "they are Israelites, and to them belong the sonship, the glory, the covenants..." (Rom 9:4).

3. This divine glory, which is manifest to Israel in a special way, is present in the whole world, as the prophet Isaiah heard the seraphim proclaim at the moment of receiving his vocation: "Holy, Holy, Holy is the Lord of hosts; the whole earth is full of His glory" (Is 6:3). Indeed, the Lord reveals His glory to all peoples, as we read in the Psalter: "all the peoples behold His glory" (Ps 97:6). Therefore, the enkindling of the light of glory is universal, so that all humanity can discover the divine presence in the cosmos.

It is especially in Christ that this revelation is fulfilled, because He "reflects the glory" of God (Heb 1:3). It is also fulfilled through His works, as the Evangelist John testifies with regard to the sign of Cana: Christ "manifested His glory; and His disciples believed in Him" (Jn 2:11). He also radiates divine glory through His word which is divine: "I have given them Your word", Jesus says to the Father; "the glory which You have given Me, I have given to them" (Jn 17:14,22). More radically, Christ manifests divine glory through His humanity, assumed in the Incarnation: "The Word became flesh and dwelt among us, full of grace and truth; we have beheld His glory, glory as of the only Son from the Father" (Jn 1:14).

4. The earthly revelation of the divine glory reaches its apex in Easter which, especially in the Johannine and Pauline writings, is treated as a glorification of Christ at the right hand of the Father (cf. Jn 12:23;13:31;17:1; Phil 2:6-11; Col 3:1; 1 Tim 3:16). Now the paschal mystery, in which "God is perfectly glorified" (Sacrosanctum Concilium, n. 7), is perpetuated in the Eucharistic sacrifice, the memorial of the death and resurrection entrusted by Christ to the Church, His beloved Spouse (cf. ibid., n. 47). With the command "Do this in remembrance of Me" (Lk 22:19), Jesus assures the presence of His paschal glory in all the Eucharistic

celebrations which will mark the flow of human history. "Through the Holy Eucharist the event of Christ's Pasch expands throughout the Church.... By communion with the Body and Blood of Christ, the faithful grow in that mysterious divinization which by the Holy Spirit makes them dwell in the Son as children of the Father" (John Paul II and Moran Mar Ignatius Zakka I Iwas, Joint Declaration, 23 June 1984, n. 6: Enchiridion Vaticanum, 9, 842).

5. It is certain that today we have the loftiest celebration of divine glory in the liturgy: "Since Christ's death on the Cross and His resurrection constitute the content of the daily life of the Church and the pledge of His eternal Passover, the liturgy has as its first task to lead us untiringly back to the Easter pilgrimage initiated by Christ, in which we accept death in order to enter into life" (Apostolic Letter Vicesimus quintus annus, n. 6). Now, this task is exercised first of all through the Eucharistic celebration which makes present Christ's Passover and communicates its dynamism to the faithful. Thus Christian worship is the most vivid expression of the encounter between divine glory and the glorification which rises from human lips and hearts. The way we "glorify the Lord generously" (Sir 35: 8) must correspond to "the glory of the Lord that filled the tabernacle" (cf. Ex 40:34).

6. As St Paul recalls, we must also glorify God in our bodies, that is, in our whole existence, because our bodies are temples of the Spirit who is within us (cf. 1 Cor 6:19,20). In this light one can also speak of a cosmic celebration of divine glory. The world created, "so often disfigured by selfishness and greed", has in itself a "Eucharistic potential": it is "destined to be assumed in the Eucharist of the Lord, in His Passover, present in the sacrifice of the altar" (Orientale lumen, n. 11). The choral praise of creation will then respond, in harmonious counterpoint, to the breath of the glory of the Lord which is "above the heavens" (Ps 113:4) and shines down on the world in order that "in everything God may be glorified through Jesus Christ. To Him belong glory and dominion for ever and ever. Amen!" (1 Pt 4:11).

2. Eucharist: Memorial of God's Mighty Works

GENERAL AUDIENCE
Wednesday 4 October 2000

1. Prominent among the many aspects of the Eucharist is that of "memorial", which is related to a biblical theme of primary importance. We read, for example, in the Book of Exodus: "God remembered his covenant with Abraham and Jacob" (Ex 2:24). In Deuteronomy, however, it says: "You shall remember what the Lord your God did ..." (7:18). In the Bible, the remembrance of God and the remembrance of man are interwoven and form a fundamental element in the life of God's People. However, this is not the mere commemoration of a past that is no more, but a zikkarôn, that is, a "memorial". It "is not merely the recollection of past events, but the proclamation of the mighty works wrought by God for men. In the liturgical celebration of these events, they become in a certain way present and real" (CCC, n. 1363). The memorial recalls the bond of an unfailing covenant: "The Lord has been mindful of us; He will bless us" (Ps 115:12). Biblical faith thus implies the effective recollection of the works of salvation. They are professed in the "Great Hallel", Psalm 136, which - after proclaiming creation and the salvation offered to Israel in the Exodus - concludes: "It is He who remembered us in our low estate, for His steadfast love endures for ever; and rescued us ...; He who gives food to all flesh, for His steadfast love endures for ever" (Ps 136:23-25). We find similar words in the Gospel on the lips of Mary and Zechariah: "He has helped His servant Israel, in remembrance of His mercy ... to remember His holy covenant" (Lk 1:54,72).

2. In the Old Testament, the "memorial" par excellence of God's works in history was the Passover liturgy of the Exodus: every time the people of Israel celebrated the Passover, God effectively offered them the gifts of freedom and salvation. In the Passover rite, therefore, the two remembrances converge: the divine and the human, that is, saving grace and grateful faith. "This day shall be for you a memorial day, and you shall keep it as a feast to the Lord....

It shall be to you as a sign on your hand and as a memorial between your eyes, that the law of the Lord may be in your mouth; for with a strong hand the Lord has brought you out of Egypt" (Ex 12:14;13:9). By virtue of this event, as a Jewish philosopher said, Israel will always be "a community based on remembrance" (M. Buber).

3. The interweaving of God's remembrance with that of man is also at the center of the Eucharist, which is the "memorial" par excellence of the Christian Passover. For "anamnesis", i.e., the act of remembrance, is the heart of the celebration: Christ's sacrifice, a unique event done ephapax, that is, "once for all" (Heb 7:27;9:12,26;10:12), extends its saving presence in the time and space of human history. This is expressed in the last command, which Luke and Paul record in the account of the Last Supper: "This is My Body which is for you. Do this in remembrance of Me.... This cup is the new covenant in My Blood. Do this, as often as you drink it, in remembrance of Me" (1 Cor 11:24-25; cf. Lk 22:19). The past of the "Body given for us" on the Cross is presented alive today and, as Paul declares, opens onto the future of the final redemption: "As often as you eat this bread and drink the cup, you proclaim the Lord's death until He comes" (1 Cor 11:26). The Eucharist is thus the memorial of Christ's death, but it is also the presence of His sacrifice and the anticipation of His glorious coming. It is the sacrament of the risen Lord's continual saving closeness in history.

Thus we can understand Paul's exhortation to Timothy: "Remember Jesus Christ, risen from the dead, descended from David" (2 Tim 2:8). In the Eucharist this remembrance is alive and at work in a special way.

4. The Evangelist John explains to us the deep meaning of the "memorial" of Christ's words and events. When Jesus cleanses the temple of the merchants and announces that it will be destroyed and rebuilt in three days, John remarks: "When He was raised from the dead, His disciples remembered that He had said this; and they believed the scripture and the word which Jesus had spoken"

(Jn 2:22). This memorial which produces and nourishes faith is the work of the Holy Spirit, "whom the Father will send in the name" of Christ: "He will teach you all things, and bring to your remembrance all that I have said to you" (Jn 14:26). Thus there is an effective remembrance: one that is interior and leads to an understanding of the Word of God, and a sacramental one, which takes place in the Eucharist. These are the two realities of salvation which Luke combined in his splendid account of the disciples of Emmaus, structured around the explanation of the Scriptures and the "breaking of the bread" (cf. Lk 24:13-55).

5. "To remember" is therefore "to bring back to the heart" in memory and affection, but it is also to celebrate a presence. "Only the Eucharist, the true memorial of Christ's paschal mystery, is capable of keeping alive in us the memory of His love. It is, therefore, the secret of the vigilance of the Church: it would be too easy for her, otherwise, without the divine efficacy of this continual and very sweet incentive, without the penetrating power of this look of her Bridegroom fixed on her, to fall into forgetfulness, insensitivity and unfaithfulness" (Apostolic Letter Patres Ecclesiae, III: Ench. Vat., 7, 33). This call to vigilance opens our Eucharistic liturgies to the full coming of the Lord, to the appearance of the heavenly Jerusalem. In the Eucharist Christians nurture the hope of the definitive encounter with their Lord.

3. Eucharist: A Perfect Sacrifice of Praise

GENERAL AUDIENCE
Wednesday 11 October 2000

Eucharist is perfect sacrifice of praise

1. "Through Him, with Him, in Him, in the unity of the Holy Spirit, all glory and honor is Yours, almighty Father". This proclamation of Trinitarian praise seals the prayer of the Canon at every Eucharistic celebration. The Eucharist, in fact, is the perfect "sacrifice of praise", the highest glorification that rises from earth to heaven, "the source and summit of the Christian life in which (the children

of God) offer the divine victim (to the Father) and themselves along with it" (Lumen Gentium, n. 11). In the New Testament, the Letter to the Hebrews teaches us that the Christian liturgy is offered by "a high priest, holy, blameless, unstained, separated from sinners, exalted above the heavens", who achieved a unique sacrifice once and for all by "offering up Himself" (cf. Heb 7:26-27). "Through Him then", the Letter says, "let us continually offer up a sacrifice of praise to God" (Heb 3:15). Today let us briefly recall the two themes of sacrifice and praise which are found in the Eucharist, sacrificium laudis.

2. First of all the sacrifice of Christ becomes present in the Eucharist. Jesus is really present under the appearances of bread and wine, as He Himself assures us: "This is My Body ... this is My Blood" (Mt 26:26,28). But the Christ present in the Eucharist is the Christ now glorified, who on Good Friday offered Himself on the cross. This is what is emphasized by the words He spoke over the cup of wine: "This is My Blood of the covenant, which is poured out for many" (Mt 26:28; cf. Mk 14:24; Lk 22:20). If these words are examined in the light of their biblical import, two significant references appear. The first consists of the expression "blood poured out" which, as the biblical language attests (cf. Gen 9:6), is synonymous with violent death. The second is found in the precise statement "for many", regarding those for whom this blood is poured out. The allusion here takes us back to a fundamental text for the Christian interpretation of Scripture, the fourth song of Isaiah: by his sacrifice, the Servant of the Lord "poured out his soul to death", and "bore the sin of many" (Is 53:12; cf. Heb 9:28; 1 Pt 2:24).

3. The same sacrificial and redemptive dimension of the Eucharist is expressed by Jesus' words over the bread at the Last Supper, as they are traditionally related by Luke and Paul: "This is My Body which is given for you" (Lk 22:19; cf. 1 Cor 11:24). Here too there is a reference to the sacrificial self-giving of the Servant of the Lord according to the passage from Isaiah already mentioned (53:12): "He poured out his soul to death...; he bore the sin of many, and made intercession for the transgressors". "The Eucharist is

above all else a sacrifice. It is the sacrifice of the Redemption and also the sacrifice of the New Covenant, as we believe and as the Eastern Churches clearly profess: 'Today's sacrifice', the Greek Church stated centuries ago [at the Synod of Constantinople against Sotericus in 1156-57], 'is like that offered once by the Only-begotten Incarnate Word; it is offered by Him (now as then), since it is one and the same sacrifice'" (Apostolic Letter Dominicae Cenae, n. 9).

4. The Eucharist, as the sacrifice of the New Covenant, is the development and fulfillment of the covenant celebrated on Sinai when Moses poured half the blood of the sacrificial victims on the altar, the symbol of God, and half on the assembly of the children of Israel (cf. Ex 24:5-8). This "blood of the covenant" closely united God and man in a bond of solidarity. With the Eucharist the intimacy becomes total; the embrace between God and man reaches its apex. This is the fulfillment of that "new covenant" which Jeremiah had foretold (cf. 31: 31-34): a pact in the spirit and in the heart, which the Letter to the Hebrews extols precisely by taking the prophet's oracle and linking it to Christ's one definitive sacrifice (cf. Heb 10:14-17).

5. At this point we can illustrate the other affirmation: the Eucharist is a sacrifice of praise. Essentially oriented to full communion between God and man, "the Eucharistic sacrifice is the source and summit of the whole of the Church's worship and of the Christian life. The faithful participate more fully in this sacrament of thanksgiving, propitiation, petition and praise, not only when they wholeheartedly offer the sacred victim, and in it themselves, to the Father with the priest, but also when they receive this same victim sacramentally" (Sacred Congregation of Rites, Eucharisticum Mysterium, n. 3e).

As the term itself originally says in Greek, Eucharist means "thanksgiving"; in it the Son of God unites redeemed humanity to Himself in a hymn of thanksgiving and praise. Let us remember that the Hebrew word todah, translated "praise", also means "thanksgiving". The sacrifice of praise was a sacrifice of thanksgiving (cf.

Ps 50 [49]: 14, 23). At the Last Supper, in order to institute the Eucharist, Jesus gave thanks to His Father (cf. Mt 26:26-27 and parallels); this is the origin of the name of this sacrament. 6. "In the Eucharistic sacrifice the whole of creation loved by God is presented to the Father through the death and the Resurrection of Christ" (CCC, n. 1359). Uniting herself to Christ's sacrifice, the Church in the Eucharist voices the praise of all creation. The commitment of every believer to offer his existence, his "body", as Paul says, as a "living sacrifice, holy and acceptable to God" (Rom 12:1), in full communion with Christ, must correspond to this. In this way, one life unites God and man, Christ crucified and raised for us all and the disciple who is called to give himself entirely to Him.

The French poet Paul Claudel sings of this intimate communion of love, putting these words on Christ's lips: "Come with Me, where I Am, in yourself, / and I will give you the key to life. / Where I Am, there eternally / is the secret of your origin ... / .... Where are your hands that are not Mine? And your feet that are not nailed to the same cross? I died and rose once and for all! We are very close to one another / .... How can you separate yourself from Me / without breaking My heart?" (La Messe là-bas).

4. Eucharist: Banquet of Communion With God

GENERAL AUDIENCE
Wednesday 18 October 2000

Eucharist, banquet of communion with God

1. "We have become Christ. For if He is the head we are the members; He and we together are the whole man" (Augustine, Tractatus in Joh., 21,8). St Augustine's bold words extol the intimate communion that is created between God and man in the mystery of the Church, a communion which, on our journey through history, finds its supreme sign in the Eucharist. The commands, "Take, eat ... Drink of it ..." (Mt 26:26-27), which Jesus gives His disciples in that room on the upper floor of a house in Jerusalem on the last evening of His earthly life (cf. Mk 14:15), are rich in meaning. The

universal symbolic value of the banquet offered in bread and wine (cf. Is 25:6) already suggests communion and intimacy. Other more explicit elements extol the Eucharist as a banquet of friendship and covenant with God. For, as the Catechism of the Catholic Church recalls, it is "at the same time, and inseparably, the sacrificial memorial in which the sacrifice of the cross is perpetuated, and the sacred banquet of communion with the Lord's Body and Blood" (CCC, n. 1382).

2. Just as in the Old Testament the movable shrine in the desert was called the "tent of meeting", that is, of the encounter between God and His people and of brethren in faith among themselves, the ancient Christian tradition called the Eucharistic celebration the "synaxis", i.e., "meeting". In it "the Church's inner nature is revealed, a community of those summoned to the synaxis to celebrate the gift of the One who is offering and offered: participating in the Holy Mysteries, they become 'kinsmen' of Christ, anticipating the experience of divinization in the now inseparable bond linking divinity and humanity in Christ" (Orientale lumen, n. 10).

If we wish to reflect more deeply on the genuine meaning of this mystery of communion between God and the faithful, we must return to Jesus' words at the Last Supper. They refer to the biblical category of "covenant", recalled precisely through the connection between Christ's Blood and the sacrificial blood poured out on Sinai: "This is My Blood of the covenant" (Mk 14:24). Moses had said: "Behold the blood of the covenant" (Ex 24:8). The covenant on Sinai which united Israel to the Lord with a bond of blood, foretold the new covenant which would give rise - to use an expression of the Greek Fathers - to a kinship as it were betweeen Christ and the faithful (cf. Cyril of Alexandria, In Johannis Evangelium, XI; John Chrysostom, In Matthaeum hom., LXXXII, 5).

3. It is especially in the Johannine and Pauline theologies that the believer's communion with Christ in the Eucharist is extolled. In His discourse at the synagogue in Capernaum Jesus says explicitly: "I am the living bread which came down from heaven; if anyone eats of this bread, he will live for ever" (Jn 6:51). The entire

text of this discourse is meant to emphasize the vital communion which is established in faith between Christ, the Bread of life, and whoever eats it. In particular, we find the Greek verb menein, "to abide, to dwell", which is typically used in the Fourth Gospel to indicate the mystical intimacy between Christ and the disciple: "He who eats My Flesh and drinks My Blood abides in Me, and I in him" (Jn 6:56; cf. 15:4-9).

4. Then the Greek word for "communion", koinonia, is used in the reflection of the First Letter to the Corinthians, where Paul speaks of the sacrificial banquets of idolatry, calling them the "table of demons" (10:21), while expressing a valid principle for all sacrifices: "Those who eat the sacrifices are partners in the altar" (10:18). The Apostle applies this principle in a clear and positive way to the Eucharist: "The cup of blessing which we bless, is it not a participation (koinonia) in the Blood of Christ? The bread which we break, is it not a participation (koinonia) in the Body of Christ?... We all partake of the one bread" (10:16-17). "Sharing in the Eucharist, the sacrament of the New Covenant, is the culmination of our assimilation to Christ, the source of "eternal life', the source and power of that complete gift of self" (Veritatis splendor, n. 21).

5. This communion with Christ thus produces an inner transformation of the believer. St Cyril of Alexandria effectively describes this event, showing its resonance in life and in history: "Christ forms us in His image so that the features of His divine nature will shine in us through sanctification, justice and a good life in conformity with virtue. The beauty of this image shines in us who are in Christ, when we show ourselves to be good people through our deeds" (Tractatus ad Tiberium Diaconum sociosque, II, Responsiones ad Tiberium Diaconum sociosque, in In divi Johannis Evangelium, vol. III, Brussels 1965, p. 590). "By sharing in the sacrifice of the Cross, the Christian partakes of Christ's self-giving love and is equipped and committed to live this same charity in all his thoughts and deeds. In the moral life the Christian's royal service is also made evident and effective" (Veritatis splendor, n. 107). This royal service is rooted in Baptism and blossoms in Eucharistic

communion. The way of holiness, love and truth is therefore the revelation to the world of our intimacy with God, expressed in the Eucharistic banquet.

Let us express our desire for the divine life offered in Christ in the warm tones of a great theologian of the Armenian Church, Gregory of Narek (10th century): "It is not for His gifts, but for the Giver that I always long. It is not glory to which I aspire, but the Glorified One whom I desire to embrace.... It is not rest that I seek, but the face of the One who gives rest that I implore. It is not for the wedding feast, but for desire of the Bridegroom that I languish" (XII Prayer).

5. Eucharist: "A Taste of Eternity in Time"

GENERAL AUDIENCE
Wednesday 25 October 2000

The Eucharist, "a taste of eternity in time'
1. "In the earthly liturgy we share, by way of foretaste, in that heavenly liturgy" (Sacrosanctum Concilium, n. 8; cf. Gaudium et Spes, n. 38). These limpid and essential words of the Second Vatican Council show us a fundamental dimension of the Eucharist: its being a "futurae gloriae pignus", a pledge of future glory, as beautifully expressed by the Christian tradition (cf. Sacrosanctum Concilium, n. 47). "This sacrament", St Thomas Aquinas notes, "does not admit us at once to glory, but bestows on us the power of coming into glory and, therefore, is called viaticum" (Summa Theol., III, 79, 2, ad 1). The communion with Christ that we enjoy now while we are pilgrims and wayfarers on the paths of history anticipates that supreme encounter on the day when "we shall be like Him, for we shall see Him as He is" (1 Jn 3:2). Elijah, who collapsed helplessly under a broom tree during his journey in the wilderness and was strengthened by a mysterious bread until he reached the summit of his encounter with God (cf. 1 Kgs 19:1-8), is a traditional symbol of the journey of the faithful, who find strength in the Eucharistic bread to advance towards the shining goal of the holy city.

2. This is also the profound meaning of the manna prepared by God on the steppes of Sinai, the "food of angels", providing every pleasure and suited to every taste, a manifestation of God's sweetness toward His children (cf. Wis 16:20-21). Christ Himself will be the one to shed light on this spiritual significance of the Exodus event. He is the one who enables us to taste in the Eucharist the twofold savior of the pilgrim's food and the food of messianic fullness in eternity (cf. Is 25:6).

To borrow a phrase from the Jewish Sabbath liturgy, the Eucharist is a "taste of eternity in time" (A. J. Heschel). Just as Christ lived in the flesh while remaining in the glory of God's Son, so the Eucharist is a divine and transcendent presence, a communion with the eternal, a sign that "the earthly city and the heavenly city penetrate one another" (Gaudium et Spes, n. 40). The Eucharist, memorial of Christ's Passover, is by its nature the bearer of the eternal and the infinite in human history.

3. This aspect, which opens the Eucharist to God's future while leaving it anchored to present reality, is illustrated by the words Jesus spoke over the cup of wine at the Last Supper (cf. Lk 22:20; 1 Cor 11:25). With these same words Mark and Matthew evoke the covenant in the blood of the sacrifices on Sinai (cf. Mk 14:24; Mt 26:28; Ex 24:8). Luke and Paul, however, reveal the fulfillment of the "new covenant" foretold by the prophet Jeremiah: "Behold, the days are coming, says the Lord, when I will make a new covenant with the house of Israel and the house of Judah, not like the covenant I made with their fathers" (Jer 31:31-32). Jesus, in fact, declares: "This cup is the new covenant in My Blood". In biblical language "new" usually means progress, final perfection.

It is also Luke and Paul who stress that the Eucharist is an anticipation of the horizon of glorious light belonging to the kingdom of God. Before the Last Supper Jesus said: "I have earnestly desired to eat this Passover with you before I suffer; for I tell you I shall not eat it until it is fulfilled in the kingdom of God. And He took a cup, and when He had given thanks He said, "Take this, and divide it among yourselves; for I tell you that from now on I shall not drink of the fruit of the vine until the kingdom of God comes'"

(Lk 22:15-18). And Paul explicitly recalls that the Eucharistic supper looks forward to the Lord's final coming: "As often as you eat this bread and drink the cup, you proclaim the Lord's death until He comes" (1 Cor 11:26).

4. The fourth Evangelist, John, extols this orientation of the Eucharist towards the fullness of God's kingdom in the well-known discourse on the "bread of life" that Jesus gave at the synagogue in Capernaum. The symbol he used as a biblical reference was, as was already mentioned, the manna offered by God to Israel on its pilgrimage through the desert. Regarding the Eucharist, Jesus solemnly declared: "If anyone eats of this bread, he will live for ever.... He who eats My Flesh and drinks My Blood has eternal life, and I will raise him up at the last day.... This is the bread which came down from heaven, not such as the fathers ate and died; he who eats this bread will live for ever" (Jn 6:51,54,58). In the language of the fourth Gospel, "eternal life" is the divine life itself which transcends the bounds of time. Being a communion with Christ, the Eucharist is thus a sharing in God's life, which is eternal and conquers death. Jesus therefore says: "This is the will of Him who sent Me, that I should lose nothing of all that He has given Me, but raise it up at the last day. For this is the will of My Father, that everyone who sees the Son and believes in Him should have eternal life; and I will raise him up at the last day" (Jn 6:39-40).

5. In this light - as a Russian theologian, Sergei Bulgakov, evocatively said - "the liturgy is heaven on earth". For this reason, in the Apostolic Letter Dies Domini I quoted the words of Paul VI, urging Christians not to neglect "this encounter, this banquet which Christ prepares for us in His love.

May our sharing in it be most worthy and joyful! It is Christ, crucified and glorified, who comes among His disciples, to lead them all together into the newness of His Resurrection. This is the climax, here below, of the covenant of love between God and His people: the sign and source of Christian joy, a stage on the way to the eternal feast" (n. 58; cf. Gaudete in Domino, conclusion).

6. Eucharist: A Sacrament of the Church's Unity

GENERAL AUDIENCE
Wednesday 8 November 2000

Eucharist is sacrament of the Church's unity

1. "O sacrament of devotion! O sign of unity! O bond of charity!". St Augustine's exclamation in his commentary on the Gospel of John (In Joannis Evangelium, 26, 13) captures the theme and sums up the words that Paul addressed to the Corinthians and we have just heard: "Because there is one bread, we who are many are one body, for we all partake of the one bread" (1 Cor 10:17). The Eucharist is the sacrament and source of the Church's unity. This has been stressed since the beginnings of the Christian tradition and is based on the sign of the bread and wine. This is how it is stated in the Didache, a writing composed at the dawn of Christianity: "Just as this broken bread was first scattered on the mountains and, after being harvested, became one reality, so may your Church be gathered from the ends of the earth into your kingdom" (9, 1).

2. St Cyprian, Bishop of Carthage, echoed these words in the third century, saying: "The sacrifices of the Lord themselves highlight the unanimity of Christians strengthened by solid, indivisible charity. For when the Lord calls the bread formed of the union of many grains His Body, and when He calls the wine pressed from many clusters of grapes and poured together His Blood, in the same way He indicates our flock formed of a multitude united together" (Ep. ad Magnum, 6).

This Eucharistic symbolism of the Church's unity returns frequently in the Fathers and Scholastic theologians. "The Council of Trent summarized the doctrine, teaching that our Savior left the Eucharist to his Church "as a symbol of her unity and of the charity with which He wanted all Christians to be closely united with one another'; and for this reason it is "a symbol of that one body of which he is the head'" (Paul VI, Mysterium fidei: Ench. Vat., 2, 424; cf. Council of Trent, Decr. de SS. Eucharistia, introd. and ch. 2). The Catechism of the Catholic Church sums it up very effectively: "Those who receive the Eucharist are united more closely to Christ. Through it Christ unites them to all the faithful in one body - the Church" (CCC, 1396).

3. This traditional doctrine is deeply rooted in Scripture. Paul develops it in the passage already cited from the First Letter to the Corinthians, taking koinonia as the basic theme, that is, the communion which is established between the faithful and Christ in the Eucharist. "The cup of blessing which we bless, is it not a participation (koinonia) in the Blood of Christ? The bread which we break, is it not a participation (koinonia) in the Body of Christ?" (10:16). This communion is more precisely described in John's Gospel as an extraordinary relationship of "mutual interiority": "He in me and I in Him". Jesus, in fact, says at the synagogue in Capernaum: "He who eats My Flesh and drinks My Blood abides in Me, and I in him" (Jn 6:56).

It is a theme that will also be underscored in the discourses at the Last Supper with the symbol of the vine: the branch is verdant and fruitful only if it is grafted on to the vine stem, from which it receives sap and support (Jn 15: 1-7). Otherwise it is just a withered branch to be thrown into the fire: aut vitis aut ignis, "either the vine or the fire", St Augustine succinctly comments (In Johannis Evangelium, 81, 3). Here we see a unity, a communion, which is realized between the faithful and Christ present in the Eucharist, on the basis of the principle that Paul expresses this way: "Those who eat the sacrifices are partners in the altar" (1 Cor 10:18).

4. Because this type of "vertical" communion-koinonia makes us one with the divine mystery, it produces at the same time a communion-koinonia we could call "horizontal", or ecclesial, fraternal, capable of uniting all who partake of the same table in a bond of love. "We who are many are one body", Paul reminds us, "for we all partake of the one bread" (1 Cor 10:17). The discourse on the Eucharist anticipates the great ecclesial reflection which the Apostle will develop in chapter 12 of the same Letter, when he will speak of the Body of Christ in its unity and multiplicity. The well-known description of the Jerusalem Church offered by Luke in the

Acts of the Apostles also outlines this fraternal unity or koinonia, connecting it with the breaking of bread, that is, the Eucharistic celebration (cf. Acts 2:42). This communion is realized in concrete historical reality:

"They devoted themselves to the Apostles' teaching and fellowship (koinonia), to the breaking of bread and the prayers.... All who believed were together and had all things in common" (Acts 2:42-44). 5. The profound meaning of the Eucharist is thus denied when it is celebrated without taking into account the demands of charity and communion. Paul is severe with the Corinthians because when they meet together, "it is not the Lord's supper that you eat" (1 Cor 11:20), as a result of their divisions, injustices and selfishness. In this case, the Eucharist is no longer agape, that is, the expression and source of love. And whoever partakes of it unworthily, without making it bear fruit in fraternal charity, "eats and drinks judgment upon himself" (1 Cor 11:29). "In fact Christian life is expressed in the fulfilling of the greatest commandment, that is to say in the love of God and neighbor, and this love finds its source in the Blessed Sacrament, which is commonly called the sacrament of love" (Dominicae cenae, n. 5). The Eucharist recalls, makes present and brings about this charity.

Let us then answer the appeal of the Bishop and martyr Ignatius, who exhorted the faithful of Philadelphia in Asia Minor to unity: "One is the Flesh of our Lord Jesus Christ, one is the chalice in the unity of His Blood, one is the altar, just as one is the Bishop" (Ep. ad Philadelphenses, 4). And let us pray with the liturgy to God the Father: "Grant that we, who are nourished by His Body and Blood, may be filled with His Holy Spirit, and become one body, one spirit in Christ" (Eucharistic Prayer III).

7. Word, Eucharist and Divided Christians

GENERAL AUDIENCE
Wednesday 15 November 2000

Word, Eucharist and divided Christians

1. In the program for this Jubilee Year we could not omit the dimension of ecumenical and interreligious dialogue, as I had indicated earlier in Tertio millennio adveniente (cf. nn. 53 and 55). The Trinitarian and Eucharistic line we developed in our previous catecheses now prompts us to reflect on this aspect, examining first of all the problem of restoring unity among Christians. We do so in the light of the Gospel account of the disciples of Emmaus (cf. Lk 24:13-35), observing the way that the two disciples who were leaving the community were spurred to reverse their direction to rediscover it.

2. The two disciples turned their backs on the place where Jesus had been crucified, because the event had been a cruel disappointment to them. For this very reason they were leaving the other disciples and returning, as it were, to individualism. "They were talking with each other about all these things that had happened" (Lk 24:14), without understanding their meaning. They did not realize that Jesus had died "to gather into one the children of God who are scattered" (Jn 11:52).

They only saw the tremendously negative aspect of the cross, which had destroyed their hopes: "We had hoped that He was the one to redeem Israel" (Lk 24:21). The risen Jesus comes up and walks beside them, "but their eyes were kept from recognizing Him" (Lk 24:16), because from the spiritual standpoint they were in the darkest shadows. Then Jesus, with wonderful patience, endeavors to bring them back into the light of faith through a long biblical catechesis: "Beginning with Moses and all the prophets, He interpreted to them in all the Scriptures the things concerning Himself" (Lk 24:27). Their hearts began to burn (cf. Lk 24:32). They begged their mysterious companion to stay with them. "When He was at table with them, He took the bread and blessed and broke it, and gave it to them. And their eyes were opened and they recognized Him; and He vanished out of their sight" (Lk 24:30-31). Thanks to the clear explanation of the Scriptures, they emerged from the gloom of incomprehension into the light of faith and were able to recognize the risen Christ "in the breaking of the bread" (Lk 24:35).

The effect of this profound change was an impulse to set out again without delay and return to Jerusalem to join "the Eleven gathered together and those who were with them" (Lk 24:33). The journey of faith had made fraternal union possible.

3. The connection between the interpretation of the word of God and the Eucharist also appears in other parts of the New Testament. In his gospel, John links this word with Eucharist, when in the discourse at Capernaum he presents Jesus recalling the gift of manna in the wilderness and reinterpreting it in a Eucharistic key (cf. Jn 6:32-58). In the Church of Jerusalem, diligent listening to the didache, that is, the apostolic teaching based on the word of God, preceded participation in the "breaking of bread" (Acts 2:42).

At Troas, when the Christians gathered around Paul "to break bread", Luke relates that the gathering began with a long speech by the Apostle (cf. Acts 20:7), which was certainly intended to nurture their faith, hope and charity. It is clear from all this that unity in faith is the necessary condition for common participation in the Eucharist.

With the Liturgy of the Word and the Eucharist - as the Second Vatican Council reminds us, citing St John Chrysostom (In Joh. hom., 46) - "the faithful, united with their Bishops, have access to God the Father through the Son, the Word made flesh who suffered and was glorified, in the outpouring of the Holy Spirit. And so, made "sharers of the divine nature' (2 Pt 1:4), they enter into communion with the most holy Trinity. Hence, through the celebration of the Eucharist of the Lord in each of these Churches, the Church of God is built up and grows in stature, and through concelebration their communion with one another is made manifest" (Unitatis redintegratio, n. 15). This link with the mystery of divine unity thus produces a bond of communion and love among those seated at the one table of the Word and of the Eucharist. The one table is a sign and expression of unity.

"Thus Eucharistic communion is inseparably linked to full ecclesial communion and its visible expression" (Directory for the Application of the Principles and Norms of Ecumenism, 1993, n. 129).

4. In this light we can understand how the doctrinal divisions between the disciples of Christ grouped in the various Churches and Ecclesial Communities limit full sacramental sharing. Baptism, however, is the deep root of a basic unity that links Christians despite their divisions. Therefore, although Christians who are still separated are excluded from participation in the same Eucharist, it is possible to introduce into the Eucharistic celebration, in specific cases provided for in the Ecumenical Directory, certain signs of participation that express the unity already existing and move in the direction of the full communion of the Churches around the table of the Word and of the Lord's Body and Blood. Consequently, "on exceptional occasions and for a just cause, the bishop of the diocese may permit a member of another Church or Ecclesial Community to take on the task of reader" during a Eucharistic celebration in the Catholic Church (n. 133).

Likewise, "whenever necessity requires or a genuine spiritual advantage suggests, and provided that the danger of error or indifferentism is avoided", a certain reciprocity regarding the sacraments of Penance, the Eucharist and the Anointing of the Sick is lawful between Catholics and Eastern Christians (cf. nn. 123-131). 5. Nevertheless, the tree of unity must grow to its full extent, as Christ implored in His great prayer in the Upper Room, proclaimed here at the start of our meeting (cf. Jn 17:20-26; Unitatis Redintegratio, n. 22). The limits to intercommunion at the table of the Word and of the Eucharist must become a call to purification, to dialogue and to the ecumenical progress of the Churches.

They are limits that make us feel all the more strongly, in the Eucharistic celebration itself, the weight of our divisions and contradictions. The Eucharist is thus a challenge and a summons in the very heart of the Church to remind us of Christ's intense, final desire: "that they may be one" (Jn 17:11,21).

The Church must not be a body of divided and suffering members, but a strong, living organism that moves onward, sustained by the divine bread as prefigured in Elijah's journey (cf. 1 Kgs 19:1-8), to the summit of the definitive encounter with God. There, at last, will be the vision of Revelation: "And I saw the holy city, the new Jerusalem, coming down out of heaven from God, prepared as a bride adorned for her husband" (Rev 21:2).

8. Love Binds All Christian Communities

GENERAL AUDIENCE
Wednesday 22 November 2000

Love binds all Christian communities

1. Faith, hope and love are like three stars that rise in the sky of our spiritual life to guide us to God. They are the theological virtues par excellence: they put us in communion with God and lead us to Him. They form a triptych, whose apex is found in love, the agape excellently praised by Paul in a hymn of the First Letter to the Corinthians. It is sealed by the following declaration: "So faith, hope, love abide, these three; but the greatest of these is love" (13:13).

To the extent that they enliven the disciples of Christ, the three theological virtues spur them on towards unity, in accordance with Paul's words which we heard at the beginning: "One body ..., one hope ..., one Lord ..., one faith ..., one God and Father" (Eph 4:4-6). Continuing to reflect on the ecumenical perspective discussed in the preceding catechesis, today we want to look more closely at the role of the theological virtues in the journey that leads to full communion with God, with the Trinity and with others.

2. In the passage quoted from the Letter to the Ephesians, the Apostle primarily extols the unity of faith. This unity has its source in the word of God, which all the Churches and Ecclesial Communities consider a light for the steps of their journey in history (cf. Ps 119:105). Together the Churches and the Ecclesial Communities profess their faith in "one Lord", Jesus Christ true God and true

man, and in "one God and Father of us all" (Eph 4:5-6).

This fundamental unity, together with that constituted by the one Baptism, is clearly apparent in the many documents of the ecumenical dialogue, even when there remain reasons for reservation on this or that point. Thus we read, for example, in a document of the World Council of Churches: "Christians believe that the 'only true God' who made Himself known to Israel was revealed in 'Him whom you have sent', Jesus Christ (Jn 17:3); that in Christ, God reconciled the world to Himself (2 Cor 5:19) and that, through His Holy Spirit, God brings new and eternal life to all those who, through Christ, entrust themselves to Him" (WCC, Confessare una sola fede, 1992, n. 6).

The Churches and Ecclesial Communities all have a common reference-point in the ancient Creeds and the definitions of the early Ecumenical Councils. However, certain doctrinal divergences remain to be overcome, so that the journey towards unity of faith can reach the fullness indicated by the promise of Christ: "They will heed My voice. So there shall be one flock, one shepherd" (Jn 10:16).

3. Paul, in the text of the Letter to the Ephesians that we have taken as the emblem of our meeting, also speaks about one hope to which we have been called (cf. 4:4). It is a hope that is expressed in our common commitment, through prayer and an actively consistent life, to the coming of the kingdom of God. Within this vast horizon, the ecumenical movement has been oriented towards basic goals that are interrelated as objectives of one hope: the unity of the Church, the evangelization of the world, liberation and peace in the human community. The ecumenical journey has also taken advantage of the dialogue with the earthly and humanistic hopes of our time, even with the hidden hope, apparently defeated, of the "hopeless". In the face of these many expressions of hope in our time, Christians, despite the tensions among them and the trial of division, have been impelled to discover and bear witness to "a common reason for hope" (WCC, Faith and Order Commission, Sharing in One Hope, Bangalore, 1978), recognizing in Christ the indestructible foundation.

A French poet wrote: "To hope is difficult ... to despair is easy and is the great temptation" (Charles Péguy, Le porche du mystère de la deuxième vertu, ed. Pléiade, p. 538). But for us Christians, St Peter's exhortation always to account for the hope that is in us remains ever valid (cf. 1 Pt 3:15).

4. At the apex of the three theological virtues is love, which Paul compares in a way to a golden knot that holds all the Christian communities in perfect harmony: "And above all these put on love, which binds everything together in perfect harmony" (Col 3:14). Christ, in the solemn prayer for the disciples' unity, reveals the profound theological basis: "That the love with which you, [O Father], have loved me may be in them, and I in them" (Jn 17:26). It is this very love, accepted and made to grow, which composes the Church in a single body, as Paul again indicates: "Speaking the truth in love, we are to grow up in every way into Him who is the head, into Christ, from whom the whole body, joined and knit together by every joint with which it is supplied, when each part is working properly, makes bodily growth and upbuilds itself in love" (Eph 4:15-16).

5. The ecclesial goal of love, and at the same time its inexhaustible source, is the Eucharist, communion with the Body and Blood of the Lord, an anticipation of perfect intimacy with God.

Unfortunately, as I recalled in our previous catechesis, in the relations between divided Christians, "due to disagreements in matters of faith, it is not yet possible to celebrate together the same Eucharistic Liturgy. And yet we do have a burning desire to join in celebrating the one Eucharist of the Lord, and this desire itself is already a common prayer of praise, a single supplication. Together we speak to the Father and increasingly we do so "with one heart"" (Ut Unum Sint, n. 45). The Council has reminded us that "this holy objective - the reconciliation of all Christians in the unity of the one and only Church of Christ - transcends human powers and gifts". We must therefore put all our hope "in the prayer of Christ for the Church, in the love of the Father for us, and in the power of the Holy Spirit" (Unitatis Redintegratio, n. 24).

9. Interreligious Dialogue

GENERAL AUDIENCE
Wednesday 29 November 2000

God the Father offers salvation to all nations
1. The great fresco just offered to us in the Book of Revelation is filled not only with the people of Israel, symbolically represented by the 12 tribes, but also with that great multitude of nations from every land and culture, all clothed in the white robes of a luminous and blessed eternity. I begin with this evocative image to call attention to inter-religious dialogue, a subject that has become very timely in our day.

All the just of the earth sing their praise to God, having reached the goal of glory after traveling the steep and tiring road of earthly life. They have passed "through the great tribulation" and have been purified by the Blood of the Lamb, "poured out for many for the forgiveness of sins" (Mt 26:28). They all share, then, in the same source of salvation which God has poured out upon humanity. For "God sent the Son into the world not to condemn the world, but that the world might be saved through Him" (Jn 3:17).

2. Salvation is offered to all nations, as was already shown by the covenant with Noah (cf. Gen 9:8-17), testifying to the universality of God's manifestation and the human response in faith (cf. CCC, n. 58). In Abraham, then, "all the families of the earth shall bless themselves" (Gen 12:3). They are on the way to the holy city in order to enjoy that peace which will change the face of the world, when swords are beaten into ploughshares and spears into pruning hooks (cf. Is 2:2-5).

It is moving to read these words in Isaiah: "The Egyptians will worship [the Lord] with the Assyrians ... whom the Lord of hosts has blessed, saying, "Blessed be Egypt My people, and Assyria the work of My hands, and Israel My heritage'" (Is 19:23,25). "The princes of the peoples", the Psalmist sings, "are gathered together with the people of the God of Abraham. For God's are the guardians of the earth; He is supreme" (Ps 47:10). Indeed, the prophet

Malachi hears as it were a sigh of adoration and praise rising to God from the whole breadth of humanity: "From the rising of the sun to its setting My name is great among the nations, says the Lord of hosts" (Mal 1:11). The same prophet, in fact, wonders: "Have we not all one Father? Has not one God created us?" (Mal 2:10).

3. A certain form of faith thus begins when God is called upon, even if His face is "unknown" (cf. Acts 17:23). All humanity seeks authentic adoration of God and the fraternal communion of men and women under the influence of the "Spirit of truth operating outside the visible confines of the Mystical Body" of Christ (Redemptor hominis, n. 6).

In this connection St Irenaeus recalls that God established four covenants with humanity: in Adam, Noah, Moses and Christ (cf. Adversus Haereses, 3, 11, 8). The first three aim in spirit at the fullness of Christ and mark the stages of God's dialogue with His creatures, an encounter of disclosure and love, of enlightenment and grace, which the Son gathers in unity, seals in truth and brings to perfection.

4. In this light the faith of all peoples blossoms in hope. It is not yet enlightened by the fullness of revelation, which relates it to the divine promises and makes it a "theological" virtue. The sacred books of other religions, however, are open to hope to the extent that they disclose a horizon of divine communion, point to a goal of purification and salvation for history, encourage the search for truth and defend the values of life, holiness, justice, peace and freedom. With this profound striving, which withstands even human contradictions, religious experience opens people to the divine gift of charity and its demands.

The inter-religious dialogue which the Second Vatican Council encouraged should be seen in this perspective (cf. Nostra aetate, n. 2). This dialogue is expressed in the common efforts of all believers for justice, solidarity and peace. It is also expressed in cultural relations, which sow the seed of idealism and transcendence on the often arid ground of politics, the economy and social welfare. It has a significant role in the religious dialogue in which Christians bear complete witness to their faith in Christ, the only Savior of the world. By this same faith they realize that the way to the fullness of truth (cf. Jn 16:13) calls for humble listening, in order to discover and appreciate every ray of light, which is always the fruit of Christ's Spirit, from wherever it comes.

5. "The Church's mission is to foster "the kingdom of our Lord and His Christ' (Rev 11:15), at whose service she is placed. Part of her role consists in recognizing that the inchoate reality of this kingdom can be found also beyond the confines of the Church, for example, in the hearts of the followers of other religious traditions, insofar as they live evangelical values and are open to the action of the Spirit" (Pontifical Council for Interreligious Dialogue and Congregation for the Evangelization of Peoples, Dialogue and Proclamation, n. 35).

This applies especially - as the Second Vatican Council told us in the Declaration Nostra Aetate - to the monotheistic religions of Judaism and Islam. In this spirit I expressed the following wish in the Bull of Indiction of the Jubilee Year: "May the Jubilee serve to advance mutual dialogue until the day when all of us together - Jews, Christians and Moslems - will exchange the greeting of peace in Jerusalem" (Incarnationis mysterium, n. 2). I thank the Lord for having given me, during my recent pilgrimage to the Holy Places, the joy of this greeting, the promise of relations marked by an ever deeper and more universal peace.

APOSTOLIC LETTER
DIES DOMINI

OF THE HOLY FATHER JOHN PAUL II
TO THE BISHOPS, CLERGY AND FAITHFUL
OF THE CATHOLIC CHURCH
ON KEEPING THE LORD'S DAY HOLY

My esteemed Brothers in the Episcopate and the Priesthood, Dear Brothers and Sisters!

1. The Lord's Day — as Sunday was called from Apostolic times[1] — has always been accorded special attention in the history of the Church because of its close connection with the very core of the Christian mystery. In fact, in the weekly reckoning of time Sunday recalls the day of Christ's Resurrection. It is Easter which returns week by week, celebrating Christ's victory over sin and death, the fulfillment in Him of the first creation and the dawn of "the new creation" (cf. *2 Cor* 5:17). It is the day which recalls in grateful adoration the world's first day and looks forward in active hope to "the last day", when Christ will come in glory (cf. *Acts* 1:11; *1 Th* 4:13-17) and all things will be made new (cf. *Rev* 21:5).

Rightly, then, the Psalmist's cry is applied to Sunday: "This is the day which the Lord has made: let us rejoice and be glad in it" (*Ps* 118:24). This invitation to joy, which the Easter liturgy makes its own, reflects the astonishment which came over the women who, having seen the crucifixion of Christ, found the tomb empty when they went there "very early on the first day after the Sabbath" (*Mk* 16:2). It is an invitation to relive in some way the experience of the two disciples of Emmaus, who felt their hearts "burn within them" as the Risen One walked with them on the road, explaining the Scriptures and revealing Himself in "the breaking of the bread" (cf. *Lk* 24:32,35). And it echoes the joy — at first uncertain and then overwhelming — which the Apostles experienced on the evening of that same day, when they were visited by the Risen Jesus and received the gift of His peace and of His Spirit (cf. *Jn* 20:19-23).

2. The Resurrection of Jesus is the fundamental event upon which Christian faith rests (cf. *1 Cor* 15:14). It is an astonishing reality, fully grasped in the light of faith, yet historically attested to by those who were privileged to see the Risen Lord. It is a wondrous event which is not only absolutely unique in human history, but which lies at the very heart of the mystery of time. In fact, "all time belongs to [Christ] and all the ages", as the evocative liturgy of the Easter Vigil recalls in preparing the Paschal Candle. Therefore, in commemorating the day of Christ's Resurrection not just once a year but every Sunday, the Church seeks to indicate to every generation the true fulcrum of history, to which the mystery of the world's origin and its final destiny leads.

It is right, therefore, to claim, in the words of a fourth century homily, that "the Lord's Day" is "the lord of days".[2] Those who have received the grace of faith in the Risen Lord cannot fail to grasp the significance of this day of the week with the same deep emotion which led Saint Jerome to say: "Sunday is the day of the Resurrection, it is the day of Christians, it is our day".[3] For Christians, Sunday is "the fundamental feastday",[4] established not only to mark the succession of time but to reveal time's deeper meaning.

3. The fundamental importance of Sunday has been recognized through two thousand years of history and was emphatically restated by the Second Vatican Council: "Every seven days, the Church celebrates the Easter mystery. This is a tradition going back to the Apostles, taking its origin from the actual day of Christ's Resurrection — a day thus appropriately designated 'the Lord's Day' ."[5] Paul VI emphasized this importance once more when he approved the new General Roman Calendar and the Universal Norms which regulate the ordering of the Liturgical Year.[6] The coming of the Third Millennium, which calls believers to reflect upon the course of history in the light of Christ, also invites them to rediscover with new intensity the meaning of Sunday: its "mystery", its celebration, its significance for Christian and human life.

I note with pleasure that in the years since the Council this important theme has prompted not only many interventions by you, dear Brother Bishops, as teachers of the faith, but also different pastoral strategies which — with the support of your clergy — you have developed either individually or jointly. On the threshold of the Great Jubilee of the Year 2000, it has been my wish to offer you this Apostolic Letter in order to support your pastoral efforts in this vital area. But at the same time I wish to turn to all of you, Christ's faithful, as though I were spiritually present in all the communities in which you gather with your Pastors each Sunday to celebrate the Eucharist and "the Lord's Day". Many of the insights and intuitions which prompt this Apostolic Letter have grown from my episcopal service in Krakow and, since the time when I assumed the ministry of Bishop of Rome and Successor of Peter, in the visits to the Roman parishes which I have made regularly on the Sundays of the different seasons of the Liturgical Year. I see this Letter as continuing the lively exchange which I am always happy to have with the faithful, as I reflect with you on the meaning of Sunday and underline the reasons for living Sunday as truly "the Lord's Day", also in the changing circumstances of our own times.

4. Until quite recently, it was easier in traditionally Christian countries to keep Sunday holy because it was an almost universal practice and because, even in the organization of civil society, Sunday rest was considered a fixed part of the work schedule. Today, however, even in those countries which give legal sanction to the festive character of Sunday, changes in socioeconomic conditions have often led to profound modifications of social behavior and hence of the character of Sunday. The custom of the "weekend" has become more widespread, a weekly period of respite, spent perhaps far from home and often involving participation in cultural, political or sporting activities which are usually held on free days. This social and cultural phenomenon is by no means without its positive aspects if, while respecting true values, it can contribute to people's development and to the advancement of the life of society as a whole. All of this responds not only to the need for rest, but also to the need for celebration which is inherent in our humanity.

Unfortunately, when Sunday loses its fundamental meaning

and becomes merely part of a "weekend", it can happen that people stay locked within a horizon so limited that they can no longer see "the heavens".[7] Hence, though ready to celebrate, they are really incapable of doing so.

The disciples of Christ, however, are asked to avoid any confusion between the celebration of Sunday, which should truly be a way of keeping the Lord's Day holy, and the "weekend", understood as a time of simple rest and relaxation. This will require a genuine spiritual maturity, which will enable Christians to "be what they are", in full accordance with the gift of faith, always ready to give an account of the hope which is in them (cf. *1 Pt* 3:15). In this way, they will be led to a deeper understanding of Sunday, with the result that, even in difficult situations, they will be able to live it in complete docility to the Holy Spirit.

5. From this perspective, the situation appears somewhat mixed. On the one hand, there is the example of some young Churches, which show how fervently Sunday can be celebrated, whether in urban areas or in widely scattered villages. By contrast, in other parts of the world, because of the sociological pressures already noted, and perhaps because the motivation of faith is weak, the percentage of those attending the Sunday liturgy is strikingly low. In the minds of many of the faithful, not only the sense of the centrality of the Eucharist but even the sense of the duty to give thanks to the Lord and to pray to Him with others in the community of the Church, seems to be diminishing.

It is also true that both in mission countries and in countries evangelized long ago the lack of priests is such that the celebration of the Sunday Eucharist cannot always be guaranteed in every community.

6. Given this array of new situations and the questions which they prompt, it seems more necessary than ever to recover the deep doctrinal foundations underlying the Church's precept, so that the abiding value of Sunday in the Christian life will be clear to all the faithful. In doing this, we follow in the footsteps of the age-old tradition of the Church, powerfully restated by the Second Vatican

Council in its teaching that on Sunday "Christian believers should come together, in order to commemorate the suffering, Resurrection and glory of the Lord Jesus, by hearing God's Word and sharing the Eucharist, and to give thanks to God who has given them new birth to a living hope through the Resurrection of Jesus Christ from the dead (cf. *1 Pt* 1:3)".[8]

7. The duty to keep Sunday holy, especially by sharing in the Eucharist and by relaxing in a spirit of Christian joy and fraternity, is easily understood if we consider the many different aspects of this day upon which the present Letter will focus our attention.

Sunday is a day which is at the very heart of the Christian life. From the beginning of my Pontificate, I have not ceased to repeat: "Do not be afraid! Open, open wide the doors to Christ!".[9] In the same way, today I would strongly urge everyone to rediscover Sunday: Do not be afraid to give your time to Christ! Yes, let us open our time to Christ, that He may cast light upon it and give it direction. He is the One who knows the secret of time and the secret of eternity, and He gives us "His day" as an ever new gift of His love. The rediscovery of this day is a grace which we must implore, not only so that we may live the demands of faith to the full, but also so that we may respond concretely to the deepest human yearnings. Time given to Christ is never time lost, but is rather time gained, so that our relationships and indeed our whole life may become more profoundly human.

CHAPTER I

DIES DOMINI

The Celebration of the Creator's Work

"Through Him all things were made" (Jn 1:3)

8. For the Christian, Sunday is above all an Easter celebration, wholly illumined by the glory of the Risen Christ. It is the festival of the "new creation". Yet, when understood in depth, this aspect is inseparable from what the first pages of Scripture tell us of the plan of God in the creation of the world. It is true that the Word was made flesh in "the fullness of time" (*Gal* 4:4); but it is also true that, in virtue of the mystery of His identity as the eternal Son of the Father, He is the origin and end of the universe. As John writes in the Prologue of his Gospel: "Through Him all things were made, and without Him was made nothing that was made" (1:3). Paul, too, stresses this in writing to the Colossians: "In Him all things were created, in heaven and on earth, visible and invisible .... All things were created through Him and for Him" (1:16). This active presence of the Son in the creative work of God is revealed fully in the Paschal Mystery, in which Christ, rising as "the first fruits of those who had fallen asleep" (*1 Cor* 15:20), established the new creation and began the process which He Himself will bring to completion when He returns in glory to "deliver the kingdom to God the Father ..., so that God may be everything to everyone" (*1 Cor* 15:24,28).

Already at the dawn of creation, therefore, the plan of God implied Christ's "cosmic mission". This Christocentric perspective, embracing the whole arc of time, filled God's well-pleased gaze when, ceasing from all His work, He "blessed the seventh day and made it holy" (Gn 2:3). According to the Priestly writer of the first biblical creation story, then was born the "Sabbath", so characteristic of the first Covenant, and which in some ways foretells the sacred day of the new and final Covenant. The theme of "God's rest" (cf. Gn 2:2) and the rest which He offered to the people of the Exodus when they entered the Promised Land (cf. *Ex* 33:14; *Deut*

3:20; 12:9; *Jos* 21:44; *Ps* 95:11) is re-read in the New Testament in the light of the definitive "Sabbath rest" (*Heb* 4:9) into which Christ Himself has entered by His Resurrection. The People of God are called to enter into this same rest by persevering in Christ's example of filial obedience (cf. *Heb* 4:3-16). In order to grasp fully the meaning of Sunday, therefore, we must re-read the great story of creation and deepen our understanding of the theology of the "Sabbath".

"In the beginning, God created the heavens and the earth" (Gen 1:1)

9. The poetic style of the Genesis story conveys well the awe which people feel before the immensity of creation and the resulting sense of adoration of the One who brought all things into being from nothing. It is a story of intense religious significance, a hymn to the Creator of the universe, pointing to Him as the only Lord in the face of recurring temptations to divinize the world itself. At the same time, it is a hymn to the goodness of creation, all fashioned by the mighty and merciful hand of God.

"God saw that it was good" (*Gen* 1:10,12, etc.). Punctuating the story as it does, this refrain sheds a positive light upon every element of the universe and reveals the secret for a proper understanding of it and for its eventual regeneration: the world is good insofar as it remains tied to its origin and, after being disfigured by sin, it is again made good when, with the help of grace, it returns to the One who made it. It is clear that this process directly concerns not inanimate objects and animals but human beings, who have been endowed with the incomparable gift and risk of freedom. Immediately after the creation stories, the Bible highlights the dramatic contrast between the grandeur of man, created in the image and likeness of God, and the fall of man, which unleashes on the world the darkness of sin and death (cf. *Gen* 3).

10. Coming as it does from the hand of God, the cosmos bears the imprint of His goodness. It is a beautiful world, rightly moving us to admiration and delight, but also calling for cultivation and

development. At the "completion" of God's work, the world is ready for human activity. "On the seventh day God finished His work which He had done, and He rested on the seventh day from all His work which He had done" (*Gen* 2:2). With this anthropomorphic image of God's "work", the Bible not only gives us a glimpse of the mysterious relationship between the Creator and the created world, but also casts light upon the task of human beings in relation to the cosmos.

The "work" of God is in some ways an example for man, called not only to inhabit the cosmos, but also to "build" it and thus become God's "co-worker". As I wrote in my Encyclical *Laborem Exercens*, the first chapters of Genesis constitute in a sense the first "gospel of work".[10] This is a truth which the Second Vatican Council also stressed: "Created in God's image, man was commissioned to subdue the earth and all it contains, to rule the world in justice and holiness, and, recognizing God as the creator of all things, to refer himself and the totality of things to God so that with everything subject to God, the divine name would be glorified in all the earth".[11]

The exhilarating advance of science, technology and culture in their various forms — an ever more rapid and today even overwhelming development — is the historical consequence of the mission by which God entrusts to man and woman the task and responsibility of filling the earth and subduing it by means of their work, in the observance of God's Law.

"Shabbat": the Creator's joyful rest

11. If the first page of the Book of Genesis presents God's "work" as an example for man, the same is true of God's "rest":"On the seventh day God finished His work which He had done" (*Gen* 2:2). Here too we find an anthropomorphism charged with a wealth of meaning.

It would be banal to interpret God's "rest" as a kind of divine "inactivity". By its nature, the creative act which founds the world is unceasing and God is always at work, as Jesus himself declares in speaking of the Sabbath precept: "My Father is working still, and I am working" (Jn 5:17). The divine rest of the seventh day does not allude to an inactive God, but emphasizes the fullness of what has been accomplished. It speaks, as it were, of God's lingering before the "very good" work (*Gen* 1:31) which His hand has wrought, in order to cast upon it a gaze full of joyous delight. This is a "contemplative" gaze which does not look to new accomplishments but enjoys the beauty of what has already been achieved. It is a gaze which God casts upon all things, but in a special way upon man, the crown of creation. It is a gaze which already discloses something of the nuptial shape of the relationship which God wants to establish with the creature made in His own image, by calling that creature to enter a pact of love. This is what God will gradually accomplish, in offering salvation to all humanity through the saving covenant made with Israel and fulfilled in Christ. It will be the Word Incarnate, through the eschatological gift of the Holy Spirit and the configuration of the Church as His Body and Bride, who will extend to all humanity the offer of mercy and the call of the Father's love.

12. In the Creator's plan, there is both a distinction and a close link between the order of creation and the order of salvation. This is emphasized in the Old Testament, when it links the "*shabbat*" commandment not only with God's mysterious "rest" after the days of creation (cf. *Ex* 20:8-11), but also with the salvation which He offers to Israel in the liberation from the slavery of Egypt (cf. *Deut* 5:12-15). The God who rests on the seventh day, rejoicing in His creation, is the same God who reveals His glory in liberating His children from Pharaoh's oppression. Adopting an image dear to the Prophets, one could say that in both cases God reveals Himself as the bridegroom before the bride (cf. *Hos* 2:16-24; *Jer* 2:2; *Is* 54:4-8).

As certain elements of the same Jewish tradition suggest,[12] to reach the heart of the "*shabbat*", of God's "rest", we need to recognize in both the Old and the New Testament the nuptial intensity which marks the relationship between God and His people. Hosea, for instance, puts it thus in this marvelous passage: "I will make for you a covenant on that day with the beasts of the field, the birds of the air, and the creeping things of the ground; and I will abolish the bow, the sword, and war from the land; and I will make you lie down in safety. And I will betroth you to Me for ever; I will betroth you to Me in righteousness and in justice, in steadfast love and in mercy. I will betroth you to Me in faithfulness; and you shall know the Lord" (2:18-20).

"God blessed the seventh day and made it holy" (Gen 2:3)
13. The Sabbath precept, which in the first Covenant prepares for the Sunday of the new and eternal Covenant, is therefore rooted in the depths of God's plan. This is why, unlike many other precepts, it is set not within the context of strictly cultic stipulations but within the Decalogue, the "ten words" which represent the very pillars of the moral life inscribed on the human heart. In setting this commandment within the context of the basic structure of ethics, Israel and then the Church declare that they consider it not just a matter of community religious discipline but a defining and indelible expression of our relationship with God, announced and expounded by biblical revelation. This is the perspective within which Christians need to rediscover this precept today. Although the precept may merge naturally with the human need for rest, it is faith alone which gives access to its deeper meaning and ensures that it will not become banal and trivialized.

14. In the first place, therefore, Sunday is the day of rest because it is the day "blessed" by God and "made holy" by Him, set apart from the other days to be, among all of them, "the Lord's Day".
    In order to grasp fully what the first of the biblical creation accounts means by keeping the Sabbath "holy", we need to consider the whole story, which shows clearly how every reality, without exception, must be referred back to God. Time and space belong to him. He is not the God of one day alone, but the God of all the days of humanity.
    Therefore, if God "sanctifies" the seventh day with a special blessing and makes it "His day" par excellence, this must be understood within the deep dynamic of the dialogue of the Covenant, indeed the dialogue of "marriage". This is the dialogue of love which knows no interruption, yet is never monotonous. In fact, it

employs the different registers of love, from the ordinary and indirect to those more intense, which the words of Scripture and the witness of so many mystics do not hesitate to describe in imagery drawn from the experience of married love.

15. All human life, and therefore all human time, must become praise of the Creator and thanksgiving to Him. But man's relationship with God also demands times of explicit prayer, in which the relationship becomes an intense dialogue, involving every dimension of the person. "The Lord's Day" is the day of this relationship par excellence when men and women raise their song to God and become the voice of all creation.

This is precisely why it is also the day of rest. Speaking vividly as it does of "renewal" and "detachment", the interruption of the often oppressive rhythm of work expresses the dependence of man and the cosmos upon God. Everything belongs to God! The Lord's Day returns again and again to declare this principle within the weekly reckoning of time. The "Sabbath" has therefore been interpreted evocatively as a determining element in the kind of "sacred architecture" of time which marks biblical revelation.[13] It recalls that the universe and history belong to God; and without a constant awareness of that truth, man cannot serve in the world as co-worker of the Creator.

To "keep holy" by "remembering"

16. The commandment of the Decalogue by which God decrees the Sabbath observance is formulated in the Book of Exodus in a distinctive way: "Remember the Sabbath day in order to keep it holy" (20:8). And the inspired text goes on to give the reason for this, recalling as it does the work of God: "For in six days the Lord made heaven and earth, the sea, and all that is in them, and rested on the seventh day; therefore the Lord blessed the Sabbath day and made it holy" (v. 11). Before decreeing that something be done, the commandment urges that something be remembered. It is a call to awaken remembrance of the grand and fundamental work of God which is creation, a remembrance which must inspire the entire religious life of man and then fill the day on which man is

called to rest.

Rest therefore acquires a sacred value: the faithful are called to rest not only as God rested, but to rest in the Lord, bringing the entire creation to Him, in praise and thanksgiving, intimate as a child and friendly as a spouse.

17. The connection between Sabbath rest and the theme of "remembering" God's wonders is found also in the Book of Deuteronomy (5:12-15), where the precept is grounded less in the work of creation than in the work of liberation accomplished by God in the Exodus: "You shall remember that you were a slave in the land of Egypt, and the Lord your God brought you out from there with mighty hand and outstretched arm; therefore the Lord your God commanded you to keep the Sabbath day" (*Deut* 5:15).

This formulation complements the one we have already seen; and taken together, the two reveal the meaning of "the Lord's Day" within a single theological vision which fuses creation and salvation. Therefore, the main point of the precept is not just any kind of interruption of work, but the celebration of the marvels which God has wrought. Insofar as this "remembrance" is alive, full of thanksgiving and of the praise of God, human rest on the Lord's Day takes on its full meaning. It is then that man enters the depths of God's "rest" and can experience a tremor of the Creator's joy when, after the creation, He saw that all He had made "was very good" (*Gen* 1:31).

From the Sabbath to Sunday

18. Because the Third Commandment depends upon the remembrance of God's saving works and because Christians saw the definitive time inaugurated by Christ as a new beginning, they made the first day after the Sabbath a festive day, for that was the day on which the Lord rose from the dead. The Paschal Mystery of Christ is the full revelation of the mystery of the world's origin, the climax of the history of salvation and the anticipation of the eschatological fulfillment of the world. What God accomplished in Creation and wrought for His People in the Exodus has found its fullest expression in Christ's Death and Resurrection, though its

definitive fulfillment will not come until the *Parousia*, when Christ returns in glory. In Him, the "spiritual" meaning of the Sabbath is fully realized, as Saint Gregory the Great declares: "For us, the true Sabbath is the person of our Redeemer, our Lord Jesus Christ".[14]

This is why the joy with which God, on humanity's first Sabbath, contemplates all that was created from nothing, is now expressed in the joy with which Christ, on Easter Sunday, appeared to His disciples, bringing the gift of peace and the gift of the Spirit (cf. *Jn* 20:19-23). It was in the Paschal Mystery that humanity, and with it the whole creation, "groaning in birth-pangs until now" (*Rom* 8:22), came to know its new "exodus" into the freedom of God's children who can cry out with Christ, "Abba, Father!" (*Rom* 8:15; *Gal* 4:6). In the light of this mystery, the meaning of the Old Testament precept concerning the Lord's Day is recovered, perfected and fully revealed in the glory which shines on the face of the Risen Christ (cf. *2 Cor* 4:6). We move from the "Sabbath" to the "first day after the Sabbath", from the seventh day to the first day: the *dies Domini becomes the dies Christi!*

CHAPTER II

DIES CHRISTI

The Day of the Risen Lord and of the Gift of the Holy Spirit

The weekly Easter

19. "We celebrate Sunday because of the venerable Resurrection of our Lord Jesus Christ, and we do so not only at Easter but also at each turning of the week": so wrote Pope Innocent I at the beginning of the fifth century,[15] testifying to an already well established practice which had evolved from the early years after the Lord's Resurrection. Saint Basil speaks of "holy Sunday, honored by the Lord's Resurrection, the first fruits of all the other days";[16] and Saint Augustine calls Sunday "a sacrament of Easter".[17]

The intimate bond between Sunday and the Resurrection of the Lord is strongly emphasized by all the Churches of East and West. In the tradition of the Eastern Churches in particular, every Sunday is the *anastàsimos hemèra,* the day of Resurrection,[18] and this is why it stands at the heart of all worship.

In the light of this constant and universal tradition, it is clear that, although the Lord's Day is rooted in the very work of creation and even more in the mystery of the biblical "rest" of God, it is nonetheless to the Resurrection of Christ that we must look in order to understand fully the Lord's Day. This is what the Christian Sunday does, leading the faithful each week to ponder and live the event of Easter, true source of the world's salvation.

20. According to the common witness of the Gospels, the Resurrection of Jesus Christ from the dead took place on "the first day after the Sabbath" (*Mk* 16:2,9; *Lk* 24:1; *Jn* 20:1). On the same day, the Risen Lord appeared to the two disciples of Emmaus (cf. *Lk* 24:13-35) and to the eleven Apostles gathered together (cf. *Lk* 24:36; *Jn* 20:19). A week later — as the Gospel of John recounts (cf. 20:26) — the disciples were gathered together once again, when Jesus appeared to them and made Himself known to Thomas by

showing him the signs of His Passion. The day of Pentecost — the first day of the eighth week after the Jewish Passover (cf. *Acts* 2:1), when the promise made by Jesus to the Apostles after the Resurrection was fulfilled by the outpouring of the Holy Spirit (cf. *Lk* 24:49; *Acts* 1:4-5) — also fell on a Sunday. This was the day of the first proclamation and the first baptisms: Peter announced to the assembled crowd that Christ was risen and "those who received his word were baptized" (*Acts* 2:41). This was the epiphany of the Church, revealed as the people into which are gathered in unity, beyond all their differences, the scattered children of God.

The first day of the week
21. It was for this reason that, from Apostolic times, "the first day after the Sabbath", the first day of the week, began to shape the rhythm of life for Christ's disciples (cf. *1 Cor* 16:2). "The first day after the Sabbath" was also the day upon which the faithful of Troas were gathered "for the breaking of bread", when Paul bade them farewell and miraculously restored the young Eutychus to life (cf. *Acts* 20:7-12). The Book of Revelation gives evidence of the practice of calling the first day of the week "the Lord's Day" (1:10). This would now be a characteristic distinguishing Christians from the world around them. As early as the beginning of the second century, it was noted by Pliny the Younger, governor of Bithynia, in his report on the Christian practice "of gathering together on a set day before sunrise and singing among themselves a hymn to Christ as to a god".[19] And when Christians spoke of the "Lord's Day", they did so giving to this term the full sense of the Easter proclamation: "Jesus Christ is Lord" (*Phil* 2:11; cf. *Acts* 2:36; *1 Cor* 12:3). Thus Christ was given the same title which the Septuagint used to translate what in the revelation of the Old Testament was the unutterable name of God: *YHWH*.

22. In those early Christian times, the weekly rhythm of days was generally not part of life in the regions where the Gospel spread, and the festive days of the Greek and Roman calendars did not coincide with the Christian Sunday. For Christians, therefore, it was very difficult to observe the Lord's Day on a set day each

week. This explains why the faithful had to gather before sunrise.[20] Yet fidelity to the weekly rhythm became the norm, since it was based upon the New Testament and was tied to Old Testament revelation. This is eagerly underscored by the Apologists and the Fathers of the Church in their writings and preaching where, in speaking of the Paschal Mystery, they use the same Scriptural texts which, according to the witness of Saint Luke (cf. 24:27, 44-47), the Risen Christ Himself would have explained to the disciples. In the light of these texts, the celebration of the day of the Resurrection acquired a doctrinal and symbolic value capable of expressing the entire Christian mystery in all its newness.

Growing distinction from the Sabbath

23. It was this newness which the catechesis of the first centuries stressed as it sought to show the prominence of Sunday relative to the Jewish Sabbath. It was on the Sabbath that the Jewish people had to gather in the synagogue and to rest in the way prescribed by the Law. The Apostles, and in particular Saint Paul, continued initially to attend the synagogue so that there they might proclaim Jesus Christ, commenting upon "the words of the prophets which are read every Sabbath" (*Acts* 13:27). Some communities observed the Sabbath while also celebrating Sunday. Soon, however, the two days began to be distinguished ever more clearly, in reaction chiefly to the insistence of those Christians whose origins in Judaism made them inclined to maintain the obligation of the old Law.

Saint Ignatius of Antioch writes: "If those who were living in the former state of things have come to a new hope, no longer observing the Sabbath but keeping the Lord's Day, the day on which our life has appeared through Him and His death ..., that mystery from which we have received our faith and in which we persevere in order to be judged disciples of Christ, our only Master, how could we then live without Him, given that the prophets too, as His disciples in the Spirit, awaited Him as master?".[21] Saint Augustine notes in turn: "Therefore the Lord too has placed His seal on His day, which is the third after the Passion. In the weekly cycle, however, it is the eighth day after the seventh, that is after the Sabbath, and the first day of the week".[22] The distinction of Sunday from the Jewish Sabbath grew ever stronger in the mind of the Church, even though there have been times in history when, because the obligation of Sunday rest was so emphasized, the Lord's Day tended to become more like the Sabbath. Moreover, there have always been groups within Christianity which observe both the Sabbath and Sunday as "two brother days".[23]

The day of the new creation
24. A comparison of the Christian Sunday with the Old Testament vision of the Sabbath prompted theological insights of great interest. In particular, there emerged the unique connection between the Resurrection and Creation. Christian thought spontaneously linked the Resurrection, which took place on "the first day of the week", with the first day of that cosmic week (cf. *Gen* 1:1 - 2:4) which shapes the creation story in the Book of Genesis: the day of the creation of light (cf. 1:3-5). This link invited an understanding of the Resurrection as the beginning of a new creation, the first fruits of which is the glorious Christ, "the first born of all creation" (*Col* 1:15) and "the first born from the dead" (Col 1:18).

25. In effect, Sunday is the day above all other days which summons Christians to remember the salvation which was given to them in baptism and which has made them new in Christ. "You were buried with Him in baptism, in which you were also raised with Him through faith in the working of God, who raised Him from the dead" (*Col* 2:12; cf. *Rom* 6:4-6). The liturgy underscores this baptismal dimension of Sunday, both in calling for the celebration of baptisms — as well as at the Easter Vigil — on the day of the week "when the Church commemorates the Lord's Resurrection",[24] and in suggesting as an appropriate penitential rite at the start of Mass the sprinkling of holy water, which recalls the moment of Baptism in which all Christian life is born.[25]

The eighth day: image of eternity
26. By contrast, the Sabbath's position as the seventh day of the week suggests for the Lord's Day a complementary symbolism, much loved by the Fathers. Sunday is not only the first day, it is

also "the eighth day", set within the sevenfold succession of days in a unique and transcendent position which evokes not only the beginning of time but also its end in "the age to come". Saint Basil explains that Sunday symbolizes that truly singular day which will follow the present time, the day without end which will know neither evening nor morning, the imperishable age which will never grow old; Sunday is the ceaseless foretelling of life without end which renews the hope of Christians and encourages them on their way.[26] Looking towards the last day, which fulfils completely the eschatological symbolism of the Sabbath, Saint Augustine concludes the Confessions describing the *Eschaton* as "the peace of quietness, the peace of the Sabbath, a peace with no evening".[27] In celebrating Sunday, both the "first" and the "eighth" day, the Christian is led towards the goal of eternal life.[28]

The day of Christ-Light
27. This Christocentric vision sheds light upon another symbolism which Christian reflection and pastoral practice ascribed to the Lord's Day. Wise pastoral intuition suggested to the Church the christianization of the notion of Sunday as "the day of the sun", which was the Roman name for the day and which is retained in some modern languages.[29] This was in order to draw the faithful away from the seduction of cults which worshipped the sun, and to direct the celebration of the day to Christ, humanity's true "sun". Writing to the pagans, Saint Justin uses the language of the time to note that Christians gather together "on the day named after the sun",[30] but for believers the expression had already assumed a new meaning which was unmistakably rooted in the Gospel.[31]

Christ is the light of the world (cf. *Jn* 9:5; also 1:4-5,9), and, in the weekly reckoning of time, the day commemorating His Resurrection is the enduring reflection of the epiphany of His glory. The theme of Sunday as the day illuminated by the triumph of the Risen Christ is also found in the Liturgy of the Hours[32] and is given special emphasis in the *Pannichida*, the vigil which in the Eastern liturgies prepares for Sunday. From generation to generation as she gathers on this day, the Church makes her own the wonderment of Zechariah as he looked upon Christ, seeing in Him the dawn which gives "light to those who sit in darkness and in the shadow of death" (*Lk* 1:78-79), and she echoes the joy of Simeon when he takes in his arms the divine Child who has come as the "light to enlighten the Gentiles" (*Lk* 2:32).

The Day of the Gift of the Spirit

28. Sunday, the day of light, could also be called the day of "fire", in reference to the Holy Spirit. The light of Christ is intimately linked to the "fire" of the Spirit, and the two images together reveal the meaning of the Christian Sunday.[33] When He appeared to the Apostles on the evening of Easter, Jesus breathed upon them and said: "Receive the Holy Spirit. If you forgive the sins of any, they are forgiven; if you retain the sins of any, they are retained" (*Jn* 20:22-23). The outpouring of the Spirit was the great gift of the Risen Lord to His disciples on Easter Sunday. It was again Sunday when, fifty days after the Resurrection, the Spirit descended in power, as "a mighty wind" and "fire" (*Acts* 2:2-3), upon the Apostles gathered with Mary. Pentecost is not only the founding event of the Church, but is also the mystery which for ever gives life to the Church.[34] Such an event has its own powerful liturgical moment in the annual celebration which concludes "the great Sunday",[35] but it also remains a part of the deep meaning of every Sunday, because of its intimate bond with the Paschal Mystery. The "weekly Easter" thus becomes, in a sense, the "weekly Pentecost", when Christians relive the Apostles' joyful encounter with the Risen Lord and receive the life-giving breath of His Spirit.

The Day of Faith

29. Given these different dimensions which set it apart, Sunday appears as the supreme day of faith. It is the day when, by the power of the Holy Spirit, who is the Church's living "memory" (cf. *Jn* 14:26), the first appearance of the Risen Lord becomes an event renewed in the "today" of each of Christ's disciples. Gathered in His presence in the Sunday assembly, believers sense themselves called like the Apostle Thomas: "Put your finger here, and see My hands. Put out your hand, and place it in My side. Doubt no longer, but believe" (*Jn* 20:27). Yes, Sunday is the day of faith. This is

stressed by the fact that the Sunday Eucharistic liturgy, like the liturgy of other solemnities, includes the Profession of Faith. Recited or sung, the Creed declares the baptismal and Paschal character of Sunday, making it the day on which in a special way the baptized renew their adherence to Christ and His Gospel in a rekindled awareness of their baptismal promises. Listening to the word and receiving the Body of the Lord, the baptized contemplate the Risen Jesus present in the "holy signs" and confess with the Apostle Thomas: "My Lord and my God!" (*Jn* 20:28).

An Indispensable Day!
30. It is clear then why, even in our own difficult times, the identity of this day must be protected and above all must be lived in all its depth. An Eastern writer of the beginning of the third century recounts that as early as then the faithful in every region were keeping Sunday holy on a regular basis.[36] What began as a spontaneous practice later became a juridically sanctioned norm. The Lord's Day has structured the history of the Church through two thousand years: how could we think that it will not continue to shape her future?

The pressures of today can make it harder to fulfill the Sunday obligation; and, with a mother's sensitivity, the Church looks to the circumstances of each of her children. In particular, she feels herself called to a new catechetical and pastoral commitment, in order to ensure that, in the normal course of life, none of her children is deprived of the rich outpouring of grace which the celebration of the Lord's Day brings. It was in this spirit that the Second Vatican Council, making a pronouncement on the possibility of reforming the Church calendar to match different civil calendars, declared that the Church "is prepared to accept only those arrangements which preserve a week of seven days with a Sunday".[37] Given its many meanings and aspects, and its link to the very foundations of the faith, the celebration of the Christian Sunday remains, on the threshold of the Third Millennium, an indispensable element of our Christian identity.

CHAPTER III

DIES ECCLESIAE

The Eucharistic Assembly: Heart of Sunday

The Presence of the Risen Lord

31. "I am with you always, to the end of the age" (*Mt* 28:20). This promise of Christ never ceases to resound in the Church as the fertile secret of her life and the wellspring of her hope. As the day of Resurrection, Sunday is not only the remembrance of a past event: it is a celebration of the living presence of the Risen Lord in the midst of His own people.

For this presence to be properly proclaimed and lived, it is not enough that the disciples of Christ pray individually and commemorate the death and Resurrection of Christ inwardly, in the secrecy of their hearts. Those who have received the grace of baptism are not saved as individuals alone, but as members of the Mystical Body, having become part of the People of God.[38] It is important therefore that they come together to express fully the very identity of the Church, the *ekklesia*, the assembly called together by the Risen Lord who offered His life "to reunite the scattered children of God" (*Jn* 11:52). They have become "one" in Christ (cf. Gal 3:28) through the gift of the Spirit. This unity becomes visible when Christians gather together: it is then that they come to know vividly and to testify to the world that they are the people redeemed, drawn "from every tribe and language and people and nation" (*Rev* 5:9). The assembly of Christ's disciples embodies from age to age the image of the first Christian community which Luke gives as an example in the Acts of the Apostles, when he recounts that the first baptized believers "devoted themselves to the apostles' teaching and fellowship, to the breaking of bread and the prayers" (2:42).

The Eucharistic Assembly

32. The Eucharist is not only a particularly intense expression of the reality of the Church's life, but also in a sense its

"fountain-head".[39] The Eucharist feeds and forms the Church: "Because there is one bread, we who are many are one body, for we all partake of the one bread" (*1 Cor* 10:17). Because of this vital link with the sacrament of the Body and Blood of the Lord, the mystery of the Church is savored, proclaimed, and lived supremely in the Eucharist.[40]

This ecclesial dimension intrinsic to the Eucharist is realized in every Eucharistic celebration. But it is expressed most especially on the day when the whole community comes together to commemorate the Lord's Resurrection. Significantly, the Catechism of the Catholic Church teaches that "the Sunday celebration of the Lord's Day and His Eucharist is at the heart of the Church's life".[41]

33. At Sunday Mass, Christians relive with particular intensity the experience of the Apostles on the evening of Easter when the Risen Lord appeared to them as they were gathered together (cf. *Jn* 20:19). In a sense, the People of God of all times were present in that small nucleus of disciples, the first fruits of the Church. Through their testimony, every generation of believers hears the greeting of Christ, rich with the messianic gift of peace, won by His Blood and offered with His Spirit: "Peace be with you!" Christ's return among them "a week later" (*Jn* 20:26) can be seen as a radical prefiguring of the Christian community's practice of coming together every seven days, on "the Lord's Day" or Sunday, in order to profess faith in His Resurrection and to receive the blessing which He had promised: "Blessed are those who have not seen and yet believe" (*Jn* 20:29). This close connection between the appearance of the Risen Lord and the Eucharist is suggested in the Gospel of Luke in the story of the two disciples of Emmaus, whom Christ approached and led to understand the Scriptures and then sat with them at table. They recognized Him when He "took the bread, said the blessing, broke it and gave it to them" (24:30). The gestures of Jesus in this account are His gestures at the Last Supper, with the clear allusion to the "breaking of bread", as the Eucharist was called by the first generation of Christians.

The Sunday Eucharist

34. It is true that, in itself, the Sunday Eucharist is no different from the Eucharist celebrated on other days, nor can it be separated from liturgical and sacramental life as a whole. By its very nature, the Eucharist is an epiphany of the Church;[42] and this is most powerfully expressed when the diocesan community gathers in prayer with its Pastor: "The Church appears with special clarity when the holy People of God, all of them, are actively and fully sharing in the same liturgical celebrations — especially when it is the same Eucharist — sharing one prayer at one altar, at which the Bishop is presiding, surrounded by his presbyters and his ministers".[43] This relationship with the Bishop and with the entire Church community is inherent in every Eucharistic celebration, even when the Bishop does not preside, regardless of the day of the week on which it is celebrated. The mention of the Bishop in the Eucharistic Prayer is the indication of this.

But because of its special solemnity and the obligatory presence of the community, and because it is celebrated "on the day when Christ conquered death and gave us a share in his immortal life",[44] the Sunday Eucharist expresses with greater emphasis its inherent ecclesial dimension. It becomes the paradigm for other Eucharistic celebrations. Each community, gathering all its members for the "breaking of the bread", becomes the place where the mystery of the Church is concretely made present. In celebrating the Eucharist, the community opens itself to communion with the universal Church,[45] imploring the Father to "remember the Church throughout the world" and make her grow in the unity of all the faithful with the Pope and with the Pastors of the particular Churches, until love is brought to perfection.

The day of the Church

35. Therefore, the *dies Domini* is also the *dies Ecclesiae*. This is why on the pastoral level the community aspect of the Sunday celebration should be particularly stressed. As I have noted elsewhere, among the many activities of a parish, "none is as vital or as community-forming as the Sunday celebration of the Lord's Day and his Eucharist".[46] Mindful of this, the Second Vatican Council re-

called that efforts must be made to ensure that there is "within the parish, a lively sense of community, in the first place through the community celebration of Sunday Mass".[47] Subsequent liturgical directives made the same point, asking that on Sundays and holy days the Eucharistic celebrations held normally in other churches and chapels be coordinated with the celebration in the parish church, in order "to foster the sense of the Church community, which is nourished and expressed in a particular way by the community celebration on Sunday, whether around the Bishop, especially in the Cathedral, or in the parish assembly, in which the pastor represents the Bishop".[48]

36. The Sunday assembly is the privileged place of unity: it is the setting for the celebration of the *sacramentum unitatis* which profoundly marks the Church as a people gathered "by" and "in" the unity of the Father, of the Son and of the Holy Spirit.[49] For Christian families, the Sunday assembly is one of the most outstanding expressions of their identity and their "ministry" as "domestic churches",[50] when parents share with their children at the one Table of the Word and of the Bread of Life. We do well to recall in this regard that it is first of all the parents who must teach their children to participate in Sunday Mass; they are assisted in this by catechists, who are to see to it that initiation into the Mass is made a part of the formation imparted to the children entrusted to their care, explaining the important reasons behind the obligatory nature of the precept. When circumstances suggest it, the celebration of Masses for Children, in keeping with the provisions of the liturgical norms,[51] can also help in this regard.

At Sunday Masses in parishes, insofar as parishes are "Eucharistic communities",[52] it is normal to find different groups, movements, associations and even the smaller religious communities present in the parish. This allows everyone to experience in common what they share most deeply, beyond the particular spiritual paths which, by discernment of Church authority,[53] legitimately distinguish them. This is why on Sunday, the day of gathering, small group Masses are not to be encouraged: it is not only a question of ensuring that parish assemblies are not without the necessary ministry of priests, but also of ensuring that the life and unity of the Church community are fully safeguarded and promoted.[54] Authorization of possible and clearly restricted exceptions to this general guideline will depend upon the wise discernment of the Pastors of the particular Churches, in view of special needs in the area of formation and pastoral care, and keeping in mind the good of individuals or groups — especially the benefits which such exceptions may bring to the entire Christian community.

A pilgrim people
37. As the Church journeys through time, the reference to Christ's Resurrection and the weekly recurrence of this solemn memorial help to remind us of the pilgrim and eschatological character of the People of God. Sunday after Sunday the Church moves towards the final "Lord's Day", that Sunday which knows no end. The expectation of Christ's coming is inscribed in the very mystery of the Church[55] and is evidenced in every Eucharistic celebration. But, with its specific remembrance of the glory of the Risen Christ, the Lord's Day recalls with greater intensity the future glory of His "return". This makes Sunday the day on which the Church, showing forth more clearly her identity as "Bride", anticipates in some sense the eschatological reality of the heavenly Jerusalem. Gathering her children into the Eucharistic assembly and teaching them to wait for the "divine Bridegroom", she engages in a kind of "exercise of desire",[56] receiving a foretaste of the joy of the new heavens and new earth, when the holy city, the new Jerusalem, will come down from God, "prepared as a bride adorned for her husband" (*Rev* 21:2).

The Day of Hope
38. Viewed in this way, Sunday is not only the day of faith, but is also the day of Christian hope. To share in "the Lord's Supper" is to anticipate the eschatological feast of the "marriage of the Lamb" (*Rev* 19:9). Celebrating this memorial of Christ, risen and ascended into heaven, the Christian community waits "in joyful hope for the coming of our Savior, Jesus Christ".[57] Renewed and nourished by

this intense weekly rhythm, Christian hope becomes the leaven and the light of human hope. This is why the Prayer of the Faithful responds not only to the needs of the particular Christian community but also to those of all humanity; and the Church, coming together for the Eucharistic celebration, shows to the world that she makes her own "the joys and hopes, the sorrows and anxieties of people today, especially of the poor and all those who suffer".[58] With the offering of the Sunday Eucharist, the Church crowns the witness which her children strive to offer every day of the week by proclaiming the Gospel and practicing charity in the world of work and in all the many tasks of life; thus she shows forth more plainly her identity "as a sacrament, or sign and instrument of intimate union with God and of the unity of the entire human race".[59]

The Table of the Word

39. As in every Eucharistic celebration, the Risen Lord is encountered in the Sunday assembly at the twofold Table of the Word and of the Bread of Life. The Table of the Word offers the same understanding of the history of salvation and especially of the Paschal Mystery which the Risen Jesus Himself gave to His disciples: it is Christ who speaks, present as He is in His word "when Sacred Scripture is read in the Church".[60] At the table of the Bread of Life, the Risen Lord becomes really, substantially and enduringly present through the memorial of His Passion and Resurrection, and the Bread of Life is offered as a pledge of future glory.

The Second Vatican Council recalled that "the Liturgy of the Word and the Liturgy of the Eucharist are so closely joined together that they form a single act of worship".[61] The Council also urged that "the table of the word of God be more lavishly prepared for the faithful, opening to them more abundantly the treasures of the Bible".[62] It then decreed that, in Masses of Sunday and holy days of obligation, the homily should not be omitted except for serious reasons.[63] These timely decrees were faithfully embodied in the liturgical reform, about which Paul VI wrote, commenting upon the richer offering of biblical readings on Sunday and holy days: "All this has been decreed so as to foster more and more in the faithful 'that hunger for hearing the word of the Lord' (Am

8:11) which, under the guidance of the Holy Spirit, spurs the People of the New Covenant on towards the perfect unity of the Church".[64]

40. In considering the Sunday Eucharist more than thirty years after the Council, we need to assess how well the word of God is being proclaimed and how effectively the People of God have grown in knowledge and love of Sacred Scripture.[65] There are two aspects of this — that of celebration and that of personal appropriation — and they are very closely related. At the level of celebration, the fact that the Council made it possible to proclaim the word of God in the language of the community taking part in the celebration must awaken a new sense of responsibility towards the word, allowing "the distinctive character of the sacred text" to shine forth "even in the mode of reading or singing".[66] At the level of personal appropriation, the hearing of the word of God proclaimed must be well prepared in the souls of the faithful by an apt knowledge of Scripture and, where pastorally possible, by special initiatives designed to deepen understanding of the biblical readings, particularly those used on Sundays and holy days. If Christian individuals and families are not regularly drawing new life from the reading of the sacred text in a spirit of prayer and docility to the Church's interpretation,[67] then it is difficult for the liturgical proclamation of the word of God alone to produce the fruit we might expect. This is the value of initiatives in parish communities which bring together during the week those who take part in the Eucharist — priest, ministers and faithful[68] — in order to prepare the Sunday liturgy, reflecting beforehand upon the word of God which will be proclaimed.

The objective sought here is that the entire celebration — praying, singing, listening, and not just the preaching — should express in some way the theme of the Sunday liturgy, so that all those taking part may be penetrated more powerfully by it. Clearly, much depends on those who exercise the ministry of the word. It is their duty to prepare the reflection on the word of the Lord by prayer and study of the sacred text, so that they may then express its contents faithfully and apply them to people's concerns and to their daily lives.

41. It should also be borne in mind that the liturgical proclamation of the word of God, especially in the Eucharistic assembly, is not so much a time for meditation and catechesis as a dialogue between God and His People, a dialogue in which the wonders of salvation are proclaimed and the demands of the Covenant are continually restated. On their part, the People of God are drawn to respond to this dialogue of love by giving thanks and praise, also by demonstrating their fidelity to the task of continual "conversion". The Sunday assembly commits us therefore to an inner renewal of our baptismal promises, which are in a sense implicit in the recitation of the Creed, and are an explicit part of the liturgy of the Easter Vigil and whenever Baptism is celebrated during Mass. In this context, the proclamation of the word in the Sunday Eucharistic celebration takes on the solemn tone found in the Old Testament at moments when the Covenant was renewed, when the Law was proclaimed and the community of Israel was called — like the People in the desert at the foot of Sinai (cf. *Ex* 19:7-8; 24:3,7) — to repeat its "yes", renewing its decision to be faithful to God and to obey His commandments. In speaking His word, God awaits our response: a response which Christ has already made for us with His "Amen" (cf. *2 Cor* 1:20-22), and which echoes in us through the Holy Spirit so that what we hear may involve us at the deepest level.[(69)]

The Table of the Body of Christ

42. The table of the word leads naturally to the table of the Eucharistic Bread and prepares the community to live its many aspects, which in the Sunday Eucharist assume an especially solemn character. As the whole community gathers to celebrate "the Lord's Day", the Eucharist appears more clearly than on other days as the great "thanksgiving" in which the Spirit-filled Church turns to the Father, becoming one with Christ and speaking in the name of all humanity. The rhythm of the week prompts us to gather up in grateful memory the events of the days which have just passed, to review them in the light of God and to thank him for His countless gifts, glorifying Him "through Christ, with Christ and in Christ, in the unity of the Holy Spirit". The Christian community thus comes

to a renewed awareness of the fact that all things were created through Christ (cf. *Col* 1:16; Jn 1:3), and that in Christ, who came in the form of a slave to take on and redeem our human condition, all things have been restored (cf. *Eph* 1:10), in order to be handed over to God the Father, from whom all things come to be and draw their life. Then, giving assent to the Eucharistic doxology with their "Amen", the People of God look in faith and hope towards the eschatological end, when Christ "will deliver the kingdom to God the Father ... so that God may be everything to everyone" (*1 Cor* 15:24,28).

43. This "ascending" movement is inherent in every Eucharistic celebration and makes it a joyous event, overflowing with gratitude and hope. But it emerges particularly at Sunday Mass because of its special link with the commemoration of the Resurrection. By contrast, this "Eucharistic" rejoicing which "lifts up our hearts" is the fruit of God's "descending" movement towards us, which remains for ever etched in the essential sacrificial element of the Eucharist, the supreme expression and celebration of the mystery of the kenosis, the descent by which Christ "humbled Himself, and became obedient unto death, even death on a Cross" (*Phil* 2:8).

The Mass in fact truly makes present the sacrifice of the Cross. Under the species of bread and wine, upon which has been invoked the outpouring of the Spirit who works with absolutely unique power in the words of consecration, Christ offers Himself to the Father in the same act of sacrifice by which He offered Himself on the Cross. "In this divine sacrifice which is accomplished in the Mass, the same Christ who offered Himself once and for all in a bloody manner on the altar of the Cross is contained and is offered in an unbloody manner".[70] To His sacrifice Christ unites the sacrifice of the Church: "In the Eucharist the sacrifice of Christ becomes also the sacrifice of the members of His Body.

The lives of the faithful, their praise, sufferings, prayer and work, are united with those of Christ and with His total offering, and so acquire a new value".[71] The truth that the whole community shares in Christ's sacrifice is especially evident in the Sunday gathering, which makes it possible to bring to the altar the week that has passed, with all its human burdens.

Easter Banquet and Fraternal Gathering

44. The communal character of the Eucharist emerges in a special way when it is seen as the Easter banquet, in which Christ Himself becomes our nourishment. In fact, "for this purpose Christ entrusted to the Church this sacrifice: so that the faithful might share in it, both spiritually, in faith and charity, and sacramentally, in the banquet of Holy Communion. Sharing in the Lord's Supper is always communion with Christ, who offers Himself for us in sacrifice to the Father".[72] This is why the Church recommends that the faithful receive communion when they take part in the Eucharist, provided that they are properly disposed and, if aware of grave sin, have received God's pardon in the Sacrament of Reconciliation,[73] in the spirit of what Saint Paul writes to the community at Corinth (cf. *1 Cor* 11:27-32). Obviously, the invitation to Eucharistic communion is more insistent in the case of Mass on Sundays and holy days.

It is also important to be ever mindful that communion with Christ is deeply tied to communion with our brothers and sisters. The Sunday Eucharistic gathering is an experience of brotherhood, which the celebration should demonstrate clearly, while ever respecting the nature of the liturgical action. All this will be helped by gestures of welcome and by the tone of prayer, alert to the needs of all in the community. The sign of peace — in the Roman Rite significantly placed before Eucharistic communion — is a particularly expressive gesture which the faithful are invited to make as a manifestation of the People of God's acceptance of all that has been accomplished in the celebration[74] and of the commitment to mutual love which is made in sharing the one bread, with the demanding words of Christ in mind: "If you are offering your gift at the altar, and there remember that your brother has something against you, leave your gift there before the altar and go; first be reconciled with your brother, and then come and offer your gift" (*Mt* 5:23-24).

From Mass to "Mission"

45. Receiving the Bread of Life, the disciples of Christ ready themselves to undertake with the strength of the Risen Lord and His Spirit the tasks which await them in their ordinary life. For the faithful who have understood the meaning of what they have done, the Eucharistic celebration does not stop at the church door. Like the first witnesses of the Resurrection, Christians who gather each Sunday to experience and proclaim the presence of the Risen Lord are called to evangelize and bear witness in their daily lives. Given this, the Prayer after Communion and the Concluding Rite — the Final Blessing and the Dismissal — need to be better valued and appreciated, so that all who have shared in the Eucharist may come to a deeper sense of the responsibility which is entrusted to them.

Once the assembly disperses, Christ's disciples return to their everyday surroundings with the commitment to make their whole life a gift, a spiritual sacrifice pleasing to God (cf. *Rom* 12:1). They feel indebted to their brothers and sisters because of what they have received in the celebration, not unlike the disciples of Emmaus who, once they had recognized the Risen Christ "in the breaking of the bread" (cf. *Lk* 24:30-32), felt the need to return immediately to share with their brothers and sisters the joy of meeting the Lord (cf. *Lk* 24:33-35).

The Sunday obligation

46. Since the Eucharist is the very heart of Sunday, it is clear why, from the earliest centuries, the Pastors of the Church have not ceased to remind the faithful of the need to take part in the liturgical assembly. "Leave everything on the Lord's Day", urges the third century text known as the *Didascalia,* "and run diligently to your assembly, because it is your praise of God. Otherwise, what excuse will they make to God, those who do not come together on the Lord's Day to hear the word of life and feed on the divine nourishment which lasts forever?".[75] The faithful have generally accepted this call of the Pastors with conviction of soul and, although there have been times and situations when this duty has not been perfectly met, one should never forget the genuine heroism of priests and faithful who have fulfilled this obligation even when faced

with danger and the denial of religious freedom, as can be documented from the first centuries of Christianity up to our own time.

In his first Apology addressed to the Emperor Antoninus and the Senate, Saint Justin proudly described the Christian practice of the Sunday assembly, which gathered in one place Christians from both the city and the countryside.[76] When, during the persecution of Diocletian, their assemblies were banned with the greatest severity, many were courageous enough to defy the imperial decree and accepted death rather than miss the Sunday Eucharist. This was the case of the martyrs of Abitina, in Proconsular Africa, who replied to their accusers: "Without fear of any kind we have celebrated the Lord's Supper, because it cannot be missed; that is our law"; "We cannot live without the Lord's Supper". As she confessed her faith, one of the martyrs said: "Yes, I went to the assembly and I celebrated the Lord's Supper with my brothers and sisters, because I am a Christian".[77]

47. Even if in the earliest times it was not judged necessary to be prescriptive, the Church has not ceased to confirm this obligation of conscience, which rises from the inner need felt so strongly by the Christians of the first centuries. It was only later, faced with the half-heartedness or negligence of some, that the Church had to make explicit the duty to attend Sunday Mass: more often than not, this was done in the form of exhortation, but at times the Church had to resort to specific canonical precepts. This was the case in a number of local Councils from the fourth century onwards (as at the Council of Elvira of 300, which speaks not of an obligation but of penalties after three absences)[78] and most especially from the sixth century onwards (as at the Council of Agde in 506).[79] These decrees of local Councils led to a universal practice, the obligatory character of which was taken as something quite normal.[80]

The Code of Canon Law of 1917 for the first time gathered this tradition into a universal law.[81] The present Code reiterates this, saying that "on Sundays and other holy days of obligation the faithful are bound to attend Mass".[82] This legislation has normally been understood as entailing a grave obligation: this is the teaching of the Catechism of the Catholic Church,[83] and it is easy to understand why if we keep in mind how vital Sunday is for the Christian life.

48. Today, as in the heroic times of the beginning, many who wish to live in accord with the demands of their faith are being faced with difficult situations in various parts of the world. They live in surroundings which are sometimes decidedly hostile and at other times — more frequently in fact — indifferent and unresponsive to the Gospel message. If believers are not to be overwhelmed, they must be able to count on the support of the Christian community. This is why they must be convinced that it is crucially important for the life of faith that they should come together with others on Sundays to celebrate the Passover of the Lord in the sacrament of the New Covenant. It is the special responsibility of the Bishops, therefore, "to ensure that Sunday is appreciated by all the faithful, kept holy and celebrated as truly 'the Lord's Day', on which the Church comes together to renew the remembrance of the Easter mystery in hearing the word of God, in offering the sacrifice of the Lord, in keeping the day holy by means of prayer, works of charity and abstention from work".[84]

49. Because the faithful are obliged to attend Mass unless there is a grave impediment, Pastors have the corresponding duty to offer to everyone the real possibility of fulfilling the precept. The provisions of Church law move in this direction, as for example in the faculty granted to priests, with the prior authorization of the diocesan Bishop, to celebrate more than one Mass on Sundays and holy days,[85] the institution of evening Masses[86] and the provision which allows the obligation to be fulfilled from Saturday evening onwards, starting at the time of First Vespers of Sunday.[87] From a liturgical point of view, in fact, holy days begin with First Vespers.[88] Consequently, the liturgy of what is sometimes called the "Vigil Mass" is in effect the "festive" Mass of Sunday, at which the celebrant is required to preach the homily and recite the Prayer of the Faithful.

Moreover, Pastors should remind the faithful that when they are away from home on Sundays they are to take care to attend Mass wherever they may be, enriching the local community with their personal witness. At the same time, these communities should show a warm sense of welcome to visiting brothers and sisters, especially in places which attract many tourists and pilgrims, for whom it will often be necessary to provide special religious assistance.[89]

Joyful Celebration in Song

50. Given the nature of Sunday Mass and its importance in the lives of the faithful, it must be prepared with special care. In ways dictated by pastoral experience and local custom in keeping with liturgical norms, efforts must be made to ensure that the celebration has the festive character appropriate to the day commemorating the Lord's Resurrection. To this end, it is important to devote attention to the songs used by the assembly, since singing is a particularly apt way to express a joyful heart, accentuating the solemnity of the celebration and fostering the sense of a common faith and a shared love. Care must be taken to ensure the quality, both of the texts and of the melodies, so that what is proposed today as new and creative will conform to liturgical requirements and be worthy of the Church's tradition which, in the field of sacred music, boasts a priceless heritage.

A Celebration Involving All

51. There is a need too to ensure that all those present, children and adults, take an active interest, by encouraging their involvement at those points where the liturgy suggests and recommends it.[90] Of course, it falls only to those who exercise the priestly ministry to effect the Eucharistic Sacrifice and to offer it to God in the name of the whole people.[91] This is the basis of the distinction, which is much more than a matter of discipline, between the task proper to the celebrant and that which belongs to deacons and the non-ordained faithful.[92] Yet the faithful must realize that, because of the common priesthood received in Baptism, "they participate in the offering of the Eucharist".[93] Although there is a distinction of roles, they still "offer to God the divine victim and themselves with Him. Offering the sacrifice and receiving holy communion, they take part actively in the liturgy",[94] finding in it light and strength to live

their baptismal priesthood and the witness of a holy life.

Other Moments of the Christian Sunday

52. Sharing in the Eucharist is the heart of Sunday, but the duty to keep Sunday holy cannot be reduced to this. In fact, the Lord's Day is lived well if it is marked from beginning to end by grateful and active remembrance of God's saving work. This commits each of Christ's disciples to shape the other moments of the day — those outside the liturgical context: family life, social relationships, moments of relaxation — in such a way that the peace and joy of the Risen Lord will emerge in the ordinary events of life. For example, the relaxed gathering of parents and children can be an opportunity not only to listen to one another but also to share a few formative and more reflective moments. Even in lay life, when possible, why not make provision for special times of prayer — especially the solemn celebration of Vespers, for example — or moments of catechesis, which on the eve of Sunday or on Sunday afternoon might prepare for or complete the gift of the Eucharist in people's hearts?

This rather traditional way of keeping Sunday holy has perhaps become more difficult for many people; but the Church shows her faith in the strength of the Risen Lord and the power of the Holy Spirit by making it known that, today more than ever, she is unwilling to settle for minimalism and mediocrity at the level of faith. She wants to help Christians to do what is most correct and pleasing to the Lord. And despite the difficulties, there are positive and encouraging signs. In many parts of the Church, a new need for prayer in its many forms is being felt; and this is a gift of the Holy Spirit. There is also a rediscovery of ancient religious practices, such as pilgrimages; and often the faithful take advantage of Sunday rest to visit a Shrine where, with the whole family perhaps, they can spend time in a more intense experience of faith. These are moments of grace which must be fostered through evangelization and guided by genuine pastoral wisdom.

Sunday Assemblies Without a Priest

53. There remains the problem of parishes which do not have the

ministry of a priest for the celebration of the Sunday Eucharist. This is often the case in young Churches, where one priest has pastoral responsibility for faithful scattered over a vast area. However, emergency situations can also arise in countries of long-standing Christian tradition, where diminishing numbers of clergy make it impossible to guarantee the presence of a priest in every parish community. In situations where the Eucharist cannot be celebrated, the Church recommends that the Sunday assembly come together even without a priest,[95] in keeping with the indications and directives of the Holy See which have been entrusted to the Episcopal Conferences for implementation.[96] Yet the objective must always remain the celebration of the Sacrifice of the Mass, the one way in which the Passover of the Lord becomes truly present, the only full realization of the Eucharistic assembly over which the priest presides *in persona Christi*, breaking the bread of the word and the Eucharist. At the pastoral level, therefore, everything has to be done to ensure that the Sacrifice of the Mass is made available as often as possible to the faithful who are regularly deprived of it, either by arranging the presence of a priest from time to time, or by taking every opportunity to organize a gathering in a central location accessible to scattered groups.

Radio and Television

54. Finally, the faithful who, because of sickness, disability or some other serious cause, are prevented from taking part, should as best they can unite themselves with the celebration of Sunday Mass from afar, preferably by means of the readings and prayers for that day from the Missal, as well as through their desire for the Eucharist.[97] In many countries, radio and television make it possible to join in the Eucharistic celebration broadcast from some sacred place.[98] Clearly, this kind of broadcast does not in itself fulfil the Sunday obligation, which requires participation in the fraternal assembly gathered in one place, where Eucharistic communion can be received. But for those who cannot take part in the Eucharist and who are therefore excused from the obligation, radio and television are a precious help, especially if accompanied by the generous service of extraordinary ministers who bring the Eucharist to

the sick, also bringing them the greeting and solidarity of the whole community. Sunday Mass thus produces rich fruits for these Christians too, and they are truly enabled to experience Sunday as "the Lord's Day" and "the Church's day".

CHAPTER IV

DIES HOMINIS

Sunday: Day of Joy, Rest and Solidarity

The "Full Joy" of Christ

55. "Blessed be He who has raised the great day of Sunday above all other days. The heavens and the earth, angels and of men give themselves over to joy".[99] This cry of the Maronite liturgy captures well the intense acclamations of joy which have always characterized Sunday in the liturgy of both East and West. Moreover, historically — even before it was seen as a day of rest, which in any case was not provided for in the civil calendar — Christians celebrated the weekly day of the Risen Lord primarily as a day of joy. "On the first day of the week, you shall all rejoice", urges the *Didascalia*. [100] This was also emphasized by liturgical practice, through the choice of appropriate gestures. [101] Voicing an awareness widespread in the Church, Saint Augustine describes the joy of the weekly Easter: "Fasting, is set aside and prayers are said standing, as a sign of the Resurrection, which is also why the Alleluia is sung on every Sunday". [102]

56. Beyond particular ritual forms, which can vary in time depending upon Church discipline, there remains the fact that Sunday, as a weekly echo of the first encounter with the Risen Lord, is unfailingly marked by the joy with which the disciples greeted the Master: "The disciples rejoiced to see the Lord" (*Jn* 20:20). This was the confirmation of the words which Jesus spoke before the Passion and which resound in every Christian generation: "You will be sorrowful, but your sorrow will turn to joy" (*Jn* 16:20). Had not He Himself prayed for this, that the disciples would have "the fullness of His joy" (cf. Jn 17:13)? The festive character of the Sunday Eucharist expresses the joy that Christ communicates to his Church through the gift of the Spirit. Joy is precisely one of the fruits of the Holy Spirit (cf. *Rom* 14:17; *Gal* 5:22).

57. Therefore, if we wish to rediscover the full meaning of Sunday, we must rediscover this aspect of the life of faith. Certainly, Christian joy must mark the whole of life, and not just one day of the week. But in virtue of its significance as the day of the Risen Lord, celebrating God's work of creation and "new creation", Sunday is the day of joy in a very special way, indeed the day most suitable for learning how to rejoice and to rediscover the true nature and deep roots of joy. This joy should never be confused with shallow feelings of satisfaction and pleasure, which inebriate the senses and emotions for a brief moment, but then leave the heart unfulfilled and perhaps even embittered. In the Christian view, joy is much more enduring and consoling; as the saints attest, it can hold firm even in the dark night of suffering. [103] It is, in a certain sense, a "virtue" to be nurtured.

58. Yet there is no conflict whatever between Christian joy and true human joys, which in fact are exalted and find their ultimate foundation precisely in the joy of the glorified Christ, the perfect image and revelation of man as God intended. As my revered predecessor Paul VI wrote in his Exhortation on Christian joy: "In essence, Christian joy is a sharing in the unfathomable joy, at once divine and human, found in the heart of the glorified Christ". [104] Pope Paul concluded his Exhortation by asking that, on the Lord's Day, the Church should witness powerfully to the joy experienced by the Apostles when they saw the Lord on the evening of Easter. To this end, he urged pastors to insist "upon the need for the baptized to celebrate the Sunday Eucharist in joy. How could they neglect this encounter, this banquet which Christ prepares for us in His love? May our sharing in it be most worthy and joyful! It is Christ, crucified and glorified, who comes among His disciples, to lead them all together into the newness of His Resurrection. This is the climax, here below, of the covenant of love between God and His people: the sign and source of Christian joy, a stage on the way to the eternal feast". [105] This vision of faith shows the Christian Sunday to be a true "time for celebration", a day given by God to men and women for their full human and spiritual growth.

The Fulfillment of the Sabbath

59. This aspect of the Christian Sunday shows in a special way how it is the fulfillment of the Old Testament Sabbath. On the Lord's Day, which — as we have already said — the Old Testament links to the work of creation (cf. *Gen* 2:1-3; *Ex* 20:8-11) and the Exodus (cf. Dt 5:12-15), the Christian is called to proclaim the new creation and the new covenant brought about in the Paschal Mystery of Christ. Far from being abolished, the celebration of creation becomes more profound within a Christocentric perspective, being seen in the light of the God's plan "to unite all things in [Christ], things in heaven and things on earth" (Eph 1:10). The remembrance of the liberation of the Exodus also assumes its full meaning as it becomes a remembrance of the universal redemption accomplished by Christ in His Death and Resurrection. More than a "replacement" for the Sabbath, therefore, Sunday is its fulfillment, and in a certain sense its extension and full expression in the ordered unfolding of the history of salvation, which reaches its culmination in Christ.

60. In this perspective, the biblical theology of the "Sabbath" can be recovered in full, without compromising the Christian character of Sunday. It is a theology which leads us ever anew and in unfailing awe to the mystery of the beginning, when the eternal Word of God, by a free decision of love, created the world from nothing. The work of creation was sealed by the blessing and consecration of the day on which God ceased "from all the work which He had done in creation" (*Gen* 2:3). This day of God's rest confers meaning upon time, which in the sequence of weeks assumes not only a chronological regularity but also, in a manner of speaking, a theological resonance. The constant return of the "*shabbat*" ensures that there is no risk of time being closed in upon itself, since, in welcoming God and His *kairoi* — the moments of His grace and His saving acts — time remains open to eternity.

61. As the seventh day blessed and consecrated by God, the "*shabbat*" concludes the whole work of creation, and is therefore immediately linked to the work of the sixth day when God made

man "in His image and likeness" (cf. *Gen* 1:26). This very close connection between the "day of God" and the "day of man" did not escape the Fathers in their meditation on the biblical creation story. Saint Ambrose says in this regard: "Thanks, then, to the Lord our God who accomplished a work in which He might find rest. He made the heavens, but I do not read that He found rest there; He made the stars, the moon, the sun, and neither do I read that He found rest in them. I read instead that He made man and that then He rested, finding in man one to whom He could offer the forgiveness of sins". [106] Thus there will be for ever a direct link between the "day of God" and the "day of man". When the divine commandment declares: "Remember the Sabbath day in order to keep it holy" (*Ex* 20:8), the rest decreed in order to honor the day dedicated to God is not at all a burden imposed upon man, but rather an aid to help him to recognize his life-giving and liberating dependence upon the Creator, and at the same time his calling to cooperate in the Creator's work and to receive His grace. In honoring God's "rest", man fully discovers himself, and thus the Lord's Day bears the profound imprint of God's blessing (cf. *Gen* 2:3), by virtue of which, we might say, it is endowed in a way similar to the animals and to man himself, with a kind of "fruitfulness" (cf. *Gen* 1:22, 28). This "fruitfulness" is apparent above all in filling and, in a certain sense, "multiplying" time itself, deepening in men and women the joy of living and the desire to foster and communicate life.

62. It is the duty of Christians therefore to remember that, although the practices of the Jewish Sabbath are gone, surpassed as they are by the "fulfillment" which Sunday brings, the underlying reasons for keeping "the Lord's Day" holy — inscribed solemnly in the Ten Commandments — remain valid, though they need to be reinterpreted in the light of the theology and spirituality of Sunday: "Remember the Sabbath day to keep it holy, as the Lord your God commanded you. Six days you shall labor, and do all your work; but the seventh day is a Sabbath to the Lord your God. Then you shall do no work, you, or your son, or your daughter, or your servant, or your maid, or your ox, or your ass, or any of your beasts, or

the foreigner within your gates, that your servant and maid may rest as well as you. You shall remember that you were a servant in the land of Egypt, and the Lord your God brought you out from there with a mighty hand and an outstretched arm. Therefore the Lord your God commanded that you keep the Sabbath day" (*Deut* 5:12-15). Here the Sabbath observance is closely linked with the liberation which God accomplished for His people.

63. Christ came to accomplish a new "exodus", to restore freedom to the oppressed. He performed many healings on the Sabbath (cf. *Mt* 12:9-14 and parallels), certainly not to violate the Lord's Day, but to reveal its full meaning: "The Sabbath was made for man, not man for the Sabbath" (*Mk* 2:27). Opposing the excessively legalistic interpretation of some of His contemporaries, and developing the true meaning of the biblical Sabbath, Jesus, as "Lord of the Sabbath" (*Mk* 2:28), restores to the Sabbath observance its liberating character, carefully safeguarding the rights of God and the rights of man. This is why Christians, called as they are to proclaim the liberation won by the Blood of Christ, felt that they had the authority to transfer the meaning of the Sabbath to the day of the Resurrection. The Passover of Christ has in fact liberated man from a slavery more radical than any weighing upon an oppressed people — the slavery of sin, which alienates man from God, and alienates man from himself and from others, constantly sowing within history the seeds of evil and violence.

The Day of Rest
64. For several centuries, Christians observed Sunday simply as a day of worship, without being able to give it the specific meaning of Sabbath rest. Only in the fourth century did the civil law of the Roman Empire recognize the weekly recurrence, determining that on "the day of the sun" the judges, the people of the cities and the various trade corporations would not work. [107] Christians rejoiced to see thus removed the obstacles which until then had sometimes made observance of the Lord's Day heroic. They could now devote themselves to prayer in common without hindrance. [108]

It would therefore be wrong to see in this legislation of the rhythm of the week a mere historical circumstance with no special significance for the Church and which she could simply set aside. Even after the fall of the Empire, the Councils did not cease to insist upon the arrangements regarding Sunday rest. In countries where Christians are in the minority and where the festive days of the calendar do not coincide with Sunday, it is still Sunday which remains the Lord's Day, the day on which the faithful come together for the Eucharistic assembly. But this involves real sacrifices. For Christians it is not normal that Sunday, the day of joyful celebration, should not also be a day of rest, and it is difficult for them to keep Sunday holy if they do not have enough free time.

65. By contrast, the link between the Lord's Day and the day of rest in civil society has a meaning and importance which go beyond the distinctly Christian point of view. The alternation between work and rest, built into human nature, is willed by God Himself, as appears in the creation story in the Book of Genesis (cf. 2:2-3; *Ex* 20:8-11): rest is something "sacred", because it is man's way of withdrawing from the sometimes excessively demanding cycle of earthly tasks in order to renew his awareness that everything is the work of God. There is a risk that the prodigious power over creation which God gives to man can lead him to forget that God is the Creator upon whom everything depends. It is all the more urgent to recognize this dependence in our own time, when science and technology have so incredibly increased the power which man exercises through his work.

66. Finally, it should not be forgotten that even in our own day work is very oppressive for many people, either because of miserable working conditions and long hours — especially in the poorer regions of the world — or because of the persistence in economically more developed societies of too many cases of injustice and exploitation of man by man. When, through the centuries, she has made laws concerning Sunday rest, [109] the Church has had in mind above all the work of servants and workers, certainly not because this work was any less worthy when compared to the spiritual requirements of Sunday observance, but rather because it needed

greater regulation to lighten its burden and thus enable everyone to keep the Lord's Day holy. In this matter, my predecessor Pope Leo XIII in his Encyclical *Rerum Novarum* spoke of Sunday rest as a worker's right which the State must guarantee. [110]

In our own historical context there remains the obligation to ensure that everyone can enjoy the freedom, rest and relaxation which human dignity requires, together with the associated religious, family, cultural and interpersonal needs which are difficult to meet if there is no guarantee of at least one day of the week on which people can both rest and celebrate. Naturally, this right of workers to rest presupposes their right to work and, as we reflect on the question of the Christian understanding of Sunday, we cannot but recall with a deep sense of solidarity the hardship of countless men and women who, because of the lack of jobs, are forced to remain inactive on workdays as well.

67. Through Sunday rest, daily concerns and tasks can find their proper perspective: the material things about which we worry give way to spiritual values; in a moment of encounter and less pressured exchange, we see the true face of the people with whom we live. Even the beauties of nature — too often marred by the desire to exploit, which turns against man himself — can be rediscovered and enjoyed to the full. As the day on which man is at peace with God, with himself and with others, Sunday becomes a moment when people can look anew upon the wonders of nature, allowing themselves to be caught up in that marvelous and mysterious harmony which, in the words of Saint Ambrose, weds the many elements of the cosmos in a "bond of communion and peace" by "an inviolable law of concord and love". [111] Men and women then come to a deeper sense, as the Apostle says, that "everything created by God is good and nothing is to be rejected if it is received with thanksgiving, for then it is consecrated by the word of God and prayer" (*1 Tim* 4:4-5). If after six days of work — reduced in fact to five for many people — people look for time to relax and to pay more attention to other aspects of their lives, this corresponds to an authentic need which is in full harmony with the vision of the Gospel message. Believers are therefore called to satisfy this need

in a way consistent with the manifestation of their personal and community faith, as expressed in the celebration and sanctification of the Lord's Day.

Therefore, also in the particular circumstances of our own time, Christians will naturally strive to ensure that civil legislation respects their duty to keep Sunday holy. In any case, they are obliged in conscience to arrange their Sunday rest in a way which allows them to take part in the Eucharist, refraining from work and activities which are incompatible with the sanctification of the Lord's Day, with its characteristic joy and necessary rest for spirit and body. (112)

68. In order that rest may not degenerate into emptiness or boredom, it must offer spiritual enrichment, greater freedom, opportunities for contemplation and fraternal communion. Therefore, among the forms of culture and entertainment which society offers, the faithful should choose those which are most in keeping with a life lived in obedience to the precepts of the Gospel. Sunday rest then becomes "prophetic", affirming not only the absolute primacy of God, but also the primacy and dignity of the person with respect to the demands of social and economic life, and anticipating in a certain sense the "new heavens" and the "new earth", in which liberation from slavery to needs will be final and complete. In short, the Lord's Day thus becomes in the truest sense the day of man as well.

A Day of Solidarity

69. Sunday should also give the faithful an opportunity to devote themselves to works of mercy, charity and apostolate. To experience the joy of the Risen Lord deep within is to share fully the love which pulses in His heart: there is no joy without love! Jesus Himself explains this, linking the "new commandment" with the gift of joy: "If you keep My commandments, you will remain in My love, just as I have kept the Father's commandments and remain in His love. I have told you this that My own joy may be in you and your joy may be complete. This is My commandment: that you love one another as I have loved you" (*Jn* 15:10-12).

The Sunday Eucharist, therefore, not only does not absolve the faithful from the duties of charity, but on the contrary commits them even more "to all the works of charity, of mercy, of apostolic outreach, by means of which it is seen that the faithful of Christ are not of this world and yet are the light of the world, giving glory to the Father in the presence of men". [113]

70. Ever since Apostolic times, the Sunday gathering has in fact been for Christians a moment of fraternal sharing with the very poor. "On the first day of the week, each of you is to put aside and save whatever extra you earn" (*1 Cor* 16:2), says Saint Paul referring to the collection organized for the poor Churches of Judaea. In the Sunday Eucharist, the believing heart opens wide to embrace all aspects of the Church. But the full range of the apostolic summons needs to be accepted: far from trying to create a narrow "gift" mentality, Paul calls rather for a demanding culture of sharing, to be lived not only among the members of the community itself but also in society as a whole. [114] More than ever, we need to listen once again to the stern warning which Paul addresses to the community at Corinth, guilty of having humiliated the poor in the fraternal agape which accompanied "the Lord's Supper": "When you meet together, it is not the Lord's Supper that you eat. For in eating, each one goes ahead with his own meal, and one is hungry and another is drunk. What! Do you not have houses to eat and drink in? Or do you despise the Church of God and humiliate those who have nothing?" (*1 Cor* 11:20-22). James is equally forceful in what he writes: "If a man with gold rings and in fine clothing comes into your assembly and a poor man in shabby clothing also comes in, and you pay attention to the one who wears the fine clothing and say, 'Take a seat here, please', while you say to the poor man, 'Stand there', or, 'Sit at my feet', have you not made distinctions among yourselves, and become judges with evil thoughts?" (2:2-4).

71. The teachings of the Apostles struck a sympathetic chord from the earliest centuries, and evoked strong echoes in the preaching of the Fathers of the Church. Saint Ambrose addressed words of fire to the rich who presumed to fulfill their religious obligations by

attending church without sharing their goods with the poor, and who perhaps even exploited them: "You who are rich, do you hear what the Lord God says? Yet you come into church not to give to the poor but to take instead". [115] Saint John Chrysostom is no less demanding: "Do you wish to honor the Body of Christ? Do not ignore Him when He is naked. Do not pay Him homage in the temple clad in silk only then to neglect Him outside where He suffers cold and nakedness. He who said: 'This is My Body' is the same One who said: 'You saw Me hungry and you gave Me no food', and 'Whatever you did to the least of My brothers you did also to Me' ... What good is it if the Eucharistic table is overloaded with golden chalices, when he is dying of hunger? Start by satisfying his hunger, and then with what is left you may adorn the altar as well". [116]

These words effectively remind the Christian community of the duty to make the Eucharist the place where fraternity becomes practical solidarity, where the last are the first in the minds and attentions of the brethren, where Christ Himself — through the generous gifts from the rich to the very poor — may somehow prolong in time the miracle of the multiplication of the loaves. [117]

72. The Eucharist is an event and program of true brotherhood. From the Sunday Mass there flows a tide of charity destined to spread into the whole life of the faithful, beginning by inspiring the very way in which they live the rest of Sunday. If Sunday is a day of joy, Christians should declare by their actual behavior that we cannot be happy "on our own". They look around to find people who may need their help. It may be that in their neighborhood or among those they know there are sick people, elderly people, children or immigrants who precisely on Sundays feel more keenly their isolation, needs and suffering. It is true that commitment to these people cannot be restricted to occasional Sunday gestures. But presuming a wider sense of commitment, why not make the Lord's Day a more intense time of sharing, encouraging all the inventiveness of which Christian charity is capable? Inviting to a meal people who are alone, visiting the sick, providing food for needy families, spending a few hours in voluntary work and acts of

solidarity: these would certainly be ways of bringing into people's lives the love of Christ received at the Eucharistic table.

73. Lived in this way, not only the Sunday Eucharist but the whole of Sunday becomes a great school of charity, justice and peace. The presence of the Risen Lord in the midst of His people becomes an undertaking of solidarity, a compelling force for inner renewal, an inspiration to change the structures of sin in which individuals, communities and at times entire peoples are entangled. Far from being an escape, the Christian Sunday is a "prophecy" inscribed on time itself, a prophecy obliging the faithful to follow in the footsteps of the One who came "to preach good news to the poor, to proclaim release to captives and new sight to the blind, to set at liberty those who are oppressed, and to proclaim the acceptable year of the Lord" (*Lk* 4:18-19). In the Sunday commemoration of Easter, believers learn from Christ, and remembering His promise: "I leave you peace, My peace I give you" (*Jn* 14:27), they become in their turn builders of peace.

CHAPTER V

DIES DIERUM

Sunday: The Primordial Feast, Revealing the Meaning of Time

Christ the Alpha and Omega of Time

74. "In Christianity time has a fundamental importance. Within the dimension of time the world was created; within it the history of salvation unfolds, finding its culmination in the 'fullness of time' of the Incarnation, and its goal in the glorious return of the Son of God at the end of time. In Jesus Christ, the Word made flesh, time becomes a dimension of God, who is Himself eternal". [118]

In the light of the New Testament, the years of Christ's earthly life truly constitute the center of time; this center reaches its apex in the Resurrection. It is true that Jesus is God made man from the very moment of His conception in the womb of the Blessed Virgin, but only in the Resurrection is His humanity wholly transfigured and glorified, thus revealing the fullness of His divine identity and glory. In His speech in the synagogue at Antioch in Pisidia (cf. *Acts* 13:33), Paul applies the words of Psalm 2 to the Resurrection of Christ: "You are my Son, this day I have begotten you" (v. 7). It is precisely for this reason that, in celebrating the Easter Vigil, the Church acclaims the Risen Christ as "the Beginning and End, the Alpha and Omega". These are the words spoken by the celebrant as he prepares the Paschal candle, which bears the number of the current year. These words clearly attest that "Christ is the Lord of time; He is its beginning and its end; every year, every day and every moment are embraced by His Incarnation and Resurrection, and thus become part of the 'fullness of time'". [119]

75. Since Sunday is the weekly Easter, recalling and making present the day upon which Christ rose from the dead, it is also the day which reveals the meaning of time. It has nothing in common with the cosmic cycles according to which natural religion and human

culture tend to impose a structure on time, succumbing perhaps to the myth of eternal return. The Christian Sunday is wholly other! Springing from the Resurrection, it cuts through human time, the months, the years, the centuries, like a directional arrow which points them towards their target: Christ's Second Coming. Sunday foreshadows the last day, the day of the *Parousia*, which in a way is already anticipated by Christ's glory in the event of the Resurrection.

In fact, everything that will happen until the end of the world will be no more than an extension and unfolding of what happened on the day when the battered body of the Crucified Lord was raised by the power of the Spirit and became in turn the wellspring of the Spirit for all humanity. Christians know that there is no need to wait for another time of salvation, since, however long the world may last, they are already living in the last times. Not only the Church, but the cosmos itself and history are ceaselessly ruled and governed by the glorified Christ. It is this life-force which propels creation, "groaning in birth-pangs until now" (*Rom* 8:22), towards the goal of its full redemption. Mankind can have only a faint intuition of this process, but Christians have the key and the certainty. Keeping Sunday holy is the important witness which they are called to bear, so that every stage of human history will be upheld by hope.

Sunday in the Liturgical Year

76. With its weekly recurrence, the Lord's Day is rooted in the most ancient tradition of the Church and is vitally important for the Christian. But there was another rhythm which soon established itself: the annual liturgical cycle. Human psychology in fact desires the celebration of anniversaries, associating the return of dates and seasons with the remembrance of past events. When these events are decisive in the life of a people, their celebration generally creates a festive atmosphere which breaks the monotony of daily routine.

Now, by God's design, the great saving events upon which the Church's life is founded were closely linked to the annual Jewish feasts of Passover and Pentecost, and were prophetically foreshadowed in them. Since the second century, the annual celebration of Easter by Christians — having been added to the weekly Easter celebration — allowed a more ample meditation on the mystery of Christ crucified and risen. Preceded by a preparatory fast, celebrated in the course of a long vigil, extended into the fifty days leading to Pentecost, the feast of Easter — "solemnity of solemnities" — became the day par excellence for the initiation of catechumens. Through baptism they die to sin and rise to a new life because Jesus "was put to death for our sins and raised for our justification" (*Rom* 4:25; cf. 6:3-11). Intimately connected to the Paschal Mystery, the Solemnity of Pentecost takes on special importance, celebrating as it does the coming of the Holy Spirit upon the Apostles gathered with Mary and inaugurating the mission to all peoples. [120]

77. A similar commemorative logic guided the arrangement of the entire Liturgical Year. As the Second Vatican Council recalls, the Church wished to extend throughout the year "the entire mystery of Christ, from the Incarnation and Nativity to the Ascension, to the day of Pentecost and to the waiting in blessed hope for the return of the Lord. Remembering in this way the mysteries of redemption, the Church opens to the faithful the treasury of the Lord's power and merits, making them present in some sense to all times, so that the faithful may approach them and be filled by them with the grace of salvation". [121]

After Easter and Pentecost, the most solemn celebration is undoubtedly the Nativity of the Lord, when Christians ponder the mystery of the Incarnation and contemplate the Word of God who deigns to assume our humanity in order to give us a share in His divinity.

78. Likewise, "in celebrating this annual cycle of the mysteries of Christ, the holy Church venerates with special love the Blessed Virgin Mary, Mother of God, united forever with the saving work of her Son". [122] In a similar way, by inserting into the annual cycle the commemoration of the martyrs and other saints on the occasion of their anniversaries, "the Church proclaims the Easter mys-

tery of the saints who suffered with Christ and with Him are now glorified". (123) When celebrated in the true spirit of the liturgy, the commemoration of the saints does not obscure the centrality of Christ, but on the contrary extols it, demonstrating as it does the power of the redemption wrought by Him. As Saint Paulinus of Nola sings, "all things pass, but the glory of the saints endures in Christ, who renews all things, while He Himself remains unchanged". (124) The intrinsic relationship between the glory of the saints and that of Christ is built into the very arrangement of the Liturgical Year, and is expressed most eloquently in the fundamental and sovereign character of Sunday as the Lord's Day. Following the seasons of the Liturgical Year in the Sunday observance which structures it from beginning to end, the ecclesial and spiritual commitment of Christians comes to be profoundly anchored in Christ, in whom believers find their reason for living and from whom they draw sustenance and inspiration.

79. Sunday emerges therefore as the natural model for understanding and celebrating these feast-days of the Liturgical Year, which are of such value for the Christian life that the Church has chosen to emphasize their importance by making it obligatory for the faithful to attend Mass and to observe a time of rest, even though these feast-days may fall on variable days of the week. (125) Their number has been changed from time to time, taking into account social and economic conditions, as also how firmly they are established in tradition, and how well they are supported by civil legislation. (126)

The present canonical and liturgical provisions allow each Episcopal Conference, because of particular circumstances in one country or another, to reduce the list of Holy Days of obligation. Any decision in this regard needs to receive the special approval of the Apostolic See, (127) and in such cases the celebration of a mystery of the Lord, such as the Epiphany, the Ascension or the Solemnity of the Body and Blood of Christ, must be transferred to Sunday, in accordance with liturgical norms, so that the faithful are not denied the chance to meditate upon the mystery. (128) Pastors should also take care to encourage the faithful to attend Mass on other important feast-days celebrated during the week. (129)

80. There is a need for special pastoral attention to the many situations where there is a risk that the popular and cultural traditions of a region may intrude upon the celebration of Sundays and other liturgical feast-days, mingling the spirit of genuine Christian faith with elements which are foreign to it and may distort it. In such cases, catechesis and well-chosen pastoral initiatives need to clarify these situations, eliminating all that is incompatible with the Gospel of Christ. At the same time, it should not be forgotten that these traditions — and, by analogy, some recent cultural initiatives in civil society — often embody values which are not difficult to integrate with the demands of faith. It rests with the discernment of Pastors to preserve the genuine values found in the culture of a particular social context and especially in popular piety, so that liturgical celebration — above all on Sundays and holy days — does not suffer but rather may actually benefit. [(130)]

CONCLUSION

81. The spiritual and pastoral riches of Sunday, as it has been handed on to us by tradition, are truly great. When its significance and implications are understood in their entirety, Sunday in a way becomes a synthesis of the Christian life and a condition for living it well. It is clear therefore why the observance of the Lord's Day is so close to the Church's heart, and why in the Church's discipline it remains a real obligation. Yet more than as a precept, the observance should be seen as a need rising from the depths of Christian life. It is crucially important that all the faithful should be convinced that they cannot live their faith or share fully in the life of the Christian community unless they take part regularly in the Sunday Eucharistic assembly. The Eucharist is the full realization of the worship which humanity owes to God, and it cannot be compared to any other religious experience. A particularly efficacious expression of this is the Sunday gathering of the entire community, obedient to the voice of the Risen Lord who calls the faithful together to give them the light of his word and the nourishment of his Body as the perennial sacramental wellspring of redemption. The

grace flowing from this wellspring renews mankind, life and history.

82. It is with this strong conviction of faith, and with awareness of the heritage of human values which the observance of Sunday entails, that Christians today must face the enticements of a culture which has accepted the benefits of rest and free time, but which often uses them frivolously and is at times attracted by morally questionable forms of entertainment. Certainly, Christians are no different from other people in enjoying the weekly day of rest; but at the same time they are keenly aware of the uniqueness and originality of Sunday, the day on which they are called to celebrate their salvation and the salvation of all humanity. Sunday is the day of joy and the day of rest precisely because it is "the Lord's Day", the day of the Risen Lord.

83. Understood and lived in this fashion, Sunday in a way becomes the soul of the other days, and in this sense we can recall the insight of Origen that the perfect Christian "is always in the Lord's Day, and is always celebrating Sunday". [131] Sunday is a true school, an enduring program of Church pedagogy — an irreplaceable pedagogy, especially with social conditions now marked more and more by a fragmentation and cultural pluralism which constantly test the faithfulness of individual Christians to the practical demands of their faith. In many parts of the world, we see a "*diaspora*" Christianity, which is put to the test because the scattered disciples of Christ can no longer easily maintain contact with one another, and lack the support of the structures and traditions proper to Christian culture. In a situation of such difficulty, the opportunity to come together on Sundays with fellow believers, exchanging gifts of brotherhood, is an indispensable help.

84. Sustaining Christian life as it does, Sunday has the additional value of being a testimony and a proclamation. As a day of prayer, communion and joy, Sunday resounds throughout society, emanating vital energies and reasons for hope. Sunday is the proclamation that time, in which He who is the Risen Lord of history makes

his home, is not the grave of our illusions but the cradle of an ever new future, an opportunity given to us to turn the fleeting moments of this life into seeds of eternity. Sunday is an invitation to look ahead; it is the day on which the Christian community cries out to Christ, "*Marana tha: Come, O Lord!*" (*1 Cor* 16:22). With this cry of hope and expectation, the Church is the companion and support of human hope. From Sunday to Sunday, enlightened by Christ, she goes forward towards the unending Sunday of the heavenly Jerusalem, which "has no need of the sun or moon to shine upon it, for the glory of God is its light and its lamp is the Lamb" (*Rev* 21:23).

85. As she strains towards her goal, the Church is sustained and enlivened by the Spirit. It is He who awakens memory and makes present for every generation of believers the event of the Resurrection. He is the inward gift uniting us to the Risen Lord and to our brothers and sisters in the intimacy of a single body, reviving our faith, filling our hearts with charity and renewing our hope. The Spirit is unfailingly present to every one of the Church's days, appearing unpredictably and lavishly with the wealth of His gifts. But it is in the Sunday gathering for the weekly celebration of Easter that the Church listens to the Spirit in a special way and reaches out with Him to Christ in the ardent desire that He return in glory: "The Spirit and the Bride say, 'Come!'" (*Rev* 22:17). Precisely in consideration of the role of the Spirit, I have wished that this exhortation aimed at rediscovering the meaning of Sunday should appear in this year which, in the immediate preparation for the Jubilee, is dedicated to the Holy Spirit.

86. I entrust this Apostolic Letter to the intercession of the Blessed Virgin, that it may be received and put into practice by the Christian community. Without in any way detracting from the centrality of Christ and His Spirit, Mary is always present in the Church's Sunday. It is the mystery of Christ itself which demands this: indeed, how could she who is *Mater Domini and Mater Ecclesiae* fail to be uniquely present on the day which is both *dies Domini and dies Ecclesiae*?

As they listen to the word proclaimed in the Sunday assembly, the faithful look to the Virgin Mary, learning from her to keep it and ponder it in their hearts (cf. *Lk* 2:19). With Mary, they learn to stand at the foot of the Cross, offering to the Father the sacrifice of Christ and joining to it the offering of their own lives. With Mary, they experience the joy of the Resurrection, making their own the words of the Magnificat which extol the inexhaustible gift of divine mercy in the inexorable flow of time: "His mercy is from age to age upon those who fear Him" (*Lk* 1:50). From Sunday to Sunday, the pilgrim people follow in the footsteps of Mary, and her maternal intercession gives special power and fervor to the prayer which rises from the Church to the Most Holy Trinity.

87. Dear Brothers and Sisters, the imminence of the Jubilee invites us to a deeper spiritual and pastoral commitment. Indeed, this is its true purpose. In the Jubilee year, much will be done to give it the particular stamp demanded by the ending of the Second Millennium and the beginning of the Third since the Incarnation of the Word of God. But this year and this special time will pass, as we look to other jubilees and other solemn events. As the weekly "solemnity", however, Sunday will continue to shape the time of the Church's pilgrimage, until that Sunday which will know no evening.

Therefore, dear Brother Bishops and Priests, I urge you to work tirelessly with the faithful to ensure that the value of this sacred day is understood and lived ever more deeply. This will bear rich fruit in Christian communities, and will not fail to have a positive influence on civil society as a whole.

In coming to know the Church, which every Sunday joyfully celebrates the mystery from which she draws her life, may the men and women of the Third Millennium come to know the Risen Christ. And constantly renewed by the weekly commemoration of Easter, may Christ's disciples be ever more credible in proclaiming the Gospel of salvation and ever more effective in building the civilization of love.

My blessing to you all!
From the Vatican, on 31 May, the Solemnity of Pentecost, in the year 1998, the twentieth of my Pontificate.

Notes:

(1) Cf. Rev 1:10: *"Kyriake heméra"*; cf. also the *Didaché* 14, 1, Saint Ignatius of Antioch, To the Magnesians 9, 1-2; SC 10, 88-89.

(2) Pseudo-Eusebius of Alexandria, Sermon 16: PG 86, 416.

(3) *In Die Dominica Paschae* II, 52: CCL 78, 550.

(4) Second Vatican Ecumenical Council, Constitution on the Sacred Liturgy Sacrosanctum Concilium, 106.

(5) Ibid.

(6) Cf. *Motu Proprio Mysterii Paschalis* (14 February 1969): AAS 61 (1969), 222-226.

(7) Cf. Pastoral Note of the Italian Episcopal Conference *"Il giorno del Signore"* (15 July 1984), 5: *Enchiridion* CEI 3, 1398.

(8) Constitution on the Sacred Liturgy *Sacrosanctum Concilium*, 106.

(9) Homily for the Solemn Inauguration of the Pontificate (22 October 1978), 5: AAS 70 (1978), 947.

(10) No. 25: AAS 73 (1981), 639.

(11) Pastoral Constitution on the Church in the Modern World *Gaudium et Spes*, 34.

(12) For our Jewish brothers and sisters, a "nuptial" spirituality characterizes the Sabbath, as appears, for example, in texts of Genesis Rabbah such as X, 9 and XI, 8 (cf. J. Neusner, Genesis Rabbah, vol. I, Atlanta 1985, p. 107 and p. 117). The song *Leka Dôdi* is also nuptial in tone: *"Your God will delight in you, as the Bridegroom delights in the Bride ... In the midst of the faithful of your beloved people, come O Bride, O Shabbat Queen"* (cf. Preghiera serale del sabato, issued by A. Toaff, Rome, 1968-69, p. 3).

(13) Cf. A. J. Heschel, The Sabbath: Its Meaning for Modern Man (22nd ed., 1995), pp. 3-24.

(14) *"Verum autem sabbatum ipsum redemptorem nostrum Iesum Christum Dominum habemus"*: Epist. 13, 1: CCL 140A, 992.

(15) *Ep. ad Decentium* XXV, 4, 7: PL 20, 555.

(16) *Homiliae in Hexaemeron* II, 8: SC 26, 184.

(17) *Cf. In Io. Ev. Tractatus* XX, 20, 2: CCL 36, 203; Epist. 55, 2: CSEL 34, 170-171.

(18) The reference to the Resurrection is especially clear in Russian, which calls Sunday simply "Resurrection" (Voskresenie).

(19) *Epist.* 10, 96, 7.

(20) Cf. ibid. In reference to Pliny's letter, Tertullian also recalls the *coetus antelucani in Apologeticu*m 2, 6: CCL 1, 88; De Corona 3, 3: CCL 2, 1043.

(21) To the Magnesians 9, 1-2: SC 10, 88-89.

(22) Sermon 8 in the Octave of Easter 4: PL 46, 841. This sense of Sunday as "the first day" is clear in the Latin liturgical calendar, where Monday is called *feria secunda*, Tuesday *feria tertia* and so on. In Portuguese, the days are named in the same way.

(23)   Saint Gregory of Nyssa, *De Castigatione*: PG 46, 309. The Maronite Liturgy also stresses the link between the Sabbath and Sunday, beginning with the "mystery of Holy Saturday" (cf. M. Hayek, Maronite [Eglise], *Dictionnaire de spiritualité*, X [1980], 632-644).]

(24)   Rite of Baptism of Children, No. 9; cf. Rite of Christian Initiation of Adults, No. 59.

(25)   Cf. Roman Missal, Rite of Blessing and Sprinkling of Holy Water.

(26)   Cf. Saint Basil, On the Holy Spirit, 27, 66: SC 17, 484-485. Cf. also Letter of Barnabas 15, 8-9: SC 172, 186-189; Saint Justin, Dialogue with Trypho 24; 138: PG 6, 528, 793; Origen, Commentary on the Psalms, Psalm 118(119), 1: PG 12, 1588.

(27)   "*Domine, praestitisti nobis pacem quietis, pacem sabbati, pacem sine vespera*": Confess., 13, 50: CCL 27, 272.

(28)   Cf. Saint Augustine, Epist. 55, 17: CSEL 34, 188: "*Ita ergo erit octavus, qui primus, ut prima vita sed aeterna reddatur*".

(29)   Thus in English "Sunday" and in German "Sonntag".

(30)   Apologia I, 67: PG 6, 430.

(31)   Cf. Saint Maximus of Turin, Sermo 44, 1: CCL 23, 178; *Sermo* 53, 2: CCL 23, 219; Eusebius of Caesarea, Comm. in Ps. 91: PG 23, 1169-1173.

(32)   See, for example, the Hymn of the Office of Readings: "*Dies aetasque ceteris octava splendet sanctior in te quam, Iesu, consecras primitiae surgentium* (Week I); and also: "*Salve dies, dierum gloria, dies felix Christi victoria, dies digna iugi laetitia dies prima. Lux divina caecis irradiat, in qua Christus infernum spoliat, mortem vincit et reconciliat summis ima*" (Week II). Similar expressions are found in hymns included in the Liturgy of the Hours in various modern languages.

(33)   Cf. Clement of Alexandria, *Stromata*, VI, 138, 1-2: PG 9, 364.

(34)   Cf. John Paul II, Encyclical Letter *Dominum et Vivificantem* (18 May 1986), 22-26: AAS 78 (1986), 829-837.

(35)   Cf. Saint Athanasius of Alexandria, Sunday Letters 1, 10: PG 26, 1366.

(36)   Cf. Bardesanes, Dialogue on Destiny, 46: PS 2, 606-607.

(37)   Constitution on the Sacred Liturgy *Sacrosanctum Concilium*, Appendix: Declaration on the Reform of the Calendar.

(38)   Cf. Second Vatican Ecumenical Council, Dogmatic Constitution on the Church *Lumen Gentium*, 9.

(39)   Cf. John Paul II, Letter *Dominicae Cenae* (24 February 1980), 4: AAS 72 (1980), 120; Encyclical Letter *Dominum et Vivificantem* (18 May 1986), 62-64: AAS 78 (1986), 889-894.

(40)   Cf. John Paul II, Apostolic Letter *Vicesimus Quintus Annus* (4 December 1988), 9: AAS 81 (1989), 905-906.

(41)   No. 2177.

(42)   Cf. John Paul II, Apostolic Letter *Vicesimus Quintus Annus* (4 December 1988), 9: AAS 81 (1989), 905-906.

(43)   Second Vatican Ecumenical Council, Constitution on the Sacred Liturgy *Sacrosanctum Concilium*, 41; cf. Decree on the Pastoral Office of Bish-

ops in the Church *Christus Dominus*, 15.

(44)   These are the words of the Embolism, formulated in this or similar ways in some of the Eucharistic Prayers of the different languages. They stress powerfully the "Paschal" character of Sunday.

(45)   Cf. Congregation for the Doctrine of the Faith, Letter to the Bishops of the Catholic Church on Certain Aspects of the Church as Communion *Communionis Notio* (28 May 1992), 11-14: AAS 85 (1993), 844-847.

(46)   Speech to the Third Group of the Bishops of the United States of America (17 March 1998), 4: *L'Osservatore Romano*, 18 March 1998, 4.

(47)   Constitution on the Sacred Liturgy *Sacrosanctum Concilium*, 42.

(48)   Sacred Congregation of Rites, Instruction on the Worship of the Eucharistic Mystery *Eucharisticum Mysterium* (25 May 1967), 26: AAS 59 (1967), 555.

(49)   Cf. Saint Cyprian, De Orat. Dom. 23: PL 4, 553; *De Cath. Eccl. Unitate*, 7: CSEL 31, 215; Second Vatican Ecumenical Council, Dogmatic Constitution on the Church Lumen Gentium, 4; Constitution on the Sacred Liturgy *Sacrosanctum Concilium*, 26.

(50)   Cf. John Paul II, Apostolic Exhortation *Familiaris Consortio* (22 November 1981), 57; 61: AAS 74 (1982), 151; 154.

(51)   Cf. Sacred Congregation for Divine Worship, Directory for Masses with Children (1 November 1973): AAS 66 (1974), 30-46.

(52)   Cf. Sacred Congregation of Rites, Instruction on the Worship of the Eucharistic Mystery *Eucharisticum Mysterium* (25 May 1967), 26: AAS 59 (1967), 555-556; Sacred Congregation for Bishops, Directory for the Pastoral Ministry of Bishops *Ecclesiae Imago* (22 February 1973), 86c: *Enchiridion Vaticanum* 4, 2071.

(53)   Cf. John Paul II, Post-Synodal Apostolic Exhortation *Christifideles Laici* (30 December 1988), 30: AAS 81 (1989), 446-447.

(54)   Cf. Sacred Congregation for Divine Worship, Instruction Masses for Particular Groups (15 May 1969), 10: AAS 61 (1969), 810.

(55)   Cf. Second Vatican Ecumenical Council, Dogmatic Constitution on the Church *Lumen Gentium*, 48-51.

(56)   *"Haec est vita nostra, ut desiderando exerceamur"*: Saint Augustine, In Prima Ioan. Tract. 4, 6: SC 75, 232.

(57)   Roman Missal, Embolism after the Lord's Prayer.

(58)   Second Vatican Ecumenical Council, Pastoral Constitution on the Church in the Modern World *Gaudium et Spes*, 1.

(59)   Second Vatican Ecumenical Council, Dogmatic Constitution on the Church *Lumen Gentium*, 1; cf. John Paul II, Encyclical Letter *Dominum et Vivificantem* (18 May 1986), 61-64: AAS 78 (1986), 888-894.

(60)   Second Vatican Ecumenical Council, Constitution on the Sacred Liturgy *Sacrosanctum Concilium*, 7; cf. 33.

(61)   Ibid., 56; cf. *Ordo Lectionum Missae, Praenotanda*, No. 10.

(62)   Constitution on the Sacred Liturgy *Sacrosanctum Concilium*, 51.

(63)   Cf. ibid., 52; Code of Canon Law, Canon 767, 2; Code of Canons of the

Eastern Churches, Canon 614.

(64) Apostolic Constitution *Missale Romanum* (3 April 1969): AAS 61 (1969), 220.

(65) The Council's Constitution *Sacrosanctum Concilium* speaks of *"suavis et vivus Sacrae Scripturae affectus"* (No. 24).

(66) John Paul II, Letter *Dominicae Cenae* (24 February 1980), 10: AAS 72 (1980), 135.

(67) Cf. Second Vatican Ecumenical Council, Dogmatic Constitution on Divine Revelation *Dei Verbum*, 25.

(68) Cf. *Ordo Lectionum Missae, Praenotanda*, Chap. III.

(69) Cf. Ordo *Lectionum Missae, Praenotanda*, Chap. I, No. 6.

(70) Ecumenical Council of Trent, Session XXII, Doctrine and Canons on the Most Holy Sacrifice of the Mass, II: DS 1743; cf. Catechism of the Catholic Church, 1366.

(71) Catechism of the Catholic Church, 1368.

(72) Sacred Congregation of Rites, Instruction on the Worship of the Eucharistic Mystery *Eucharisticum Mysterium* (25 May 1967), 3b: AAS 59 (1967), 541; cf. Pius XII, Encyclical Letter Mediator Dei (20 November 1947), II: AAS 39 (1947), 564-566.

(73) Cf. Catechism of the Catholic Church, 1385; cf. also Congregation for the Doctrine of the Faith, Letter to the Bishops of the Catholic Church concerning the Reception of Eucharistic Communion by Divorced and Remarried Faithful (14 September 1994): AAS 86 (1994), 974-979.

(74) Cf. Innocent I, Epist. 25, 1 to *Decentius of Gubbio*: PL 20, 553.

(75) II, 59, 2-3: ed. F. X. Funk, 1905, pp. 170-171.

(76) Cf. Apologia I, 67, 3-5: PG 6, 430.

(77) Acta SS. *Saturnini, Dativi et aliorum plurimorum Martyrum* in Africa, 7, 9, 10: PL 8, 707, 709-710.

(78) Cf. Canon 21, *Mansi*, Conc. II, 9.

(79) Cf. Canon 47, *Mansi*, Conc. VIII, 332.

(80) Cf. the contrary proposition, condemned by Innocent XI in 1679, concerning the moral obligation to keep the feast-day holy: DS 2152.

(81) Canon 1248: *"Festis de praecepto diebus Missa audienda est"*: Canon 1247, 1: *"Dies festi sub praecepto in universa Ecclesia sunt...omnes et singuli dies dominici"*.

(82) Code of Canon Law, Canon 1247; the Code of Canons of the Eastern Churches, Canon 881, 1, prescribes that "the Christian faithful are bound by the obligation to participate on Sundays and feast days in the Divine Liturgy or, according to the prescriptions or legitimate customs of their own Church *sui iuris,* in the celebration of the divine praises".

(83) No. 2181: "Those who deliberately fail in this obligation commit a grave sin".

(84) Sacred Congregation for Bishops, Directory for the Pastoral Ministry of Bishops *Ecclesiae Imago* (22 February 1973), 86a: *Enchiridion Vaticanum* 4, 2069.

(85)   Cf. Code of Canon Law, Canon 905, 2.

(86)   Cf. Pius XII, Apostolic Constitution *Christus Dominus* (6 January 1953): AAS 45 (1953), 15-24; *Motu Proprio Sacram Communionem* (19 March 1957): AAS 49 (1957), 177-178. Congregation of the Holy Office, Instruction on the Discipline concerning the Eucharist Fast (6 January 1953): AAS 45 (1953), 47-51.

(87)   Cf. Code of Canon Law, Canon 1248, 1; Code of Canons of the Eastern Churches, Canon 881, 2.

(88)   Cf. *Missale Romanum, Normae Universales de Anno Liturgico et de Calendario*, 3.

(89)   Cf. Sacred Congregation of Bishops, Directory for the Pastoral Ministry of Bishops *Ecclesiae Imago* (22 February 1973), 86: *Enchiridion Vaticanum* 4, 2069-2073.

(90)   Cf. Second Vatican Ecumenical Council, Constitution on the Sacred Liturgy *Sacrosanctum Concilium*, 14; 26; John Paul II, Apostolic Letter *Vicesimus Quintus Annus* (4 December 1988), 4; 6; 12: AAS 81 (1989), 900-901; 902; 909-910.

(91)   Cf. Second Vatican Ecumenical Council, Dogmatic Constitution on the Church *Lumen Gentium*, 10.

(92)   Cf. Interdicasterial Instruction on Certain Questions concerning the Collaboration of Lay Faithful in the Ministry of Priests *Ecclesiae de Mysterio* (15 August 1997), 6; 8: AAS 89 (1997), 869; 870-872.

(93)   Second Vatican Ecumenical Council, Dogmatic Constitution on the Church *Lumen Gentium*, 10: "*in oblationem Eucharistiae concurrunt*".

(94)   Ibid., 11.

(95)   Cf. Code of Canon Law, Canon 1248, 2.

(96)   Cf. Sacred Congregation for Divine Worship, Directory for Sunday Celebrations in the Absence of a Priest *Christi Ecclesia* (2 June 1988): *Enchiridion Vaticanum* 11, 442-468; Interdicasterial Instruction on Certain Questions concerning the Collaboration of Lay Faithful in the Ministry of Priests *Ecclesiae de Mysterio* (15 August 1997): AAS 89 (1997), 852-877.

97)   Cf. Code of Canon Law, Canon 1248, 2; Congregation for the Doctrine of the Faith, Letter *Sacerdotium Ministeriale* (6 August 1983), III: AAS 75 (1983), 1007.

(98)   Cf. Pontifical Commission for Social Communications, *Instruction Communio et Progressio* (23 May 1971), 150-152; 157: AAS 63 (1971), 645-646; 647.

(99)   This is the Deacon's proclamation in honor of the Lord's Day: cf. the Syriac text in the Missal of the Church of Antioch of the Maronites (edition in Syriac and Arabic), Jounieh (Lebanon) 1959, p. 38.

(100) V, 20, 11: ed. F. X. Funk, 1905, p. 298; cf. *Didache* 14, 1: ed. F. X. Funk, 1901, p. 32; Tertullian, *Apologeticum* 16, 11: CCL 1, 116. See in particular the Epistle of Barnabas, 15, 9: SC 172, 188-189: "This is why we celebrate as a joyous feast the eighth day on which Jesus was raised from

the dead and, after having appeared, ascended into heaven".

(101) Tertullian for example tells us that on Sunday it was forbidden to kneel, since kneeling, which was then seen as an essentially penitential gesture, seemed unsuited to the day of joy. Cf. De Corona 3, 4: CCL 2, 1043.

(102) Ep. 55, 28: CSEL 342, 202.

(103) Cf. Saint Therese of the Child Jesus and the Holy Face, *Derniers entretiens*, 5-6 July 1897, in: *Oeuvres complètes, Cerf - Desclée de Brouwer*, Paris, 1992, pp. 1024-1025.

(104) Apostolic Exhortation, Gaudete in Domino (9 May 1975), II: AAS 67 (1975), 295.

(105) Ibid. VII, l.c., 322.

(106) Hex. 6, 10, 76: CSEL 321, 261.

(107) Cf. The Edict of Constantine, 3 July 321: Codex Theodosianus II, tit. 8, 1, ed. T. Mommsen, 12, p. 87; Codex Iustiniani, 3, 12, 2, ed. P. Krueger, p. 248.

(108) Cf. Eusebius of Caesarea, Life of Constantine, 4, 18: PG 20, 1165.

(109) The most ancient text of this kind is can. 29 of the Council of Laodicea (second half of the fourth century): Mansi, II, 569-570. From the sixth to the ninth century, many Councils prohibited *"opera ruralia"*. The legislation on prohibited activities, supported by civil laws, became increasingly detailed.

(110) Cf. Encyclical Letter *Rerum Novarum* (15 May 1891): Acta Leonis XIII 11 (1891), 127-128.

(111) Hex. 2, 1, 1: CSEL 321, 41.

(112) Cf. Code of Canon Law, Canon 1247; Code of Canons of the Eastern Churches, Canon 881, 1; 4.

(113) Second Vatican Ecumenical Council, Constitution on the Sacred Liturgy *Sacrosanctum Concilium*, 9.

(114) Cf. also Saint Justin, Apologia I, 67, 6: "Each of those who have an abundance and who wish to make an offering gives freely whatever he chooses, and what is collected is given to him who presides and he assists the orphans, the widows, the sick, the poor, the prisoners, the foreign visitors — in a word, he helps all those who are in need": PG 6, 430.

(115) De Nabuthae, 10, 45: *"Audis, dives, quid Dominus Deus dicat? Et tu ad ecclesiam venis, non ut aliquid largiaris pauperi, sed ut auferas"*: CSEL 322, 492.

(116) Homilies on the Gospel of Matthew, 50, 3-4: PG 58, 508-509.

(117) Saint Paulinus of Nola, Ep. 13, 11-12 to Pammachius: CSEL 29, 92-93. The Roman Senator is praised because, by combining participation in the Eucharist with distribution of food to the poor, he in a sense reproduced the Gospel miracle.

(118) John Paul II, Apostolic Letter *Tertio Millennio Adveniente* (10 November 1994), 10: AAS 87 (1995), 11.

(119) Ibid.

(120) Cf. Catechism of the Catholic Church, 731-732.

(121) Constitution on the Sacred Liturgy *Sacrosanctum Concilium*, 102.

(122) Ibid., 103.

(123) Ibid., 104.

(124) Carm. XVI, 3-4: *"Omnia praetereunt, sanctorum gloria durat in Christo qui cuncta novat, dum permanet ipse"*: CSEL 30, 67.

(125) Cf. Code of Canon Law, Canon 1247; Code of Canons of the Eastern Churches, Canon 881, 1; 4.

(126) By general law, the holy days of obligation in the Latin Church are the Feasts of the Nativity of the Lord, the Epiphany, the Ascension, the Body and Blood of Christ, Mary Mother of God, the Immaculate Conception, the Assumption, Saint Joseph, Saints Peter and Paul and All Saints: cf. Code of Canon Law, Canon 1246. The holy days of obligation in all the Eastern Churches are the Feasts of the Nativity of the Lord, the Epiphany, the Ascension, the Dormition of Mary Mother of God and Saints Peter and Paul: cf. Code of Canons of the Eastern Churches, Canon 880, 3.

(127) Cf. Code of Canon Law, Canon 1246, 2; for the Eastern Churches, cf. Code of Canons of the Eastern Churches, Canon 880, 3.

(128) Cf. Sacred Congregation of Rites, *Normae Universales de Anno Liturgico et de Calendario* (21 March 1969), 5, 7: *Enchiridion Vaticanum* 3, 895; 897.

(129) Cf. *Caeremoniale Episcoporum, ed. typica* 1995, No. 230.

(130) Cf. ibid., No. 233.

(131) *Contra Celsum VIII*, 22: SC 150, 222-224. m VIII, 22: SC 150, 222-224.

(131) *Contra Celsum VIII*, 22: SC 150, 222-224. *Liturgico et de Calendario* (21 March 1969), 5, 7: *Enchiridion Vaticanum* 3, 895; 897.

(129) Cf. *Caeremoniale Episcoporum, ed. typica* 1995, No. 230.

(130) Cf. ibid., No. 233.

(131) *Contra Celsum VIII*, 22: SC 150, 222-224.

The Eucharist

CATECHISM OF THE CATHOLIC CHURCH

SECOND EDITION

PART TWO
THE CELEBRATION
OF THE CHRISTIAN MYSTERY
SECTION TWO
THE SEVEN SACRAMENTS OF THE CHURCH
CHAPTER ONE
THE SACRAMENTS OF CHRISTIAN INITIATION

ARTICLE 3
THE SACRAMENT OF THE EUCHARIST

1322 The holy Eucharist completes Christian initiation. Those who have been raised to the dignity of the royal priesthood by Baptism and configured more deeply to Christ by Confirmation participate with the whole community in the Lord's own sacrifice by means of the Eucharist.

1323 "At the Last Supper, on the night he was betrayed, our Savior instituted the Eucharistic sacrifice of His Body and Blood. This He did in order to perpetuate the sacrifice of the cross throughout the ages until He should come again, and so to entrust to His beloved Spouse, the Church, a memorial of His death and resurrection: a sacrament of love, a sign of unity, a bond of charity, a Paschal banquet 'in which Christ is consumed, the mind is filled with grace, and a pledge of future glory is given to us.'"[135]

I. THE EUCHARIST - SOURCE AND SUMMIT OF ECCLESIAL LIFE

1324 The Eucharist is "the source and summit of the Christian life."[136] "The other sacraments, and indeed all ecclesiastical ministries and works of the apostolate, are bound up with the Eucharist and are oriented toward it. For in the blessed Eucharist is contained the whole spiritual good of the Church, namely Christ Himself, our Pasch."[137]

1325 "The Eucharist is the efficacious sign and sublime cause of that communion in the divine life and that unity of the People of God by which the Church is kept in being. It is the culmination both of God's action sanctifying the world in Christ and of the worship men offer to Christ and through Him to the Father in the Holy Spirit."[138]

1326 Finally, by the Eucharistic celebration we already unite ourselves with the heavenly liturgy and anticipate eternal life, when God will be all in all.[139]

1327 In brief, the Eucharist is the sum and summary of our faith: "Our way of thinking is attuned to the Eucharist, and the Eucharist in turn confirms our way of thinking."[140]

II. WHAT IS THIS SACRAMENT CALLED?

1328 The inexhaustible richness of this sacrament is expressed in the different names we give it. Each name evokes certain aspects of it. It is called: Eucharist, because it is an action of thanksgiving to God. The Greek words *eucharistein*[141] and *eulogein*[142] recall the Jewish blessings that proclaim - especially during a meal - God's works: creation, redemption, and sanctification.

1329 *The Lord's Supper*, because of its connection with the supper which the Lord took with His disciples on the eve of His Passion and because it anticipates the wedding feast of the Lamb in the heavenly Jerusalem.[143]

The *Breaking of Bread*, because Jesus used this rite, part of a Jewish meat when as master of the table He blessed and distributed the bread,[144] above all at the Last Supper.[145] It is by this action that His disciples will recognize Him after His Resurrection,[146] and it is this expression that the first Christians will use to designate their Eucharistic assemblies;[147] by doing so they signified that all who eat the one broken bread, Christ, enter into communion with Him and form but one body in Him.[148]

The *Eucharistic Assembly* (*synaxis*), because the Eucharist is celebrated amid the assembly of the faithful, the visible expression of the Church.[149]

1330 The *memorial* of the Lord's Passion and Resurrection.

The *Holy Sacrifice*, because it makes present the one sacrifice of Christ the Savior and includes the Church's offering. The terms *holy sacrifice of the Mass, "sacrifice of praise," spiritual sacrifice, pure and holy sacrifice* are also used,[150] since it completes and surpasses all the sacrifices of the Old Covenant.

The *Holy and Divine Liturgy*, because the Church's whole liturgy finds its center and most intense expression in the celebration of this sacrament; in the same sense we also call its celebration the *Sacred Mysteries*. We speak of the *Most Blessed Sacrament* because it is the Sacrament of sacraments. The Eucharistic species reserved in the tabernacle are designated by this same name.

1331 *Holy Communion*, because by this sacrament we unite ourselves to Christ, who makes us sharers in His Body and Blood to form a single body.[151] We also call it: the holy things (*ta hagia; sancta*)[152] - the first meaning of the phrase "communion of saints" in the Apostles' Creed - the bread of angels, bread from heaven, medicine of immortality,[153] viaticum. . . .

1332 *Holy Mass* (*Missa*), because the liturgy in which the mystery of salvation is accomplished concludes with the sending forth (*missio*) of the faithful, so that they may fulfill God's will in their daily lives.

III. THE EUCHARIST
IN THE ECONOMY OF SALVATION

The signs of bread and wine

1333 At the heart of the Eucharistic celebration are the bread and wine that, by the words of Christ and the invocation of the Holy Spirit, become Christ's Body and Blood. Faithful to the Lord's command the Church continues to do, in His memory and until His glorious return, what He did on the eve of His Passion: "He took bread. . . ." "He took the cup filled with wine. . . ." The signs of bread and wine become, in a way surpassing understanding, the Body and Blood of Christ; they continue also to signify the goodness of creation. Thus in the Offertory we give thanks to the Creator for bread and wine,[154] fruit of the "work of human hands," but above all as "fruit of the earth" and "of the vine" - gifts of the Creator. The Church sees in the gesture of the king-priest Melchizedek, who "brought out bread and wine," a prefiguring of her own offering.[155]

1334 In the Old Covenant bread and wine were offered in sacrifice among the first fruits of the earth as a sign of grateful acknowledgment to the Creator. But they also received a new significance in the context of the Exodus: the unleavened bread that Israel eats every year at Passover commemorates the haste of the departure that liberated them from Egypt; the remembrance of the manna in the desert will always recall to Israel that it lives by the bread of the Word of God;[156] their daily bread is the fruit of the promised land, the pledge of God's faithfulness to His promises. The "cup of blessing"[157] at the end of the Jewish Passover meal adds to the festive joy of wine an eschatological dimension: the messianic expectation of the rebuilding of Jerusalem. When Jesus instituted the Eucharist, He gave a new and definitive meaning to the blessing of the bread and the cup.

1335 The miracles of the multiplication of the loaves, when the Lord says the blessing, breaks and distributes the loaves through

His disciples to feed the multitude, prefigure the superabundance of this unique bread of His Eucharist.[(158)] The sign of water turned into wine at Cana already announces the Hour of Jesus' glorification. It makes manifest the fulfillment of the wedding feast in the Father's kingdom, where the faithful will drink the new wine that has become the Blood of Christ.[(159)]

1336 The first announcement of the Eucharist divided the disciples, just as the announcement of the Passion scandalized them: "This is a hard saying; who can listen to it?"[(160)] The Eucharist and the Cross are stumbling blocks. It is the same mystery and it never ceases to be an occasion of division. "Will you also go away?"[(161)] the Lord's question echoes through the ages, as a loving invitation to discover that only he has "the words of eternal life"[(162)] *and that to receive in faith the gift of His Eucharist is to receive the Lord Himself.*

The institution of the Eucharist

1337 The Lord, having loved those who were His own, loved them to the end. Knowing that the hour had come to leave this world and return to the Father, in the course of a meal He washed their feet and gave them the commandment of love.[(163)] In order to leave them a pledge of this love, in order never to depart from His own and to make them sharers in His Passover, He instituted the Eucharist as the memorial of His death and Resurrection, and commanded His apostles to celebrate it until His return; "thereby He constituted them priests of the New Testament."[(164)]

1338 The three synoptic Gospels and St. Paul have handed on to us the account of the institution of the Eucharist; St. John, for his part, reports the words of Jesus in the synagogue of Capernaum that prepare for the institution of the Eucharist: Christ calls Himself the bread of life, come down from heaven.[(165)]

1339 Jesus chose the time of Passover to fulfill what He had announced at Capernaum: giving His disciples His Body and His

Blood:

> Then came the day of Unleavened Bread, on which the
> passover lamb had to be sacrificed. So Jesus sent Peter and
> John, saying, "Go and prepare the passover meal for us,
> that we may eat it. . . ." They went . . . and prepared the
> passover. And when the hour came, He sat at table, and the
> apostles with Him. And He said to them, "I have earnestly
> desired to eat this passover with you before I suffer; for I
> tell you I shall not eat it again until it is fulfilled in the
> kingdom of God.". . . . And He took bread, and when He
> had given thanks He broke it and gave it to them, saying,
> "This is My Body which is given for you. Do this in re-
> membrance of Me." And likewise the cup after supper, say-
> ing, "This cup which is poured out for you is the New
> Covenant in My Blood."[166]

1340 By celebrating the Last Supper with His apostles in the course
of the Passover meal, Jesus gave the Jewish Passover its definitive
meaning. Jesus' passing over to His father by His death and Resurrection, the new Passover, is anticipated in the Supper and celebrated in the Eucharist, which fulfills the Jewish Passover and
anticipates the final Passover of the Church in the glory of the kingdom.

"Do this in memory of Me"

1341 The command of Jesus to repeat His actions and words "until He comes" does not only ask us to remember Jesus and what He
did. It is directed at the liturgical celebration, by the apostles and
their successors, of the memorial of Christ, of His life, of His death,
of His Resurrection, and of His intercession in the presence of the
Father.[167]

1342 From the beginning the Church has been faithful to the Lord's
command. Of the Church of Jerusalem it is written:

> They devoted themselves to the apostles' teaching and fel-

lowship, to the breaking of bread and the prayers. . . . Day by day, attending the temple together and breaking bread in their homes, they partook of food with glad and generous hearts.[(168)]

1343 It was above all on "the first day of the week," Sunday, the day of Jesus' resurrection, that the Christians met "to break bread."[(169)] From that time on down to our own day the celebration of the Eucharist has been continued so that today we encounter it everywhere in the Church with the same fundamental structure. It remains the center of the Church's life.

1344 Thus from celebration to celebration, as they proclaim the Paschal mystery of Jesus "until He comes," the pilgrim People of God advances, "following the narrow way of the cross,"[(170)] toward the heavenly banquet, when all the elect will be seated at the table of the kingdom.

IV. THE LITURGICAL CELEBRATION OF THE EUCHARIST

The Mass of all ages

1345 As early as the second century we have the witness of St. Justin Martyr for the basic lines of the order of the Eucharistic celebration. They have stayed the same until our own day for all the great liturgical families. St. Justin wrote to the pagan emperor Antoninus Pius (138-161) around the year 155, explaining what Christians did:

On the day we call the day of the sun, all who dwell in the city or country gather in the same place.

The memoirs of the apostles and the writings of the prophets are read, as much as time permits.

When the reader has finished, he who presides over those gathered admonishes and challenges them to imitate these beautiful things.

Then we all rise together and offer prayers* for ourselves . . .and for all others, wherever they may be, so that
we may be found righteous by our life and actions, and
faithful to the commandments, so as to obtain eternal salvation.

When the prayers are concluded we exchange the kiss.

Then someone brings bread and a cup of water and
wine mixed together to him who presides over the brethren.

He takes them and offers praise and glory to the Father of the universe, through the name of the Son and of
the Holy Spirit and for a considerable time he gives thanks
(in Greek: *eucharistian*) that we have been judged worthy
of these gifts.

When he has concluded the prayers and thanksgivings,
all present give voice to an acclamation by saying: 'Amen.'

When he who presides has given thanks and the people
have responded, those whom we call deacons give to those
present the "eucharisted" bread, wine and water and take
them to those who are absent.[(171)]

1346 The liturgy of the Eucharist unfolds according to a fundamental structure which has been preserved throughout the centuries down to our own day. It displays two great parts that form a
fundamental unity:
- the gathering, the liturgy of the Word, with readings, homily and
general intercessions;
- the liturgy of the Eucharist, with the presentation of the bread and
wine, the consecratory thanksgiving, and communion.

The liturgy of the Word and liturgy of the Eucharist together
form "one single act of worship";[(172)] the Eucharistic table set for
us is the table both of the Word of God and of the Body of the
Lord.[(173)]

1347 Is this not the same movement as the Paschal meal of the
risen Jesus with His disciples? Walking with them He explained
the Scriptures to them; sitting with them at table "He took bread,
blessed and broke it, and gave it to them."[(174)]

The movement of the celebration

1348 *All gather together.* Christians come together in one place for the Eucharistic assembly. At its head is Christ Himself, the principal agent of the Eucharist. He is high priest of the New Covenant; it is He Himself who presides invisibly over every Eucharistic celebration. It is in representing Him that the bishop or priest acting in the person of Christ the head (*in persona Christi capitis*) presides over the assembly, speaks after the readings, receives the offerings, and says the Eucharistic Prayer. All have their own active parts to play in the celebration, each in his own way: readers, those who bring up the offerings, those who give communion, and the whole people whose "Amen" manifests their participation.

1349 *The Liturgy of the Word* includes "the writings of the prophets," that is, the Old Testament, and "the memoirs of the apostles" (their letters and the Gospels). After the homily, which is an exhortation to accept this Word as what it truly is, the Word of God,[175] and to put it into practice, come the intercessions for all men, according to the Apostle's words: "I urge that supplications, prayers, intercessions, and thanksgivings be made for all men, for kings, and all who are in high positions."[176]

1350 *The presentation of the offerings* (the Offertory). Then, sometimes in procession, the bread and wine are brought to the altar; they will be offered by the priest in the name of Christ in the Eucharistic sacrifice in which they will become His Body and Blood. It is the very action of Christ at the Last Supper - "taking the bread and a cup." "The Church alone offers this pure oblation to the Creator, when she offers what comes forth from His creation with thanksgiving."[177] The presentation of the offerings at the altar takes up the gesture of Melchizedek and commits the Creator's gifts into the hands of Christ who, in His sacrifice, brings to perfection all human attempts to offer sacrifices.

1351 From the very beginning Christians have brought, along with the bread and wine for the Eucharist, gifts to share with those in need. This custom of the collection, ever appropriate, is inspired by the example of Christ who became poor to make us rich. [178] Those who are well off, and who are also willing, give as each chooses. What is gathered is given to him who presides to assist orphans and widows, those whom illness or any other cause has deprived of resources, prisoners, immigrants and, in a word, all who are in need. [179]

1352 The *anaphora*: with the Eucharistic Prayer - the prayer of thanksgiving and consecration - we come to the heart and summit of the celebration:

In the *preface*, the Church gives thanks to the Father, through Christ, in the Holy Spirit, for all His works: creation, redemption, and sanctification. The whole community thus joins in the unending praise that the Church in heaven, the angels and all the saints, sing to the thrice-holy God.

1353 In the *epiclesis*, the Church asks the Father to send His Holy Spirit (or the power of His blessing)[180] on the bread and wine, so that by His power they may become the Body and Blood of Jesus Christ and so that those who take part in the Eucharist may be one body and one spirit (some liturgical traditions put the epiclesis after the anamnesis).

In the *institution narrative*, the power of the words and the action of Christ, and the power of the Holy Spirit, make sacramentally present under the species of bread and wine Christ's Body and Blood, His sacrifice offered on the cross once for all.

1354 In the *anamnesis* that follows, the Church calls to mind the Passion, resurrection, and glorious return of Christ Jesus; she presents to the Father the offering of His Son which reconciles us with Him.

In the *intercessions*, the Church indicates that the Eucharist is celebrated in communion with the whole Church in heaven and on earth, the living and the dead, and in communion with the pastors of the Church, the Pope, the diocesan bishop, his presbyterium and his deacons, and all the bishops of the whole world together with their Churches.

1355 In the communion, preceded by the Lord's prayer and the breaking of the bread, the faithful receive "the bread of heaven" and "the cup of salvation," the Body and Blood of Christ who offered Himself "for the life of the world".[181]

> Because this bread and wine have been made Eucharist ("eucharisted," according to an ancient expression), "we call this food *Eucharist*, and no one may take part in it unless he believes that what we teach is true, has received baptism for the forgiveness of sins and new birth, and lives in keeping with what Christ taught."[182]

V. THE SACRAMENTAL SACRIFICE THANKSGIVING, MEMORIAL, PRESENCE

1356 If from the beginning Christians have celebrated the Eucharist and in a form whose substance has not changed despite the great diversity of times and liturgies, it is because we know ourselves to be bound by the command the Lord gave on the eve of His Passion: "Do this in remembrance of Me."[183]

1357 We carry out this command of the Lord by celebrating the *memorial of His sacrifice*. In so doing, we *offer to the Father* what He has Himself given us: the gifts of His creation, bread and wine which, by the power of the Holy Spirit and by the words of Christ, have become the Body and Blood of Christ. Christ is thus really and mysteriously made present.

1358 We must therefore consider the Eucharist as:
- thanksgiving and praise to the *Father*;
- the sacrificial memorial of *Christ* and His Body;
- the presence of Christ by the power of His word and of His *Spirit*.

Thanksgiving and Praise to the Father

1359 The Eucharist, the sacrament of our salvation accomplished by Christ on the cross, is also a sacrifice of praise in thanksgiving for the work of creation. In the Eucharistic sacrifice the whole of creation loved by God is presented to the Father through the death and the Resurrection of Christ. Through Christ the Church can offer the sacrifice of praise in thanksgiving for all that God has made good, beautiful, and just in creation and in humanity.

1360 The Eucharist is a sacrifice of thanksgiving to the Father, a blessing by which the Church expresses her gratitude to God for all His benefits, for all that He has accomplished through creation, redemption, and sanctification. Eucharist means first of all "thanksgiving."

1361 The Eucharist is also the sacrifice of praise by which the Church sings the glory of God in the name of all creation. This sacrifice of praise is possible only through Christ: He unites the faithful to His person, to His praise, and to His intercession, so that the sacrifice of praise to the Father is offered *through* Christ and *with* Him, to be accepted *in* Him.

The Sacrificial Memorial of Christ and of His Body, the Church

1362 The Eucharist is the memorial of Christ's Passover, the making present and the sacramental offering of His unique sacrifice, in the liturgy of the Church which is His Body. In all the Eucharistic Prayers we find after the words of institution a prayer called the anamnesis or memorial.

1363 In the sense of Sacred Scripture the memorial is not merely the recollection of past events but the proclamation of the mighty works wrought by God for men.[184] In the liturgical celebration of these events, they become in a certain way present and real. This is how Israel understands its liberation from Egypt: every time Passover is celebrated, the Exodus events are made present to the memory of believers so that they may conform their lives to them.

1364 In the New Testament, the memorial takes on new meaning.

When the Church celebrates the Eucharist, she commemorates Christ's Passover, and it is made present the sacrifice Christ offered once for all on the cross remains ever present.(185) "As often as the sacrifice of the Cross by which 'Christ our Pasch has been sacrificed' is celebrated on the altar, the work of our redemption is carried out."(186)

1365 Because it is the memorial of Christ's Passover, the Eucharist is also a sacrifice. The sacrificial character of the Eucharist is manifested in the very words of institution: "This is My Body which is given for you" and "This cup which is poured out for you is the New Covenant in My Blood."(187) In the Eucharist Christ gives us the very Body which He gave up for us on the cross, the very Blood which He "poured out for many for the forgiveness of sins."(188)

1366 The Eucharist is thus a sacrifice because it *re-presents* (makes present) the sacrifice of the cross, because it is its *memorial* and because it *applies* its fruit:

> [Christ], our Lord and God, was once and for all to offer Himself to God the Father by His death on the altar of the cross, to accomplish there an everlasting redemption. But because His priesthood was not to end with His death, at the Last Supper "on the night when He was betrayed," [He wanted] to leave to His beloved spouse the Church a visible sacrifice (as the nature of man demands) by which the bloody sacrifice which he was to accomplish once for all on the cross would be re-presented, its memory perpetuated until the end of the world, and its salutary power be applied to the forgiveness of the sins we daily commit.(189)

1367 The sacrifice of Christ and the sacrifice of the Eucharist are *one single sacrifice*: "The victim is one and the same: the same now offers through the ministry of priests, who then offered Himself on the cross; only the manner of offering is different." "And since in this divine sacrifice which is celebrated in the Mass, the same Christ who offered Himself once in a bloody manner on the altar of the cross is contained and is offered in an unbloody manner. . . this sacrifice is truly propitiatory."[190]

1368 *The Eucharist is also the sacrifice of the Church.* The Church which is the Body of Christ participates in the offering of her Head. With Him, she herself is offered whole and entire. She unites herself to His intercession with the Father for all men. In the Eucharist the sacrifice of Christ becomes also the sacrifice of the members of His Body. The lives of the faithful, their praise, sufferings, prayer, and work, are united with those of Christ and with His total offering, and so acquire a new value. Christ's sacrifice present on the altar makes it possible for all generations of Christians to be united with His offering.

In the catacombs the Church is often represented as a woman in prayer, arms outstretched in the praying position. Like Christ who stretched out His arms on the cross, through Him, with Him, and in Him, she offers herself and intercedes for all men.

1369 *The whole Church is united with the offering and intercession of Christ.* Since he has the ministry of Peter in the Church, the Pope is associated with every celebration of the Eucharist, wherein he is named as the sign and servant of the unity of the universal Church. The bishop of the place is always responsible for the Eucharist, even when a priest presides; the bishop's name is mentioned to signify his presidency over the particular Church, in the midst of his presbyterium and with the assistance of deacons. The community intercedes also for all ministers who, for it and with it, offer the Eucharistic sacrifice:

> Let only that Eucharist be regarded as legitimate, which is celebrated under [the presidency of] the bishop or him to whom he has entrusted it.[191]

> Through the ministry of priests the spiritual sacrifice of the faithful is completed in union with the sacrifice of Christ the only Mediator, which in the Eucharist is offered through the priests' hands in the name of the whole Church in an unbloody and sacramental manner until the Lord Himself comes.[192]

1370 To the offering of Christ are united not only the members still here on earth, but also those already *in the glory of heaven.* In communion with and commemorating the Blessed Virgin Mary and all the saints, the Church offers the Eucharistic sacrifice. In the Eucharist the Church is, as it were, at the foot of the cross with Mary, united with the offering and intercession of Christ.

1371 The Eucharistic sacrifice is also offered for *the faithful departed* who "have died in Christ but are not yet wholly purified,"[193] so that they may be able to enter into the light and peace of Christ:

> Put this body anywhere! Don't trouble yourselves about it! I simply ask you to remember me at the Lord's altar wherever you are.[194]

> Then, we pray [in the anaphora] for the holy fathers and bishops who have fallen asleep, and in general for all who have fallen asleep before us, in the belief that it is a great benefit to the souls on whose behalf the supplication is offered, while the holy and tremendous Victim is present. . . . By offering to God our supplications for those who have fallen asleep, if they have sinned, we . . . offer Christ sacrificed for the sins of all, and so render favorable, for them and for us, the God who loves man.[195]

1372 St. Augustine admirably summed up this doctrine that moves us to an ever more complete participation in our Redeemer's sacrifice which we celebrate in the Eucharist:

> This wholly redeemed city, the assembly and society of the saints, is offered to God as a universal sacrifice by the high priest who in the form of a slave went so far as to offer Himself for us in His Passion, to make us the Body of so great a head. . . . Such is the sacrifice of Christians: "we who are many are one Body in Christ" The Church continues to reproduce this sacrifice in the sacrament of the altar so well-known to believers wherein it is evident to them that in what she offers she herself is offered.[196]
> The presence of Christ by the power of His word and the Holy Spirit.

1373 "Christ Jesus, who died, yes, who was raised from the dead, who is at the right hand of God, who indeed intercedes for us," is present in many ways to His Church[197] in His word, in His Church's prayer, "where two or three are gathered in My name,"[198] in the poor, the sick, and the imprisoned,[199] in the sacraments of which He is the author, in the sacrifice of the Mass, and in the person of the minister. But "He is present . . . most *especially in the Eucharistic species*."[200]

1374 The mode of Christ's presence under the Eucharistic species is unique. It raises the Eucharist above all the sacraments as "the perfection of the spiritual life and the end to which all the sacraments tend."[201] In the most Blessed Sacrament of the Eucharist "the Body and Blood, together with the Soul and Divinity, of our Lord Jesus Christ and, therefore, the *whole Christ is truly, really, and substantially* contained."[202] "This presence is called 'real' - by which is not intended to exclude the other types of presence as if they could not be 'real' too, but because it is presence in the fullest sense: that is to say, it is a *substantial* presence by which Christ, God and man, makes Himself wholly and entirely present."[203]

1375 It is by the conversion of the bread and wine into Christ's Body and Blood that Christ becomes present in this sacrament. The Church Fathers strongly affirmed the faith of the Church in the efficacy of the Word of Christ and of the action of the Holy Spirit to bring about this conversion. Thus St. John Chrysostom declares:

> It is not man that causes the things offered to become the Body and Blood of Christ, but He who was crucified for us, Christ Himself. The priest, in the role of Christ, pronounces these words, but their power and grace are God's. This is My Body, he says. This word transforms the things offered.[204]

And St. Ambrose says about this conversion:

> Be convinced that this is not what nature has formed, but

what the blessing has consecrated. The power of the blessing prevails over that of nature, because by the blessing nature itself is changed. . . . Could not Christ's word, which can make from nothing what did not exist, change existing things into what they were not before? It is no less a feat to give things their original nature than to change their nature.[205]

1376 The Council of Trent summarizes the Catholic faith by declaring: "Because Christ our Redeemer said that it was truly His Body that He was offering under the species of bread, it has always been the conviction of the Church of God, and this holy Council now declares again, that by the consecration of the bread and wine there takes place a change of the whole substance of the bread into the substance of the Body of Christ our Lord and of the whole substance of the wine into the substance of His Blood. This change the holy Catholic Church has fittingly and properly called transubstantiation."[206]

1377 The Eucharistic presence of Christ begins at the moment of the consecration and endures as long as the Eucharistic species subsist. Christ is present whole and entire in each of the species and whole and entire in each of their parts, in such a way that the breaking of the bread does not divide Christ.[207]

1378 *Worship of the Eucharist.* In the liturgy of the Mass we express our faith in the real presence of Christ under the species of bread and wine by, among other ways, genuflecting or bowing deeply as a sign of adoration of the Lord. "The Catholic Church has always offered and still offers to the sacrament of the Eucharist the cult of adoration, not only during Mass, but also outside of it, reserving the consecrated hosts with the utmost care, exposing them to the solemn veneration of the faithful, and carrying them in procession."[208]

1379 The tabernacle was first intended for the reservation of the Eucharist in a worthy place so that it could be brought to the sick and those absent outside of Mass. As faith in the real presence of Christ in His Eucharist deepened, the Church became conscious of the meaning of silent adoration of the Lord present under the Eucharistic species. It is for this reason that the tabernacle should be located in an especially worthy place in the church and should be constructed in such a way that it emphasizes and manifests the truth of the real presence of Christ in the Blessed Sacrament.

1380 It is highly fitting that Christ should have wanted to remain present to His Church in this unique way. Since Christ was about to take His departure from His own in His visible form, He wanted to give us His sacramental presence; since He was about to offer himself on the cross to save us, He wanted us to have the memorial of the love with which He loved us "to the end,"[209] even to the giving of His life. In His Eucharistic presence He remains mysteriously in our midst as the one who loved us and gave Himself up for us,[210] and He remains under signs that express and communicate this love:

> The Church and the world have a great need for Eucharistic worship. Jesus awaits us in this sacrament of love. Let us not refuse the time to go to meet Him in adoration, in contemplation full of faith, and open to making amends for the serious offenses and crimes of the world. Let our adoration never cease.[211]

1381 "That in this sacrament are the true Body of Christ and His true Blood is something that 'cannot be apprehended by the senses,' says St. Thomas, 'but only by faith, which relies on divine authority.' For this reason, in a commentary on Luke 22:19 ('This is My Body which is given for you.'), St. Cyril says: 'Do not doubt whether this is true, but rather receive the words of the Savior in faith, for since He is the truth, He cannot lie.'"[212]

> *Godhead here in hiding, whom I do adore*
> *Masked by these bare shadows, shape and nothing more,*
> *See, Lord, at Thy service low lies here a heart*
> *Lost, all lost in wonder at the God Thou art.*

Seeing, touching, tasting are in Thee deceived;
How says trusty hearing? that shall be believed;
What God's Son has told me, take for truth I do;
Truth Himself speaks truly or there's nothing true.[213]

VI. THE PASCHAL BANQUET

1382 The Mass is at the same time, and inseparably, the sacrificial memorial in which the sacrifice of the cross is perpetuated and the sacred banquet of communion with the Lord's Body and Blood. But the celebration of the Eucharistic sacrifice is wholly directed toward the intimate union of the faithful with Christ through communion. To receive communion is to receive Christ Himself who has offered Himself for us.

1383 *The altar*, around which the Church is gathered in the celebration of the Eucharist, represents the two aspects of the same mystery: the altar of the sacrifice and the table of the Lord. This is all the more so since the Christian altar is the symbol of Christ Himself, present in the midst of the assembly of His faithful, both as the victim offered for our reconciliation and as food from heaven who is giving Himself to us. "For what is the altar of Christ if not the image of the Body of Christ?"[214] asks St. Ambrose. He says elsewhere, "The altar represents the Body [of Christ] and the Body of Christ is on the altar."[215] The liturgy expresses this unity of sacrifice and communion in many prayers. Thus the Roman Church prays in its anaphora:

> We entreat You, almighty God,
> that by the hands of Your holy Angel this offering may be borne to Your altar in heaven
> in the sight of Your divine majesty,
> so that as we receive in communion at this altar
> the most holy Body and Blood of Your Son,
> we may be filled with every heavenly blessing and grace.[216]

"Take this and eat it, all of you": communion

1384 The Lord addresses an invitation to us, urging us to receive Him in the sacrament of the Eucharist: "Truly, I say to you, unless you eat the Flesh of the Son of Man and drink His Blood, you have no life in you."[217]

1385 To respond to this invitation we must prepare ourselves for so great and so holy a moment. St. Paul urges us to examine our conscience: "Whoever, therefore, eats the bread or drinks the cup of the Lord in an unworthy manner will be guilty of profaning the Body and Blood of the Lord. Let a man examine himself, and so eat of the bread and drink of the cup. For any one who eats and drinks without discerning the Body eats and drinks judgment upon himself."[218] Anyone conscious of a grave sin must receive the sacrament of Reconciliation before coming to communion.

1386 Before so great a sacrament, the faithful can only echo humbly and with ardent faith the words of the Centurion: "*Domine, non sum dignus ut intres sub tectum meum, sed tantum dic verbo, et sanabitur anima mea*" ("Lord, I am not worthy that You should enter under my roof, but only say the word and my soul will be healed.").[219] And in the Divine Liturgy of St. John Chrysostom the faithful pray in the same spirit:

O Son of God, bring me into communion today with Your mystical supper. I shall not tell Your enemies the secret, nor kiss You with Judas' kiss. But like the good thief I cry, "Jesus, remember me when you come into Your kingdom."

1387 To prepare for worthy reception of this sacrament, the faithful should observe the fast required in their Church. [220] Bodily demeanor (gestures, clothing) ought to convey the respect, solemnity, and joy of this moment when Christ becomes our guest.

1388 It is in keeping with the very meaning of the Eucharist that the faithful, if they have the required dispositions, [221] *receive communion when* they participate in the Mass.[222] As the Second Vatican

Council says: "That more perfect form of participation in the Mass whereby the faithful, after the priest's communion, receive the Lord's Body from the same sacrifice, is warmly recommended."[(223)]

1389 The Church obliges the faithful to take part in the Divine Liturgy on Sundays and feast days and, prepared by the sacrament of Reconciliation, to receive the Eucharist at least once a year, if possible during the Easter season.[(224)] But the Church strongly encourages the faithful to receive the holy Eucharist on Sundays and feast days, or more often still, even daily.

1390 Since Christ is sacramentally present under each of the species, communion under the species of bread alone makes it possible to receive all the fruit of Eucharistic grace. For pastoral reasons this manner of receiving communion has been legitimately established as the most common form in the Latin rite. But "the sign of communion is more complete when given under both kinds, since in that form the sign of the Eucharistic meal appears more clearly."[(225)] This is the usual form of receiving communion in the Eastern rites.

The Fruits of Holy Communion

1391 *Holy Communion augments our union with Christ.* The principal fruit of receiving the Eucharist in Holy Communion is an intimate union with Christ Jesus. Indeed, the Lord said: "He who eats My Flesh and drinks My Blood abides in Me, and I in him."[(226)] Life in Christ has its foundation in the Eucharistic banquet: "As the living Father sent Me, and I live because of the Father, so he who eats Me will live because of Me."[(227)]

> On the feasts of the Lord, when the faithful receive the Body of the Son, they proclaim to one another the Good News that the first fruits of life have been given, as when the angel said to Mary Magdalene, "Christ is risen!" Now too are life and resurrection conferred on whoever receives Christ.[(228)]

1392 What material food produces in our bodily life, Holy Communion wonderfully achieves in our spiritual life. Communion with the flesh of the risen Christ, a flesh "given life and giving life through the Holy Spirit,"[229] preserves, increases, and renews the life of grace received at Baptism. This growth in Christian life needs the nourishment of Eucharistic Communion, the bread for our pilgrimage until the moment of death, when it will be given to us as viaticum.

1393 *Holy Communion separates us from sin.* The Body of Christ we receive in Holy Communion is "given up for us," and the Blood we drink "shed for the many for the forgiveness of sins." For this reason the Eucharist cannot unite us to Christ without at the same time cleansing us from past sins and preserving us from future sins: For as often as we eat this bread and drink the cup, we proclaim the death of the Lord. If we proclaim the Lord's death, we proclaim the forgiveness of sins. If, as often as His Blood is poured out, it is poured for the forgiveness of sins, I should always receive it, so that it may always forgive my sins. Because I always sin, I should always have a remedy.[230]

1394 As bodily nourishment restores lost strength, so the Eucharist strengthens our charity, which tends to be weakened in daily life; and this living charity *wipes away venial sins.*[231] By giving Himself to us Christ revives our love and enables us to break our disordered attachments to creatures and root ourselves in Him:

Since Christ died for us out of love, when we celebrate the memorial of His death at the moment of sacrifice we ask that love may be granted to us by the coming of the Holy Spirit. We humbly pray that in the strength of this love by which Christ willed to die for us, we, by receiving the gift of the Holy Spirit, may be able to consider the world as crucified for us, and to be ourselves as crucified to the world. . . . Having received the gift of love, let us die to sin and live for God.[232]

1395 By the same charity that it enkindles in us, the Eucharist *preserves us from future mortal sins.* The more we share the life of Christ and progress in His friendship, the more difficult it is to break away from Him by mortal sin. The Eucharist is not ordered to the forgiveness of mortal sins - that is proper to the sacrament of Reconciliation. The Eucharist is properly the sacrament of those who are in full communion with the Church.

1396 *The unity of the Mystical Body: the Eucharist makes the Church.* Those who receive the Eucharist are united more closely to Christ. Through it Christ unites them to all the faithful in one body - the Church. Communion renews, strengthens, and deepens this incorporation into the Church, already achieved by Baptism. In Baptism we have been called to form but one body.[(233)] The Eucharist fulfills this call: "The cup of blessing which we bless, is it not a participation in the Blood of Christ? The bread which we break, is it not a participation in the Body of Christ? Because there is one bread, we who are many are one body, for we all partake of the one bread:"[(234)]

> If you are the body and members of Christ, then it is your sacrament that is placed on the table of the Lord; it is your sacrament that you receive. To that which you are you respond "Amen" ("yes, it is true!") and by responding to it you assent to it. For you hear the words, "the Body of Christ" and respond "Amen." Be then a member of the Body of Christ that your *Amen* may be true.[(235)]

1397 *The Eucharist commits us to the poor.* To receive in truth the Body and Blood of Christ given up for us, we must recognize Christ in the poorest, His brethren:

> You have tasted the Blood of the Lord, yet you do not recognize your brother,. . . . You dishonor this table when you do not judge worthy of sharing your food someone judged worthy to take part in this meal. . . . God freed you from all your sins and invited you here, but you have not become more merciful.[(236)]

1398 The *Eucharist and the unity of Christians.* Before the greatness of this mystery St. Augustine exclaims, "*O sacrament of devotion! O sign of unity! O bond of charity!*"[237] The more painful the experience of the divisions in the Church which break the common participation in the table of the Lord, the more urgent are our prayers to the Lord that the time of complete unity among all who believe in Him may return.

1399 The Eastern churches that are not in full communion with the Catholic Church celebrate the Eucharist with great love. "These Churches, although separated from us, yet possess true sacraments, above all - by apostolic succession - the priesthood and the Eucharist, whereby they are still joined to us in closest intimacy." A certain communion *in sacris*, and so in the Eucharist, "given suitable circumstances and the approval of Church authority, is not merely possible but is encouraged."[238]

1400 Ecclesial communities derived from the Reformation and separated from the Catholic Church, "have not preserved the proper reality of the Eucharistic mystery in its fullness, especially because of the absence of the sacrament of Holy Orders."[239] It is for this reason that, for the Catholic Church, Eucharistic intercommunion with these communities is not possible. However these ecclesial communities, "when they commemorate the Lord's death and resurrection in the Holy Supper . . . profess that it signifies life in communion with Christ and await His coming in glory."[240]

1401 When, in the Ordinary's judgment, a grave necessity arises, Catholic ministers may give the sacraments of Eucharist, Penance, and Anointing of the Sick to other Christians not in full communion with the Catholic Church, who ask for them of their own will, provided they give evidence of holding the Catholic faith regarding these sacraments and possess the required dispositions.[241]

VII. THE EUCHARIST - "PLEDGE OF THE GLORY TO COME"

1402 In an ancient prayer the Church acclaims the mystery of the

Eucharist: "O sacred banquet in which Christ is received as food, the memory of His Passion is renewed, the soul is filled with grace and a pledge of the life to come is given to us." If the Eucharist is the memorial of the Passover of the Lord Jesus, if by our communion at the altar we are filled "with every heavenly blessing and grace,"[242] then the Eucharist is also an anticipation of the heavenly glory.

1403 At the Last Supper the Lord Himself directed His disciples' attention toward the fulfillment of the Passover in the kingdom of God: "I tell you I shall not drink again of this fruit of the vine until that day when I drink it new with you in My Father's kingdom."[243] Whenever the Church celebrates the Eucharist she remembers this promise and turns her gaze "to Him who is to come." In her prayer she calls for His coming: "*Marana tha!*" "Come, Lord Jesus!"[244] "May your grace come and this world pass away!"[245]

1404 The Church knows that the Lord comes even now in His Eucharist and that He is there in our midst. However, His presence is veiled. Therefore we celebrate the Eucharist "awaiting the blessed hope and the coming of our Savior, Jesus Christ,"[246] asking "to share in Your glory when every tear will be wiped away. On that day we shall see You, our God, as You are. We shall become like You and praise You for ever through Christ our Lord."[247]

1405 There is no surer pledge or dearer sign of this great hope in the new heavens and new earth "in which righteousness dwells,"[248] than the Eucharist. Every time this mystery is celebrated, "the work of our redemption is carried on" and we "break the one bread that provides the medicine of immortality, the antidote for death, and the food that makes us live for ever in Jesus Christ."[249]

IN BRIEF

1406 Jesus said: "I am the living bread that came down from heaven; if any one eats of this bread, he will live for ever; . . . he who eats My Flesh and drinks My Blood has eternal life and . . . abides in

Me, and I in him" (*Jn* 6:51,54,56).

1407 The Eucharist is the heart and the summit of the Church's life, for in it Christ associates His Church and all her members with His sacrifice of praise and thanksgiving offered once for all on the cross to His Father; by this sacrifice He pours out the graces of salvation on His Body which is the Church.

1408 The Eucharistic celebration always includes: the proclamation of the Word of God; thanksgiving to God the Father for all his benefits, above all the gift of His Son; the consecration of bread and wine; and participation in the liturgical banquet by receiving the Lord's Body and Blood. These elements constitute one single act of worship.

1409 The Eucharist is the memorial of Christ's Passover, that is, of the work of salvation accomplished by the life, death, and resurrection of Christ, a work made present by the liturgical action.

1410 It is Christ Himself, the eternal high priest of the New Covenant who, acting through the ministry of the priests, offers the Eucharistic sacrifice. And it is the same Christ, really present under the species of bread and wine, who is the offering of the Eucharistic sacrifice.

1411 Only validly ordained priests can preside at the Eucharist and consecrate the bread and the wine so that they become the Body and Blood of the Lord.

1412 The essential signs of the Eucharistic sacrament are wheat bread and grape wine, on which the blessing of the Holy Spirit is invoked and the priest pronounces the words of consecration spoken by Jesus during the Last Supper: "This is My Body which will be given up for you. . . . This is the cup of My Blood. . . ."

1413 By the consecration the transubstantiation of the bread and wine into the Body and Blood of Christ is brought about. Under the consecrated species of bread and wine Christ Himself, living and glorious, is present in a true, real, and substantial manner: His Body and His Blood, with His Soul and His Divinity (cf. Council of Trent: DS 1640; 1651).

1414 As sacrifice, the Eucharist is also offered in reparation for the sins of the living and the dead and to obtain spiritual or temporal benefits from God.

1415 Anyone who desires to receive Christ in Eucharistic communion must be in the state of grace. Anyone aware of having sinned mortally must not receive communion without having received absolution in the sacrament of penance.

1416 Communion with the Body and Blood of Christ increases the communicant's union with the Lord, forgives his venial sins, and preserves him from grave sins. Since receiving this sacrament strengthens the bonds of charity between the communicant and Christ, it also reinforces the unity of the Church as the Mystical Body of Christ.

1417 The Church warmly recommends that the faithful receive Holy Communion when they participate in the celebration of the Eucharist; she obliges them to do so at least once a year.

1418 Because Christ Himself is present in the sacrament of the altar, He is to be honored with the worship of adoration. "To visit the Blessed Sacrament is . . . a proof of gratitude, an expression of love, and a duty of adoration toward Christ our Lord" (Paul VI, MF 66).

1419 Having passed from this world to the Father, Christ gives us in the Eucharist the pledge of glory with Him. Participation in the Holy Sacrifice identifies us with His Heart, sustains our strength along the pilgrimage of this life, makes us long for eternal life, and unites us even now to the Church in heaven, the Blessed Virgin Mary, and all the saints.

Notes

(135) SC 47.
(136) LG 11.
(137) PO 5.
(138) Congregation of Rites, instruction, Eucharisticum mysterium, 6.
(139) Cf. I Cor 15:28.
(140) St. Irenaeus, Adv. haeres. 4, 18, 5: PG 7/l, 1028.
(141) Cf. Lk 22:19; I Cor 11:24.
(142) Cf. Mt 26:26; Mk 14:22.
(143) Cf. I Cor 11:20; Rev 19:9.
(144) Cf. Mt 14:19; 15:36; Mk 8:6, 19.
(145) Cf. Mt 26:26; I Cor 11:24.
(146) Cf. Lk 24:13-35.
(147) Cf. Acts 2:42, 46; 20:7, 11.
(148) Cf. I Cor 10:16-17.
(149) Cf. I Cor 11:17-34.
(150) Heb 13:15; cf. I Pet 2:5; Ps 116:13, 17; Mal 1:11.
(151) Cf. I Cor 10:16-17.
(152) Apostolic Constitutions 8, 13, 12 PG 1, 1108; Didache 9, 5; (10:6: SCh: 248,176- 178.
(153) St. Ignatius of Antioch, Ad Eph. 20, 2: SCh 10, 76.
(154) Cf. Ps 104:13-15.
(155) Gen 14:18; cf. Roman Missal, EP I (Roman Canon) 95.
(156) Cf. Deut 8:3.
(157) I Cor 10:16.
(158) Cf. Mt 14:13-21; 15:32-39.
(159) Cf. Jn 2:11; Mk 14:25.
(160) Jn 6:60.
(161) Jn 6:67.
(162) Jn 6:68.
(163) Cf. Jn 13:1-17; 34-35.
(164) Council of Trent (1562): DS 1740.
(165) Cf. Jn 6.
(166) Lk 22:7-20; Cf. *Mt* 26:17-29; *Mk* 14:12-25; § *Cor* 11:23-26.
(167) Cf. *1 Cor* 11:26.
(168) *Acts* 2:42, 46.
(169) *Acts* 20:7.
(170) AG 1; cf. *1 Cor* 11:26.
(171) St. Justin, Apol. 1, 65-67: PG 6, 428-429; the text before the asterisk (*) is from chap. 67.
(172) SC 56.
(173) Cf. DV 21.
(174) Cf. *Lk* 24:13-35.
(175) Cf. *1 Thess* 2:13.
(176) I Tim 2:1-2.

(177)   St. Irenaeus, *Adv. haeres.* 4, 18, 4: PG 7/1, 1027; cf. Mal 1:11.

(178)   Cf. *I Cor* 16:1; 2 Cor 8:9.

(179)   St. Justin, Apol. 1, 67: PG 6, 429.

(180)   Cf. Roman Missal, EP I (Roman Canon) 90.

(181)   Jn 6:51.

(182)   St. Justin, Apol. 1, 66, 1-2: PG 6, 428.

(183)   *I Cor* 11:24-25.

(184)   Cf. *Ex* 13:3.

(185)   Cf. *Heb* 7:25-27.

(186)   LG 3; cf. *I Cor* 5:7.

(187)   Lk 22:19-20.

(188)   Mt 26:28.

(189)   Council of Trent (1562): DS 1740; cf. I Cor 11:23; Heb 7:24, 27.

(190)   Council of Trent (1562): *Doctrina de ss. Missae sacrificio*, c. 2: DS 1743; cf. Heb 9:14, 27.

(191)   St. Ignatius of Antioch, *Ad Smyrn.* 8:1; SCh 10, 138.

(192)   PO 2 § 4.

(193)   Council of Trent (1562): DS 1743.

(194)   St. Monica, before her death, to her sons, St. Augustine and his brother; Conf. 9, 11, 27: PL 32, 775.

(195)   St. Cyril of Jerusalem, *Catech. myst.* 5, 9. 10 PG 33, 1116-1117.

(196)   St. Augustine, *De civ Dei*, 10, 6: PL 41, 283; cf. *Rom* 12:5.

(197)   *Rom* 8:34; cf. LG 48.

(198)   *Mt* 18:20.

(199)   Cf. *Mt* 25:31-46.

(200)   SC 7.

(201)   St. Thomas Aquinas, STh III, 73, 3c.

(202)   Council of Trent (1551): DS 1651.

(203)   Paul VI, MF 39.

(204)   St. John Chrysostom, prod. Jud. 1:6: PG 49, 380.

(205)   St. Ambrose, *De myst.* 9, 50; 52: PL 16, 405-407.

(206)   Council of Trent (1551): DS 1642; cf. *Mt* 26:26 ff.; *Mk* 14:22 ff.; *Lk* 22:19 ff.; *I Cor* 11:24 ff.

(20)7   Cf. Council of Trent: DS 1641.

(208)   Paul VI, MF 56.

(209)   Jn 13:1.

(210)   Cf. *Gal* 2:20.

(211)   John Paul II, *Dominicae cenae, 3.*

(212)   St. Thomas Aquinas, STh III, 75, 1; cf. Paul VI, MF 18; St. Cyril of Alexandria, In Luc. 22, 19: PG 72, 912; cf. Paul VI, MF 18.

(213)   St. Thomas Aquinas (attr.), *Adoro te devote*; tr. Gerard Manley Hopkins.

(214)   St. Ambrose, De Sacr. 5, 2, 7: PL 16, 447C.

(215)   St. Ambrose, De Sacr. 4, 2, 7: PL 16, 437D.

(216)   Roman Missal, EP I (Roman Canon) 96: *Supplices te rogamus, omnipotens Deus: iube haec perferri per manus sancti Angeli tui in sublime altare*

> *tuum, in conspectu divinae maiestatis tuae: ut, quotquot ex hac altaris participatione sacrosanctum Filii Corpus et Sanguinem sumpserimus, omni benedictione caelesti et gratia repleamur.*

(217) *Jn* 6:53.
(218) *1 Cor* 11:27-29.
(219) Roman Missal, response to the invitation to communion; cf. *Mt* 8:8.
(220) Cf. CIC, can. 919.
(22)1 Cf. CIC, can. 916.
(222) Cf. CIC, can. 917; The faithful may receive the Holy Eucharist only a second time on the same day [Cf. Pontificia Commissio Codici Iuris Canonici Authentice Intrepretando, Responsa ad proposita dubia, 1: AAS 76 (1984) 746].
(223) SC 55.
(224) Cf. OE 15; CIC, can. 920.
(225) GIRM 240.
(226) *Jn* 6:56.
(22)7 *Jn* 6:57.
(228) *Fanqith, Syriac* Office of Antioch, Vol. 1, Commun., 237 a-b.
(229) PO 5.
(230) St. Ambrose, De Sacr. 4, 6, 28: PL 16, 446; cf. I Cor 11:26.
(231) Cf. Council of Trent (1551): DS 1638.
(232) St. Fulgentius of Ruspe, Contra Fab. 28, 16-19: CCL 19A, 813-814.
(233) Cf. *1 Cor* 12:13.
(234) *1 Cor* 10:16-17.
(235) St. Augustine, *Sermo* 272: PL 38, 1247.
(236) St. John Chrysostom, *Hom. in I Cor.* 27, 4: PG 61, 229-230; cf. *Mt* 25:40.
(237) St. Augustine, In Jo. ev. 26, 13: PL 35, 1613; cf. SC 47.
(238) UR 15 § 2; cf. CIC, can. 844 § 3.
(239) UR 22 § 3.
(240) UR 22 § 3.
(241) Cf. CIC, can. 844 § 4.
(242) Roman Missal, EP I (Roman Canon) 96: *Supplices te rogamus.*
(243) *Mt* 26:29; cf. *Lk* 22:18; *Mk* 14:25.
(244) *Rev* 1:4; 22:20; *I Cor* 16 22.
(245) *Didache* 10, 6: SCh 248,180.
(246) Roman Missal 126, embolism after the Our Father: *expectantes beatam spem et adventum Salvatoris nostri Jesu Christi;* cf. Titus 2:13.
(247) EP III 116: prayer for the dead.
(248) *2 Pet* 3:13.
(249) LG 3; St. Ignatius of Antioch, Ad Eph. 20, 2: SCh 10, 76.

Part II

A Commentary on Pope John Paul II's Pastoral Plan for the New Millennium

Based on the
APOSTOLIC LETTER
NOVO MILLENNIO INEUNTE
OF HIS HOLINESS
POPE JOHN PAUL II
January 6, 2001

Preface

Something extraordinary happened on the very day that our Holy Father, Pope John Paul II closed the Holy Year door signaling the end of the Jubilee Year. On that very day, he issued a new apostolic letter for the whole world, outlining a pastoral plan for the whole world. Looking over the many graces that the world received from the Jubilee Year, the Holy Father stated, "As guidance and encouragement to everyone, I wish to indicate *certain pastoral priorities* which the experience of the great Jubilee has, in my view, brought to light."

Certain Pastoral Priorities

This is something unusual for it is the first time in my recollection that any pope has issued a pastoral plan for the world. This marvelous pope, who has been the greatest advocate and doctor of the Church, now using the full insights of his accumulated wisdom and the full tradition of our Catholic faith, is giving certain pastoral priorities for every Catholic throughout the world.

After speaking about the great graces in Section I of his new apostolic letter entitled, *As We Enter the New Millennium,* he spoke about meeting Christ, the legacy of the great Jubilee, and he thanked God for the many graces that were given during that year. In Section II, he talked about contemplating the face of Jesus, and he held up the witness of the gospel so that the face of Christ emerged with *a solid historical foundation.* He then went on to give his pastoral plan in Section III which follows.

III
STARTING AFRESH FROM CHRIST

29. "I am with you always, to the close of the age" (*Mt* 28:20). This assurance, dear brothers and sisters, has accompanied the Church for two thousand years, and has now been renewed in our hearts by the celebration of the Jubilee. From it we must gain *new impetus in Christian living,* making it the force which inspires our journey of faith. Conscious of the Risen Lord's presence among us, we ask ourselves today the same question put to Peter in Jerusalem immediately after his Pentecost speech: "What must we do?" (*Acts* 2:37).

We put the question with trusting optimism, but without underestimating the problems we face. We are certainly not seduced by the naive expectation that, faced with the great challenges of our time, we shall find some magic formula. No, we shall not be saved by a formula but by a Person, and the assurance which He gives us: *I am with you!*

It is not therefore a matter of inventing a "new program". The program already exists: it is the plan found in the Gospel and in the living Tradition, it is the same as ever. Ultimately, it has its center in Christ Himself, who is to be known, loved and imitated, so that in Him we may live the life of the Trinity, and with Him transform history until its fulfillment in the heavenly Jerusalem. This is a program which does not change with shifts of times and cultures, even though it takes account of time and culture for the sake of true dialogue and effective communication. This program for all times is our program for the Third Millennium.

But it must be translated into *pastoral initiatives adapted to the circumstances of each community.* The Jubilee has given us the extraordinary opportunity to travel together for a number of years on a journey common to the whole Church, a catechetical journey on the theme of the Trinity, accompanied by precise pastoral undertakings designed to ensure that the Jubilee would be a fruitful event. I am grateful for the sincere and widespread acceptance of what I proposed in my Apostolic Letter *Tertio Millennio Adveniente.* But now it is no longer an immediate goal that we face, but the larger and more demanding challenge of normal pastoral activity. With its universal and indispensable provisions, the program of the Gospel must continue to take root, as it has always done, in the life of the Church everywhere. It is *in the local churches* that the specific features of a detailed pastoral plan can be identified — goals and methods, formation and enrichment of the people involved, the search for the necessary resources — which will enable the proclamation of Christ to reach people, mould communities, and have a deep and incisive influence in bringing Gospel values to bear in society and culture.

I, therefore, earnestly exhort the Pastors of the particular Churches, with the help of all sectors of God's People, confidently to plan the stages of the journey ahead, harmonizing the choices of each diocesan community with those of neighboring Churches and of the universal Church.

This harmonization will certainly be facilitated by the collegial work which Bishops now regularly undertake in Episcopal Conferences and Synods. Was this not the point of the continental Assemblies of the Synod of Bishops which prepared for the Jubilee, and which forged important directives for the present-day proclamation of the Gospel in so many different settings and cultures? This rich legacy of reflection must not be allowed to disappear, but must be implemented in practical ways.

What awaits us therefore is an exciting work of pastoral

revitalization — a work involving all of us. As guidance and encouragement to everyone, I wish to indicate *certain pastoral priorities* which the experience of the Great Jubilee has, in my view, brought to light.

Pope's Seven Pastoral Priorities
to *Set Out into the Deep*

The Eucharist and the New Millennium

The Holy Father Stated in his Encyclical on the Eucharist,

"I would like to rekindle this Eucharist "amazement" by the present Encyclical Letter, in continuity with the Jubilee heritage which I have left to the Church in the Apostolic Letter Novo *Millennio Ineunte* and its Marian crowning, *Rosarium Virginis Maria*. *To contemplate the face of Christ, and to contemplate it with Mary, is the "program" which I have set before the Church at the dawn of the third millennium, summoning her to put out into the deep on the sea of history with the enthusiasm of the new evangelization.* To contemplate Christ involves being able to recognize Him wherever He manifests Himself, in His many forms of presence, but above all in the living sacrament of His Body and His Blood. The Church draws her life from Christ in the Eucharist; by Him she is fed and by Him she is enlightened."

We can see that the essence of this plan for the new millennium to contemplate the face of Christ is the Eucharist. The Holy Father gave in his apostolic letter *Novo Millennio Ineunte* seven pastoral priorities. He said, "I wish to indicate certain pastoral priorities which the experience of the great Jubilee has, in my view, brought to light."

The eighth pastoral priority, that of daily recitation of the rosary, he highlighted in his apostolic letter *Rosarium Virginis Maria,* which he called the crowning of the Jubilee heritage. What better way to contemplate the face of Jesus than by doing it in union with

His mother; and what better way of contemplating Jesus than by the recitation of the now 20 mysteries of the rosary.

Number One Priority - Holiness

Holiness
The Holy Father places as his first priority – holiness, which is nothing short of thinking, loving and acting like Jesus. He states,

> 30. "First of all, I have no hesitation in saying that all pastoral initiatives must be set in relation to *holiness*. Was this not the ultimate meaning of the Jubilee indulgence, as a special grace offered by Christ so that the life of every baptized person could be purified and deeply renewed?
>
> It is my hope that, among those who have taken part in the Jubilee, many will have benefited from this grace, in full awareness of its demands. Once the Jubilee is over, we resume our normal path, but knowing that stressing holiness remains more than ever an urgent pastoral task.
>
> It is necessary therefore to rediscover the full practical significance of Chapter 5 of the Dogmatic Constitution on the Church *Lumen Gentium*, dedicated to the "universal call to holiness". The Council Fathers laid such stress on this point, not just to embellish ecclesiology with a kind of spiritual veneer, but to make the call to holiness an intrinsic and essential aspect of their teaching on the Church. The rediscovery of the Church as "mystery", or as a people "gathered together by the unity of the Father, the Son and the Holy Spirit",[15] was bound to bring with it a rediscovery of the Church's "holiness", understood in the basic sense of belonging to Him who is in essence the Holy One, the "thrice Holy" (cf. *Is* 6:3). To profess the Church as holy means to point to her as *the Bride of Christ,* for whom He gave Himself precisely in order to make her holy (cf. *Eph* 5:25-26). This, as it were, objective gift of holiness is offered to all the baptized.
>
> But the gift in turn becomes a task, which must shape

the whole of Christian life: "This is the will of God, your sanctification" (*1 Th* 4:3). It is a duty which concerns not only certain Christians: "All the Christian faithful, of whatever state or rank, are called to the fullness of the Christian life and to the perfection of charity".[16]

31. At first glance, it might seem almost impractical to recall this elementary truth as the foundation of the pastoral planning in which we are involved at the start of the new millennium. Can holiness ever be "planned"? What might the word "holiness" mean in the context of a pastoral plan?

In fact, to place pastoral planning under the heading of holiness is a choice filled with consequences. It implies the conviction that, since Baptism is a true entry into the holiness of God through incorporation into Christ and the indwelling of His Spirit, it would be a contradiction to settle for a life of mediocrity, marked by a minimalist ethic and a shallow religiosity. To ask catechumens: "Do you wish to receive Baptism?" means at the same time to ask them: "Do you wish to become holy?" It means to set before them the radical nature of the Sermon on the Mount: "Be perfect as your heavenly Father is perfect" (*Mt* 5:48).

As the Council itself explained, this ideal of perfection must not be misunderstood as if it involved some kind of extraordinary existence, possible only for a few "uncommon heroes" of holiness. The ways of holiness are many, according to the vocation of each individual. I thank the Lord that in these years He has enabled me to beatify and canonize a large number of Christians, and among them many lay people who attained holiness in the most ordinary circumstances of life. The time has come to re-propose wholeheartedly to everyone this *high standard of ordinary Christian living:* the whole life of the Christian community and of Christian families must lead in this direction. It is also clear however that the paths to holiness are personal and call for a genuine *"training in holiness"*, adapted to people's needs. This training must integrate the resources offered to everyone with both the traditional forms of individual and group assistance, as well as the more recent forms of support offered in associations and movements recognized by the Church."

Number Two Priority – Prayer

Prayer

Since holiness is thinking, loving and acting like Jesus, we must set aside prime time every day to listen to the Father and to Jesus. Mother Teresa said, "It is not possible to engage in the direct apostolate without being a soul of prayer. We must be aware of oneness with Christ as He was aware of oneness with His Father. Therefore, love to pray. Feel often during the day the need for prayer, for prayer enlarges the heart until it is capable of containing God's gift of Himself." The Holy Father talks about the art of prayer. He states:

32. "This training in holiness calls for a Christian life distinguished above all in *the art of prayer.* The Jubilee Year has been a year of more intense prayer, both personal and communal. But we well know that prayer cannot be taken for granted. We have to learn to pray: as it were learning this art ever anew from the lips of the Divine Master Himself, like the first disciples: "Lord, teach us to pray!" (*Lk* 11:1). Prayer develops that conversation with Christ which makes us His intimate friends: "Abide in Me and I in you" (*Jn* 15:4). This reciprocity is the very substance and soul of the Christian life, and the condition of all true pastoral life. Wrought in us by the Holy Spirit, this reciprocity opens us, through Christ and in Christ, to contemplation of the Father's face. Learning this Trinitarian shape of Christian prayer and living it fully, above all in the liturgy, the summit and source of the Church's life,[17] but also in personal experience, is the secret of a truly vital Christianity, which has no reason to fear the future, because it returns continually to the sources and finds in them new life."

Widespread Demand for Spirituality

Now more than ever there is a hunger for spirituality and prayer, especially in the aftermath of the terrorist attack on September 11th. Here at our house of prayer, we see this hunger in all of its fullness. People want to be able to hear God's voice. We teach them how to pray, how to spend significant time worshiping and praising God, and how to listen to God (cf, my book, *Listening to God*). The Holy Father urges us to study the teachings of St. John of the Cross, St. Teresa of Avila, St. Therese of Liseux and St. Catherine of Sienna. He calls for genuine schools of prayer, places where people can be taught to fall in love with God and to open their hearts completely to Him.

33. "Is it not one of the 'signs of the times' that in today's world, despite widespread secularization, there is *a widespread demand for spirituality,* a demand which expresses itself in large part as *a renewed need for prayer?* Other religions, which are now widely present in ancient Christian lands, offer their own responses to this need, and sometimes they do so in appealing ways. But we who have received the grace of believing in Christ, the revealer of the Father and the Savior of the world, have a duty to show to what depths the relationship with Christ can lead.

The great mystical tradition of the Church of both East and West has much to say in this regard. It shows how prayer can progress, as a genuine dialogue of love, to the point of rendering the person wholly possessed by the divine Beloved, vibrating at the Spirit's touch, resting filially within the Father's heart. This is the lived experience of Christ's promise: "He who loves Me will be loved by My Father, and I will love him and manifest Myself to him" (*Jn* 14:21). It is a journey totally sustained by grace, which nonetheless demands an intense spiritual commitment and is no stranger to painful purifications (the "dark night"). But it leads, in various possible ways, to the ineffable joy experienced by the mystics as "nuptial union". How can we forget here, among the many shining examples, the teachings of Saint John of the Cross and Saint Teresa of Avila?

Yes, dear brothers and sisters, our Christian communities must become *genuine "schools" of prayer,* where the meeting with Christ is expressed not just in imploring help but also in thanksgiving, praise, adoration, contemplation, listening and ardent devotion, until the heart truly "falls in love". Intense prayer, yes, but it does not distract us from our commitment to history: by opening our heart to the love of God it also opens it to the love of our brothers and sisters, and makes us capable of shaping history according to God's plan.[18]

The Consecrated Life

34. "Christians who have received the gift of a vocation to the specially consecrated life are of course called to prayer in a particular way: of its nature, their consecration makes them more open to the experience of contemplation, and it is important that they should cultivate it with special care. But it would be wrong to think that ordinary Christians can be content with a shallow prayer that is unable to fill their whole life. Especially in the face of the many trials to which today's world subjects faith, they would be not only mediocre Christians but "Christians at risk". They would run the insidious risk of seeing their faith progressively undermined, and would perhaps end up succumbing to the allure of "substitutes", accepting alternative religious proposals and even indulging in far-fetched superstitions.

Wednesday Catechesis on Prayer and the Psalms

It is therefore essential that *education in prayer* should become in some way a key-point of all pastoral planning. I myself have decided to dedicate the forthcoming Wednesday catecheses to *reflection upon the Psalms,* beginning with the Psalms of Morning Prayer with which the public prayer of the Church invites us to consecrate and direct our day. How helpful it would be if not only in religious communities but also in parishes more were done to ensure an all-pervading climate of prayer. With proper discernment, this would require that popular piety be given its proper place, and that people be educated especially in liturgical prayer. Perhaps it is more thinkable than we usually presume for the average day of a Christian community to combine the many forms of pastoral life and witness in the world with the celebration of the Eucharist and even the recitation of Lauds and Vespers. The experience of many committed Christian groups, also those made up largely of lay people, is proof of this."

Priority Number Three – The Sunday Eucharist

The Holy Father had previously issued an apostolic letter entitled, *Dies Domini* in which he said, "the sharing in the Eucharist should really be the heart of Sunday for every baptized person." He reiterates that sentiment here, and encourages Catholics to make Sunday the Lord's Day. Although he does not say it directly, he infers that the fulfilling of the obligation of Sunday Mass should only by exception take place on Saturday evening. He is striving to restore Sunday as the day of the Church where the Church can effectively exercise her role as the sacrament of unity. He states:

The Sunday Eucharist

35. "It is therefore obvious that our principal attention must be given to the liturgy, 'the summit towards which the Church's action tends and at the same time the source from which comes all her strength'.[19] In the twentieth century, especially since the Council, there has been a great development in the way the Christian community celebrates the Sacraments, especially the Eucharist. It is necessary to continue in this direction, and to stress particularly *the Sunday Eucharist* and *Sunday* itself experienced as a special day of faith, the day of the Risen Lord and of the gift of the Spirit, the true weekly Easter.[20] For two thousand years, Christian time has been measured by the memory

of that "first day of the week" (*Mk* 16:2,9; *Lk* 24:1; *Jn* 20:1), when the Risen Christ gave the Apostles the gift of peace and of the Spirit (cf. *Jn* 20:19-23). The truth of Christ's Resurrection is the original fact upon which Christian faith is based (cf. *1 Cor* 15:14), an event set *at the center of the mystery of time*, prefiguring the last day when Christ will return in glory. We do not know what the new millennium has in store for us, but we are certain that it is safe in the hands of Christ, the "King of kings and Lord of lords" (*Rev* 19:16); and precisely by celebrating his Passover not just once a year but every Sunday, the Church will continue to show to every generation "the true fulcrum of history, to which the mystery of the world's origin and its final destiny leads".[21]

36. Following *Dies Domini*, I therefore wish to insist that *sharing in the Eucharist* should really be *the heart of Sunday* for every baptized person. It is a fundamental duty, to be fulfilled not just in order to observe a precept but as something felt as essential to a truly informed and consistent Christian life. We are entering a millennium which already shows signs of being marked by a profound interweaving of cultures and religions, even in countries which have been Christian for many centuries. In many regions Christians are, or are becoming, a "little flock" (*Lk* 12:32). This presents them with the challenge, often in isolated and difficult situations, to bear stronger witness to the distinguishing elements of their own identity. The duty to take part in the Eucharist every Sunday is one of these. The Sunday Eucharist which every week gathers Christians together as God's family round the table of the Word and the Bread of Life, is also the most natural antidote to dispersion. It is the privileged place where communion is ceaselessly proclaimed and nurtured. Precisely through sharing in the Eucharist, *the Lord's Day* also becomes *the Day of the Church*,[22] when she can effectively exercise her role as the sacrament of unity."

Priority Number Four – Frequent Confession

Realizing the darkness that has overcome mankind and the culture of death to which mankind has descended, this great apostle of mercy, who has already beatified Sister Faustina, encourages every baptized Catholic to go to confession frequently. For in the sacrament of confession, three awesome, wondrous miracles of grace take place. First, every bit of sin and guilt is washed clean through the Blood of the Lamb administered through the absolution of the priest. Second, all bitterness, unjust anger and resentment are let go of. Third, the penitents are given the awesome power to completely forgive themselves and get on with their lives. The Holy Father states:

The Sacrament of Reconciliation

37. "I am also asking for renewed pastoral courage in ensuring that the day-to-day teaching of Christian communities persuasively and effectively presents the practice of the Sacrament of Reconciliation. As you will recall, in 1984 I dealt with this subject in the Post-Synodal Exhortation *Reconciliatio et Paenitentia,* which synthesized the results of an Assembly of the Synod of Bishops devoted to this question. My invitation then was to make every effort to face the crisis of "the sense of sin" apparent in today's culture.[23] But I was even more insistent in calling for a rediscovery of Christ as *mysterium pietatis,* the one in whom God shows us His compassionate heart and reconciles us fully with Himself. It is this face of Christ that must be rediscovered through the Sacrament of Penance, which for the faithful is 'the ordinary way of obtaining forgiveness and the remission of serious sins committed after Baptism'".[24]

When the Synod addressed the problem, the crisis of the Sacrament was there for all to see, especially in some parts of the world. The causes of the crisis have not disappeared in the brief span of time since then. But the Jubilee Year, which has been particularly marked by a return to the Sacrament of Penance, has given us an encouraging

message, which should not be ignored: if many people,
and among them also many young people, have benefited
from approaching this Sacrament, it is probably necessary
that Pastors should arm themselves with more confidence,
creativity and perseverance in presenting it and leading
people to appreciate it. Dear brothers in the priesthood, we
must not give in to passing crises! The Lord's gifts — and
the Sacraments are among the most precious — come from
the One who well knows the human heart and is the Lord
of history."

Priority Number Five – Realize that Everything Is Grace

No pope has ever written of the primacy of grace and the role of
the Holy Spirit in the life of the Christian as has this pope. "I direct
you to read my book, *The Holy Spirit in the Writings of Pope John
Paul II*." The Holy Father reiterates what always has been doctrine
– that all is grace and that everything is gift, save sin. The Catholic
Church has always taught *sola gratia* – only grace. The Holy Father teaches, as the liturgy states, "All life, all holiness comes from
Him (the Father) through His Son Jesus Christ our Lord by the
working of the Holy Spirit." He explains:

The Primacy of Grace

38. If in the planning that awaits us we commit ourselves
more confidently to a pastoral activity that gives personal
and communal prayer its proper place, we shall be observing an essential principle of the Christian view of life: *the
primacy of grace*. There is a temptation which perennially
besets every spiritual journey and pastoral work: that of
thinking that the results depend on our ability to act and to
plan. God of course asks us really to cooperate with His
grace, and therefore invites us to invest all our resources of
intelligence and energy in serving the cause of the Kingdom. But it is fatal to forget that "without Christ we can do
nothing" (cf. *Jn* 15:5).

It is prayer which roots us in this truth. It constantly
reminds us of the primacy of Christ and, in union with

Him, the primacy of the interior life and of holiness. When this principle is not respected, is it any wonder that pastoral plans come to nothing and leave us with a disheartening sense of frustration? We then share the experience of the disciples in the Gospel story of the miraculous catch of fish: "We have toiled all night and caught nothing" (*Lk* 5:5). This is the moment of faith, of prayer, of conversation with God, in order to open our hearts to the tide of grace and allow the word of Christ to pass through us in all its power: *Duc in altum!* On that occasion, it was Peter who spoke the word of faith: "At Your word I will let down the nets" (*ibid.*). As this millennium begins, allow the Successor of Peter to invite the whole Church to make this act of faith, which expresses itself in a renewed commitment to prayer."

Priority Number Six – Listen, Discern and Obey the Word of the Lord

The Holy Father reiterates here a principle that Jesus Himself taught. Just as He always listened to and obeyed the word of His Father, so are we to do the same. Jesus said, "My meat is to do the will of Him who sent Me." One simply cannot do the will of God unless such a person knows what it is. And you cannot know what it is unless God tells you. We must take prime time every day, meditating upon the Scriptures (*lectio divina*) as well as the inspirations of the Holy Spirit. He says that prayer is inconceivable without a renewed listening to the Word of God. He emphasizes:

Listening to the Word

39. "There is no doubt that this primacy of holiness and prayer is inconceivable without a renewed *listening to the word of God.* Ever since the Second Vatican Council underlined the pre-eminent role of the word of God in the life of the Church, great progress has certainly been made in devout listening to Sacred Scripture and attentive study of it. Scripture has its rightful place of honor in the public prayer of the Church. Individuals and communities now

make extensive use of the Bible, and among lay people there are many who devote themselves to Scripture with the valuable help of theological and biblical studies. But it is above all the work of evangelization and catechesis which is drawing new life from attentiveness to the word of God. Dear brothers and sisters, this development needs to be consolidated and deepened, also by making sure that every family has a Bible. It is especially necessary that listening to the word of God should become a life-giving encounter, in the ancient and ever valid tradition of *lectio divina,* which draws from the biblical text the living word which questions, directs and shapes our lives."

Priority Number Seven – To Proclaim the Word

It is not enough to listen to the Word, we must live out the Word both by example and proclamation. We are to become what the Holy Father calls "servants of the Word," realizing that we are the holy gospel that most people will ever read. Since society is ever more unChristian, we Christians must ever be lights to a darkened world. This is all part of what the Holy Father has called his new evangelization. He entreats us:

Proclaiming the Word

40. "To nourish ourselves with the word in order to be 'servants of the word' in the work of evangelization: this is surely a priority for the Church at the dawn of the new millennium. Even in countries evangelized many centuries ago, the reality of a 'Christian society' which, amid all the frailties which have always marked human life, measured itself explicitly on Gospel values, is now gone. Today we must courageously face a situation which is becoming increasingly diversified and demanding, in the context of 'globalization' and of the consequent new and uncertain mingling of peoples and cultures. Over the years, I have often repeated the summons to the *new evangelization.* I do so again now, especially in order to insist that we must rekindle in ourselves the impetus of the beginnings

and allow ourselves to be filled with the ardor of the apostolic preaching which followed Pentecost. We must revive in ourselves the burning conviction of Paul, who cried out: 'Woe to me if I do not preach the Gospel'" (*1 Cor* 9:16).

Christian Communities

This passion will not fail to stir in the Church a new sense of mission, which cannot be left to a group of "specialists" but must involve the responsibility of all the members of the People of God. Those who have come into genuine contact with Christ cannot keep Him for themselves, they must proclaim Him. A new apostolic outreach is needed, which will be lived as *the everyday commitment of Christian communities and groups.* This should be done however with the respect due to the different paths of different people and with sensitivity to the diversity of cultures in which the Christian message must be planted, in such a way that the particular values of each people will not be rejected but purified and brought to their fullness.

Inculturation

In the Third Millennium, Christianity will have to respond ever more effectively to this *need for inculturation.* Christianity, while remaining completely true to itself, with unswerving fidelity to the proclamation of the Gospel and the tradition of the Church, will also reflect the different faces of the cultures and peoples in which it is received and takes root. In this Jubilee Year, we have rejoiced in a special way in the beauty of the Church's varied face. This is perhaps only a beginning, a barely sketched image of the future which the Spirit of God is preparing for us.

Evangelization of Youth

Christ must be presented to all people with confidence. We shall address adults, families, young people, children, without ever hiding the most radical demands of the Gospel message, but taking into account each person's needs in regard to their sensitivity and language, after the example of Paul who declared: "I have become all things to all men, that I might by all means save some" (*1 Cor* 9:22). In making these recommendations, I am thinking especially of *the pastoral care of young people*. Precisely in regard to young people, as I said earlier, the Jubilee has given us an encouraging testimony of their generous availability. We must learn to interpret that heartening response, by investing that enthusiasm like a new talent (cf. *Mt* 25:15) which the Lord has put into our hands so that we can make it yield a rich return.

The Example of Martyrs

41. May the shining example of the many witnesses to the faith whom we have remembered during the Jubilee sustain and guide us in this confident, enterprising and creative sense of mission. For the Church, the martyrs have always been a seed of life. *Sanguis martyrum semen christianorum*:[25] this famous "law" formulated by Tertullian has proved true in all the trials of history. Will this not also be the case of the century and millennium now beginning? Perhaps we were too used to thinking of the martyrs in rather distant terms, as though they were a category of the past, associated especially with the first centuries of the Christian era. The Jubilee remembrance has presented us with a surprising vista, showing us that our own time is particularly prolific in witnesses, who in different ways were able to live the Gospel in the midst of hostility and persecution, often to the point of the supreme test of shedding their blood. In them the word of God, sown in good soil, yielded a hundred fold (cf. *Mt* 13:8, 23). By their example they have shown us, and made smooth for us, so to speak, the path to the future. All that remains for us is, with God's grace, to follow in their footsteps.

IV
WITNESSES TO LOVE

The Holy Father reiterates something that he said in the prologue to the new Catechism: "The whole concern of doctrine and its teaching must be directed to the love that never ends. Whether something is proposed for belief, for hope or for action, the love of our Lord must always be made accessible, so that anyone can see that all the works of perfect Christian virtue spring from love and have no other objective than to arrive at love." He strongly tells us to love one another. Listen to his words:

42. "By this all will know that you are My disciples, if you have love for one another" (*Jn* 13:35). If we have truly contemplated the face of Christ, dear Brothers and Sisters, our pastoral planning will necessarily be inspired by the "new commandment" which He gave us: "Love one another, as I have loved you" (*Jn* 13:34).

Koinonia
This is the other important area in which there has to be commitment and planning on the part of the universal Church and the particular Churches: *the domain of communion* (*koinonia*), which embodies and reveals the very essence of the mystery of the Church. Communion is the fruit and demonstration of that love which springs from the heart of the Eternal Father and is poured out upon us through the Spirit which Jesus gives us (cf. *Rom* 5:5), to make us all "one heart and one soul" (*Acts* 4:32). It is in building this communion of love that the Church appears as "sacrament", as the "sign and instrument of intimate union with God and of the unity of the human race".[(26)]

Agape
The Lord's words on this point are too precise for us to diminish their import. Many things are necessary for the

Church's journey through history, not least in this new century; but without charity (*agape*), all will be in vain. It is again the Apostle Paul who in the *hymn to love* reminds us: even if we speak the tongues of men and of angels, and if we have faith "to move mountains", but are without love, all will come to "nothing" (cf. *1 Cor* 13:2). Love is truly the "heart" of the Church, as was well understood by Saint Thérèse of Lisieux, whom I proclaimed a Doctor of the Church precisely because she is an expert in the *scientia amoris:* "I understood that the Church had a Heart and that this Heart was aflame with Love. I understood that Love alone stirred the members of the Church to act... I understood that Love encompassed all vocations, that Love was everything".[27]

A Spirituality of Communion

The Holy Father is asking us to make the Church the home and the school of communion. We form the mystical body of Christ. We are His hands, His eyes, His feet. Christ must be able to live out His life in and through us. Meditate on his words:

43. "To make the Church *the home and the school of communion*: that is the great challenge facing us in the millennium which is now beginning, if we wish to be faithful to God's plan and respond to the world's deepest yearnings.

But what does this mean in practice? Here too, our thoughts could run immediately to the action to be undertaken, but that would not be the right impulse to follow. Before making practical plans, we need *to promote a spirituality of communion,* making it the guiding principle of education wherever individuals and Christians are formed, wherever ministers of the altar, consecrated persons, and pastoral workers are trained, wherever families and communities are being built up. A spirituality of communion indicates above all the heart's contemplation of the mystery of the Trinity dwelling in us, and whose light we must also be able to see shining on the face of the brothers and sisters around us. A spirituality of communion also means an ability to think of our brothers and sisters in faith within the profound unity of the Mystical Body, and therefore as "those who are a part of me". This makes us able to share their joys and sufferings, to sense their desires and attend to their needs, to offer them deep and genuine friendship. A spirituality of communion implies also the ability to see what is positive in others, to welcome it and prize it as a gift from God: not only as a gift for the brother or sister who has received it directly, but also as a "gift for me". A spirituality of communion means, finally, to know how to "make room" for our brothers and sisters, bearing "each other's burdens" (*Gal* 6:2) and resisting the selfish temptations which constantly beset us and provoke competition, careerism, distrust and jealousy. Let us have no illusions: unless we follow this spiritual path, external structures of communion will serve very little purpose. They would become mechanisms without a soul, "masks" of communion rather than its means of expression and growth.

Patrine and Episcopal Ministries
44. Consequently, the new century will have to see us more than ever intent on valuing and developing the forums and structures which, in accordance with the Second Vatican Council's major directives, serve to ensure and safeguard communion. How can we forget in the first place those *specific services to communion* which are *the Petrine ministry* and, closely related to it, *episcopal collegiality?* These are realities which have their foundation and substance in Christ's own plan for the Church,[28] but which need to be examined constantly in order to ensure that they follow their genuinely evangelical inspiration.

Much has also been done since the Second Vatican Council for the reform of the Roman Curia, the organization of Synods and the functioning of Episcopal Conferences. But there is certainly much more to be done, in order to realize all the potential of these instruments of communion, which are especially appropriate today in view of the need to respond promptly and effectively to the issues which the Church must face in these rapidly changing times.

Priests and Pastoral Councils

45. Communion must be cultivated and extended day by day and at every level in the structures of each Church's life. There, relations between Bishops, priests and deacons, between Pastors and the entire People of God, between clergy and Religious, between associations and ecclesial movements must all be clearly characterized by communion. To this end, the structures of participation envisaged by Canon Law, such as *the Council of Priests and the Pastoral Council,* must be ever more highly valued. These of course are not governed by the rules of parliamentary democracy, because they are consultative rather than deliberative;[29] yet this does not mean that they are less meaningful and relevant. The theology and spirituality of communion encourage a fruitful dialogue between Pastors and faithful: on the one hand uniting them *a priori* in all that is essential, and on the other leading them to pondered agreement in matters open to discussion.

The Lay Apostolate

To this end, we need to make our own the ancient pastoral wisdom which, without prejudice to their authority, encouraged Pastors to listen more widely to the entire People of God. Significant is Saint Benedict's reminder to the Abbot of a monastery, inviting him to consult even the youngest members of the community: "By the Lord's inspiration, it is often a younger person who knows what is best".[30] And Saint Paulinus of Nola urges: "Let us listen to what all the faithful say, because in every one of them the Spirit of God breathes".[31]

While the wisdom of the law, by providing precise rules for participation, attests to the hierarchical structure of the Church and averts any temptation to arbitrariness or unjustified claims, the spirituality of communion, by prompting a trust and openness wholly in accord with the dignity and responsibility of every member of the People of God, supplies institutional reality with a soul.

The diversity of vocations

Following St. Paul and reiterating a challenge that he gave in his magnificent document, *The Lay Faithful in Christ*, John Paul states: "You too go." He applies these words to every baptized Christian and says that everyone is called to continue across their time and space the redemptive healing work of Jesus. He continues:

46. "Such a vision of communion is closely linked to the Christian community's ability to make room for all the gifts of the Spirit. The unity of the Church is not uniformity, but an organic blending of legitimate diversities. It is the reality of many members joined in a single body, the one Body of Christ (cf. *1 Cor* 12:12). Therefore the Church of the Third Millennium will need to encourage all the baptized and confirmed to be aware of their active responsibility in the Church's life. Together with the ordained ministry, other ministries, whether formally instituted or simply recognized, can flourish for the good of the whole community, sustaining it in all its many needs: from catechesis to liturgy, from the education of the young to the widest array of charitable works.

Promoting Vocations to the Priesthood and Consecrated Life

Certainly, a generous commitment is needed — above all through insistent prayer to the Lord of the harvest (cf. *Mt* 9:38) — in *promoting vocations to the priesthood and consecrated life*. This is a question of great relevance for the life of the Church in every part of the world. In some traditionally Christian countries, the situation has become dramatic, due to changed social circumstances and a religious disinterest resulting from the consumer and secularist mentality. There is a pressing need to implement an extensive *plan of vocational promotion*, based on personal contact and involving parishes, schools and families in the effort to foster a more attentive reflection on life's essential values. These reach their fulfillment in the response which each person is invited to give to God's call, particularly when the call implies a total giving of self and of one's energies to the cause of the Kingdom.

It is in this perspective that we see the value of all other vocations, rooted as they are in the new life received in the Sacrament of Baptism. In a special way it will be necessary to discover ever more fully *the specific vocation of the laity*, called "to seek the kingdom of God by engaging in temporal affairs and by ordering them according to the plan of God";[32] they "have their own role to play in the mission of the whole people of God in the Church and in the world ... by their work for the evangelization and the sanctification of people".[33]

The Specific Role of the Laity
Along these same lines, another important aspect of communion is *the promotion of forms of association*, whether of the more traditional kind or the newer ecclesial movements, which continue to give the Church a vitality that is God's gift and a true "springtime of the Spirit". Obviously, associations and movements need to work in full harmony within both the universal Church and the particular Churches, and in obedience to the authoritative directives of the Pastors. But the Apostle's exacting and decisive warning applies to all: "Do not quench the Spirit, do not despise prophesying, but test everything and hold fast what is good" (*1 Th* 5:19-21).

Family Life

Following his apostolic constitution *Familiaris Consortio*, the Holy Father states that the way of the Church is the way of the family. Since God is a family of persons loving one another and deferring to one another and delighting in one another, that is what He is doing upon earth – creating family His way. He explains:

> 47. "At a time in history like the present, special attention must also be given to *the pastoral care of the family*, particularly when this fundamental institution is experiencing a radical and widespread crisis. In the Christian view of marriage, the relationship between a man and a woman — a mutual and total bond, unique and indissoluble — is part of God's original plan, obscured throughout history by our "hardness of heart", but which Christ came to restore to its pristine splendor, disclosing what had been God's will "from the beginning" (*Mt* 19:8). Raised to the dignity of a Sacrament, marriage expresses the "great mystery" of Christ's nuptial love for His Church (cf. *Eph* 5:32).
>
> On this point the Church cannot yield to cultural pressures, no matter how widespread and even militant they may be. Instead, it is necessary to ensure that through an ever more complete Gospel formation Christian families show convincingly that it is possible to live marriage fully in keeping with God's plan and with the true good of the human person — of the spouses, and of the children who are more fragile. Families themselves must become increasingly conscious of the care due to children, and play an active role in the Church and in society in safeguarding their rights."

Ecumenical commitment

Just as no man is an island, so the Church cannot be an island. It is a sacrament for the whole world. It must be ecumenical. He encourages us all to work for Christian unity, in these words:

> 48. "And what should we say of the urgent task of fostering

communion in the delicate area of *ecumenism?* Unhappily, as we cross the threshold of the new millennium, we take with us the sad heritage of the past. The Jubilee has offered some truly moving and prophetic signs, but there is still a long way to go.

By fixing our gaze on Christ, the Great Jubilee has given us a more vivid sense of the Church as a mystery of unity. "I believe in the one Church": what we profess in the Creed has *its ultimate foundation in Christ, in whom the Church is undivided* (cf. *1 Cor* 1:11-13). As His Body, in the unity which is the gift of the Spirit, she is indivisible. The reality of division among the Church's children appears at the level of history, as the result of human weakness in the way we accept the gift which flows endlessly from Christ the Head to His Mystical Body. The prayer of Jesus in the Upper Room — "as you, Father, are in Me and I in You, that they also may be one in Us" (*Jn* 17:21) — is both *revelation* and *invocation*. It reveals to us the unity of Christ with the Father as the wellspring of the Church's unity and as the gift which in Him she will constantly receive until its mysterious fulfillment at the end of time. This unity is concretely embodied in the Catholic Church, despite the human limitations of her members, and it is at work in varying degrees in all the elements of holiness and truth to be found in the other Churches and Ecclesial Communities. As gifts properly belonging to the Church of Christ, these elements lead them continuously towards full unity.[(34)]

That They May Be One

Christ's prayer reminds us that this gift needs to be received and developed ever more profoundly. The invocation "*ut unum sint*" is, at one and the same time, a binding imperative, the strength that sustains us, and a salutary rebuke for our slowness and closed-heartedness. It is on Jesus's prayer and not on our own strength that we base the hope that even within history we shall be able to reach full and visible communion with all Christians.

The Eastern Churches

In the perspective of our renewed post-Jubilee pilgrimage, I look with great hope to the *Eastern Churches,* and I pray for a full return to that exchange of gifts which enriched the Church of the first millennium. May the memory of the time when the Church breathed with "both lungs" spur Christians of East and West to walk together in unity of faith and with respect for legitimate diversity, accepting and sustaining each other as members of the one Body of Christ.

A similar commitment should lead to the fostering of ecumenical dialogue with our brothers and sisters belonging to the *Anglican Communion* and the *Ecclesial Communities born of the Reformation.* Theological discussion on essential points of faith and Christian morality, cooperation in works of charity, and above all the great ecumenism of holiness will not fail, with God's help, to bring results. In the meantime we confidently continue our pilgrimage, longing for the time when, together with each and every one of Christ's followers, we shall be able to join wholeheartedly in singing: "How good and how pleasant it is, when brothers live in unity!" (*Ps* 133:1).

Stake Everything on Charity

The Holy Father stresses that we must have a concrete love for every human being. He encourages us to reach out to the hungry, the thirsty, the sick, and the imprisoned. He encourages us to have a preferential option for the poor. And he stresses that through the incarnation, Jesus has united Himself with every human being. He teaches:

> 49. "Beginning with intra-ecclesial communion, charity of its nature opens out into a service that is universal; it inspires in us *a commitment to practical and concrete love for every human being.* This too is an aspect which must clearly mark the Christian life, the Church's whole activity and her pastoral planning. The century and the

millennium now beginning will need to see, and hopefully with still greater clarity, to what length of dedication the Christian community can go in charity towards the poorest. If we have truly started out anew from the contemplation of Christ, we must learn to see Him especially in the faces of those with whom He Himself wished to be identified: "I was hungry and you gave Me food, I was thirsty and you gave Me drink, I was a stranger and you welcomed Me, I was naked and you clothed Me, I was sick and you visited Me, I was in prison and you came to Me" (*Mt* 25:35-37). This Gospel text is not a simple invitation to charity: it is a page of Christology which sheds a ray of light on the mystery of Christ. By these words, no less than by the orthodoxy of her doctrine, the Church measures her fidelity as the Bride of Christ.

To Everyone

Certainly we need to remember that no one can be excluded from our love, since "through His Incarnation the Son of God has united Himself in some fashion with every person".[35] Yet, as the unequivocal words of the Gospel remind us, there is a special presence of Christ in the poor, and this requires the Church to make a preferential option for them. This option is a testimony to the nature of God's love, to His providence and mercy; and in some way history is still filled with the seeds of the Kingdom of God which Jesus Himself sowed during His earthly life whenever He responded to those who came to Him with their spiritual and material needs.

Marginalized

50. In our own time, there are so many needs which demand a compassionate response from Christians. Our world is entering the new millennium burdened by the contradictions of an economic, cultural and technological progress which offers immense possibilities to a fortunate few, while leaving millions of others not only on the margins of

progress but in living conditions far below the minimum demanded by human dignity. How can it be that even today there are still people dying of hunger? Condemned to illiteracy? Lacking the most basic medical care? Without a roof over their heads?

The scenario of poverty can extend indefinitely, if in addition to its traditional forms we think of its newer patterns. These latter often affect financially affluent sectors and groups which are nevertheless threatened by despair at the lack of meaning in their lives, by drug addiction, by fear of abandonment in old age or sickness, by marginalization or social discrimination. In this context Christians must learn to make their act of faith in Christ by discerning His voice in the cry for help that rises from this world of poverty. This means carrying on the tradition of charity which has expressed itself in so many different ways in the past two millennia, but which today calls for even greater resourcefulness. Now is the time for a new "creativity" in charity, not only by ensuring that help is effective but also by "getting close" to those who suffer, so that the hand that helps is seen not as a humiliating handout but as a sharing between brothers and sisters.

We must therefore ensure that in every Christian community the poor feel at home. Would not this approach be the greatest and most effective presentation of the good news of the Kingdom? Without this form of evangelization through charity and without the witness of Christian poverty the proclamation of the Gospel, which is itself the prime form of charity, risks being misunderstood or submerged by the ocean of words which daily engulfs us in today's society of mass communications. The charity of *works* ensures an unmistakable efficacy to the charity of *words*.

Today's Challenges
Following the Spirit of the Constitution on the Church in the Modern World, the Holy Father then takes on contemporary problems

created by the world in which we live. He mentions the ecological crisis, the problems of peace, the contempt for fundamental human rights, the lack of respect for life, the problems caused by the latest advance in science. He applies to all of these the Church's social doctrine. This pope has written three encyclicals concerning social problems, and here's what they are: *Res Socialis, Laborens Exerciens, Centessimus Annus.* He continues:

Justice and Peace
51. And how can we remain indifferent to the prospect of an *ecological crisis* which is making vast areas of our planet uninhabitable and hostile to humanity? Or by the *problems of peace*, so often threatened by the specter of catastrophic wars? Or by *contempt for the fundamental human rights* of so many people, especially children? Countless are the emergencies to which every Christian heart must be sensitive.

The Gospel of Life
A special commitment is needed with regard to certain aspects of the Gospel's radical message which are often less well understood, even to the point of making the Church's presence unpopular, but which nevertheless must be a part of her mission of charity. I am speaking of the duty to be committed to *respect for the life of every human being*, from conception until natural death. Likewise, the service of humanity leads us to insist, in season and out of season, that those using *the latest advances of science*, especially in the field of biotechnology, must never disregard fundamental ethical requirements by invoking a questionable solidarity which eventually leads to discriminating between one life and another and ignoring the dignity which belongs to every human being.

For Christian witness to be effective, especially in these delicate and controversial areas, it is important that special efforts be made to explain properly the reasons for the Church's position, stressing that it is not a case of imposing on non-believers a vision based on faith, but of interpreting and defending the values rooted in the very nature of the human person. In this way charity will necessarily become service to culture, politics, the economy and the family, so that the fundamental principles upon which depend the destiny of human beings and the future of civilization will be everywhere respected.

The Church's Social Doctrine
52. Clearly, all this must be done in a specifically Christian way: *the laity* especially must be present in these areas in fulfillment of their lay vocation, without ever yielding to the temptation to turn Christian communities into mere social agencies. In particular, the Church's relationship with civil society should respect the latter's autonomy and areas of competence, in accordance with the teachings of the *Church's social doctrine.*

Well known are the efforts made by the Church's teaching authority, especially in the twentieth century, to interpret social realities in the light of the Gospel and to offer in a timely and systematic way its contribution to the social question, which has now assumed a global dimension.

The ethical and social aspect of the question is an essential element of Christian witness: we must reject the temptation to offer a privatized and individualistic spirituality which ill accords with the demands of charity, to say nothing of the implications of the Incarnation and, in the last analysis, of Christianity's eschatological tension. While that tension makes us aware of the relative character of history, it in no way implies that we withdraw from "building" history. Here the teaching of the Second Vatican Council is more timely than ever: "The Christian message does not inhibit men and women from building up the world, or make them disinterested in the welfare of their fellow human beings: on the contrary it obliges them more fully to do these very things".(36)

A Practical Sign

The Holy Father calls for a practical sign, financial help for the poor. He states:

> 53. "In order to give a sign of this commitment to charity and human promotion, rooted in the most basic demands of the Gospel, I have resolved that the Jubilee year, in addition to the great harvest of charity which it has already yielded — here I am thinking in particular of the help given to so many of our poorer brothers and sisters to enable them to take part in the Jubilee — should leave *an endowment* which would in some way be *the fruit and seal of the love sparked by the Jubilee.* Many pilgrims have made an offering and many leaders in the financial sector have joined in providing generous assistance which has helped to ensure a fitting celebration of the Jubilee. Once the expenses of this year have been covered, the money saved will be dedicated to charitable purposes. It is important that such a major religious event should be completely dissociated from any semblance of financial gain. Whatever money remains will be used to continue the experience so often repeated since the very beginning of the Church, when the Jerusalem community offered non-Christians the moving sight of a spontaneous exchange of gifts, even to the point of holding all things in common, for the sake of the poor (cf. *Acts* 2:44-45).

The endowment to be established will be but a small stream flowing into the great river of Christian charity that courses through history. A small but significant stream: because of the Jubilee the world has looked to Rome, the Church "which presides in charity"[37] and has brought its gifts to Peter. Now the charity displayed at the center of Catholicism will in some way flow back to the world through this sign, which is meant to be an enduring legacy and remembrance of the communion experienced during the Jubilee.

Dialogue and Mission

54. A new century, a new millennium are opening in the light of Christ. But not everyone can see this light. Ours is the wonderful and demanding task of becoming its "reflection". This is the *mysterium lunae*, which was so much a part of the contemplation of the Fathers of the Church, who employed this image to show the Church's dependence on Christ, the Sun whose light she reflects.[38] It was a way of expressing what Christ Himself said when He called Himself the "light of the world" (*Jn* 8:12) and asked His disciples to be "the light of the world" (*Mt* 5:14).

This is a daunting task if we consider our human weakness, which so often renders us opaque and full of shadows. But it is a task which we can accomplish if we turn to the light of Christ and open ourselves to the grace which makes us a new creation.

55. It is in this context also that we should consider the great challenge of *inter-religious dialogue* to which we shall still be committed in the new millennium, in fidelity to the teachings of the Second Vatican Council.[39] In the years of preparation for the Great Jubilee the Church has sought to build, not least through a series of highly symbolic meetings, *a relationship of openness and dialogue with the followers of other religions*. This dialogue must continue. In the climate of increased cultural and religious pluralism which is expected to mark the society of the new millennium, it is obvious that this dialogue will be especially important in establishing a sure basis for peace and warding off the dread specter of those wars of religion which have so often bloodied human history. The name of the one God must become increasingly what it is: *a name of peace and a summons to peace*.

56. Dialogue, however, cannot be based on religious indifferentism, and we Christians are in duty bound, while engaging in dialogue, to bear clear witness to the hope that is

within us (cf. *1 Pt* 3:15). We should not fear that it will be considered an offence to the identity of others what is rather *the joyful proclamation of a gift* meant for all, and to be offered to all with the greatest respect for the freedom of each one: the gift of the revelation of the God who is Love, the God who "so loved the world that He gave His only Son" (*Jn* 3:16). As the recent Declaration *Dominus Iesus* stressed, this cannot be the subject of a dialogue understood as negotiation, as if we considered it a matter of mere opinion: rather, it is a grace which fills us with joy, a message which we have a duty to proclaim.

The Church therefore cannot forgo her missionary activity among the peoples of the world. It is the primary task of the *missio ad gentes* to announce that it is in Christ, "the Way, and the Truth, and the Life" (*Jn* 14:6), that people find salvation. Interreligious dialogue "cannot simply replace proclamation, but remains oriented towards proclamation".[40] This missionary duty, moreover, does not prevent us from approaching dialogue *with an attitude of profound willingness to listen*. We know in fact that, in the presence of the mystery of grace, infinitely full of possibilities and implications for human life and history, the Church herself will never cease putting questions, trusting in the help of the Paraclete, the Spirit of truth (cf. *Jn* 14:17), whose task it is to guide her "into all the truth" (*Jn* 16:13).

This is a fundamental principle not only for the endless theological investigation of Christian truth, but also for Christian dialogue with other philosophies, cultures and religions. In the common experience of humanity, for all its contradictions, the Spirit of God, who "blows where He wills" (*Jn* 3:8), not infrequently reveals signs of His presence which help Christ's followers to understand more deeply the message which they bear. Was it not with this humble and trust-filled openness that the Second Vatican Council sought to read "the signs of the times"?[41] Even as she engages in an active and watchful discernment aimed at understanding the "genuine signs of the presence or the purpose of God",(42) the Church acknowledges that she has not only given, but has also "received from the history and from the development of the human race".⁽⁴³⁾ This attitude of openness, combined with careful discernment, was adopted by the Council also in relation to other religions. It is our task to follow with great fidelity the Council's teaching and the path which it has traced.

In the light of the Council

57. What a treasure there is, dear brothers and sisters, in the guidelines offered to us by the Second Vatican Council! For this reason I asked the Church, as a way of preparing for the Great Jubilee, to *examine herself on the reception given to the Council*.⁽⁴⁴⁾ Has this been done? The Congress held here in the Vatican was such a moment of reflection, and I hope that similar efforts have been made in various ways in all the particular Churches. With the passing of the years, *the Council documents have lost nothing of their value or brilliance*. They need to be read correctly, to be widely known and taken to heart as important and normative texts of the Magisterium, within the Church's Tradition. Now that the Jubilee has ended, I feel more than ever in duty bound to point to the Council as *the great grace bestowed on the Church in the twentieth century:* there we find a sure compass by which to take our bearings in the century now beginning.

CONCLUSION
DUC IN ALTUM!

58. Let us go forward in hope! A new millennium is opening before the Church like a vast ocean upon which we shall venture, relying on the help of Christ. The Son of God, who became incarnate two thousand years ago out of love for humanity, is at work even today: we need discerning eyes to see this and, above all, a generous heart to become the instruments of His work. Did we not celebrate the Jubilee Year in order to refresh our contact with this

living source of our hope? Now, the Christ whom we have contemplated and loved bids us to set out once more on our journey: "Go therefore and make disciples of all nations, baptizing them in the name of the Father, and of the Son and of the Holy Spirit" (*Mt* 28:19). The missionary mandate accompanies us into the Third Millennium and urges us to share the enthusiasm of the very first Christians: we can count on the power of the same Spirit who was poured out at Pentecost and who impels us still today to start out anew, sustained by the hope "which does not disappoint" (*Rom* 5:5).

At the beginning of this new century, our steps must quicken as we travel the highways of the world. Many are the paths on which each one of us and each of our Churches must travel, but there is no distance between those who are united in the same communion, the communion which is daily nourished at the table of the Eucharistic Bread and the Word of Life. Every Sunday, the Risen Christ asks us to meet Him as it were once more in the Upper Room where, on the evening of "the first day of the week" (*Jn* 20:19) He appeared to His disciples in order to "breathe" on them His life-giving Spirit and launch them on the great adventure of proclaiming the Gospel.

On this journey we are accompanied by the Blessed Virgin Mary to whom, a few months ago, in the presence of a great number of Bishops assembled in Rome from all parts of the world, I entrusted the Third Millennium. During this year I have often invoked her as the "Star of the New Evangelization". Now I point to Mary once again as the radiant dawn and sure guide for our steps. Once more, echoing the words of Jesus himself and giving voice to the filial affection of the whole Church, I say to her: "Woman, behold your children"(cf. *Jn* 19:26).

59. Dear brothers and sisters! The symbol of the Holy Door now closes behind us, but only in order to leave more fully open the living door which is Christ. After the enthusiasm

of the Jubilee, it is not to a dull everyday routine that we return. On the contrary, if ours has been a genuine pilgrimage, it will have as it were stretched our legs for the journey still ahead. We need to imitate the zeal of the Apostle Paul: "Straining forward to what lies ahead, I press on towards the goal for the prize of the upward call of God in Christ Jesus" (*Phil* 3:13-14). Together, we must all imitate the contemplation of Mary, who returned home to Nazareth from her pilgrimage to the Holy City of Jerusalem, treasuring in her heart the mystery of her Son (cf. *Lk* 2:51).

The Risen Jesus accompanies us on our way and enables us to recognize Him, as the disciples of Emmaus did, "in the breaking of the bread" (*Lk* 24:35). May He find us watchful, ready to recognize His face and run to our brothers and sisters with the good news: "We have seen the Lord!" (*Jn* 20:25).

This will be the much desired fruit of the Jubilee of the Year 2000, the Jubilee which has vividly set before our eyes once more the mystery of Jesus of Nazareth, the Son of God and the Redeemer of man.

As the Jubilee now comes to a close and points us to a future of hope, may the praise and thanksgiving of the whole Church rise to the Father, through Christ, in the Holy Spirit.

In pledge of this, I impart to all of you my heartfelt Blessing.

From the Vatican, on 6 January, the Solemnity of the Epiphany, in the year 2001, the twenty-third of my Pontificate.

Invoking Mary's Help

The Holy Father has given to us a practical plan to live out the message of Jesus in the world of today. Let us be resolved to listen to the Father, to love with the Son and to live in the Spirit so that we may think, love and act like Jesus and continue across our time and space His redemptive, sanctifying, evangelizing, and healing work in union with Mary, our mother – the Mother of the Church, the Mother of Jesus and the Merciful Mother of all men and women.

Notes

(15) Saint Cyprian, *De Oratione Dominica*, 23: *PL* 4, 553; cf. *Lumen Gentium*, 4.

(16) Second Vatican Ecumenical Council, Dogmatic Constitution on the Church *Lumen Gentium*, 40.

(17) Cf. Second Vatican Ecumenical Council, Constitution on the Sacred Liturgy *Sacrosanctum Concilium*, 10.

(18) Cf. Congregation for the Doctrine of the Faith, Letter on Certain Aspects of Christian Meditation *Orationis Formas* (15 October 1989): *AAS* 82 (1990), 362-379.

(19) Second Vatican Ecumenical Council, Constitution on the Sacred Liturgy *Sacrosanctum Concilium*, 10.

(20) John Paul II, Apostolic Letter *Dies Domini* (31 May 1998), 19: *AAS* 90 (1998), 724.

(21) *Ibid.*, 2: *loc. cit.*, 714.

(22) Cf. *ibid.*, 35: *loc. cit.*, 734.

(23) Cf. No. 18: *AAS* 77 (1985), 224.

(24) *Ibid.*, 31: *loc. cit.*, 258.

(25) Tertullian, *Apologeticum*, 50, 13: *PL* 1, 534.

(26) Second Vatican Ecumenical Council, Dogmatic Constitution on the Church *Lumen Gentium*, 1.

(27) *Manuscript B,* 3vo: *Êuvres complètes* (Paris, 1996), p. 226.

(28) Cf. Second Vatican Ecumenical Council, Dogmatic Constitution on the Church *Lumen Gentium,* Chapter III.

(29) Cf. Congregation for the clergy et al., Instruction on Certain Questions regarding the Collaboration of the Non-ordained Faithful in the Sacred Ministry of Priests *Ecclesiae de Mysterio* (15 August 1997): *AAS* 89 (1997), 852-877, especially Article 5: "The Structures of Collaboration in the Particular Church".

(30) *Regula*, III, 3: "*Ideo autem omnes ad consilium vocari diximus, quia saepe iuniori Dominus revelat quod melius est*".

(31) "*De omnium fidelium ore pendeamus, quia in omnem fidelem Spiritus Dei spirat*": *Epistola* 23, 36 to Sulpicius Severus: *CSEL* 29, 193.

(32) Second Vatican Ecumenical Council, Dogmatic Constitution on the Church *Lumen Gentium*, 31.

(33) Second Vatican Ecumenical Council, Decree on the Apostolate of the Laity *Apostolicam Actuositatem*, 2.

(34) Cf. Second Vatican Ecumenical Council, Dogmatic Constitution on the Church *Lumen Gentium*, 8.

(35) Second Vatican Ecumenical Council, Pastoral Constitution on the Church in the Modern World *Gaudium et Spes*, 22.

(36)   Pastoral Constitution on the Church in the Modern World *Gaudium et Spes*, 34.

(37)   Cf. Saint Ignatius of Antioch, *Letter to the Romans*, Preface, ed. Funk, I, 252.

(38)   Thus, for example, SAINT AUGUSTINE: *"Luna intellegitur Ecclesia, quod suum lumen non habeat, sed ab Unigenito Dei Filio, qui multis locis in Sanctis Scripturis allegorice sol appellatus est"*: *Enarrationes in Psalmos,* 10, 3: *CCL* 38, 42.

(39)   Cf. Declaration on the Relationship of the Church to Non-Christian Religions *Nostra Aetate*.

(40)   Congregation for the Evangelization of Peoples and Pontifical Council for Interreligious Dialogue, Instruction on the Proclamation of the Gospel and Interreligious Dialogue *Dialogue and Proclamation: Reflections and Orientations* (19 May 1991), 82: *AAS* 84 (1992), 444.

(41)   Cf. Pastoral Constitution on the Church in the Modern World *Gaudium et Spes*, 4.

(42)   *Ibid.*, 11.

(43)   *Ibid.*, 44.

The Rosary

Seven Plus One

In his apostolic letter on the rosary, the Holy Father added
another of his pastoral priorities, namely frequent recitation of
the rosary.

APOSTOLIC LETTER
ROSARIUM VIRGINIS MARIAE
OF THE SUPREME PONTIFF JOHN PAUL II
TO THE BISHOPS, CLERGY AND FAITHFUL
ON THE MOST HOLY ROSARY

INTRODUCTION

1. The Rosary of the Virgin Mary, which gradually took form in
the second millennium under the guidance of the Spirit of God, is
a prayer loved by countless Saints and encouraged by the
Magisterium. Simple yet profound, it still remains, at the dawn of
this third millennium, a prayer of great significance, destined to
bring forth a harvest of holiness. It blends easily into the spiritual
journey of the Christian life, which, after two thousand years, has
lost none of the freshness of its beginnings and feels drawn by the
Spirit of God to "set out into the deep" (*duc in altum!*) in order
once more to proclaim, and even cry out, before the world that
Jesus Christ is Lord and Savior, "the Way, and the Truth and the
Life" (Jn 14:6), "the goal of human history and the point on which
the desires of history and civilization turn".[1]

The Rosary, though clearly Marian in character, is at heart a
Christocentric prayer. In the sobriety of its elements, it has all the
depth of the Gospel message in its entirety, of which it can be said
to be a compendium.[2] It is an echo of the prayer of Mary, her
perennial Magnificat for the work of the redemptive Incarnation
which began in her virginal womb. With the Rosary, the Christian
people sits at the school of Mary and is led to contemplate the
beauty on the face of Christ and to experience the depths of His

love. Through the Rosary the faithful receive abundant grace, as though from the very hands of the Mother of the Redeemer.

The Popes and the Rosary

2. Numerous predecessors of mine attributed great importance to this prayer. Worthy of special note in this regard is Pope Leo XIII who on 1 September 1883 promulgated the Encyclical *Supremi Apostolatus Officio*,[3] a document of great worth, the first of his many statements about this prayer, in which he proposed the Rosary as an effective spiritual weapon against the evils afflicting society. Among the more recent Popes who, from the time of the Second Vatican Council, have distinguished themselves in promoting the Rosary I would mention Blessed John XXIII[4] and above all Pope Paul VI, who in his Apostolic Exhortation *Marialis Cultus* emphasized, in the spirit of the Second Vatican Council, the Rosary's evangelical character and its Christocentric inspiration. I myself have often encouraged the frequent recitation of the Rosary. From my youthful years this prayer has held an important place in my spiritual life. I was powerfully reminded of this during my recent visit to Poland, and in particular at the Shrine of Kalwaria. The Rosary has accompanied me in moments of joy and in moments of difficulty. To it I have entrusted any number of concerns; in it I have always found comfort.

Twenty-four years ago, on 29 October 1978, scarcely two weeks after my election to the See of Peter, I frankly admitted: "The Rosary is my favorite prayer. A marvelous prayer! Marvelous in its simplicity and its depth. [...]. It can be said that the Rosary is, in some sense, a prayer-commentary on the final chapter of the Vatican II Constitution *Lumen Gentium*, a chapter which discusses the wondrous presence of the Mother of God in the mystery of Christ and the Church. Against the background of the words Ave Maria the principal events of the life of Jesus Christ pass before the eyes of the soul. They take shape in the complete series of the joyful, sorrowful and glorious mysteries, and they put us in living communion with Jesus through – we might say – the heart of his Mother. At the same time our heart can embrace in the decades of the Rosary all the events that make up the lives of individuals, families, nations, the Church, and all mankind. Our personal concerns and those of our neighbor, especially those who are closest to us, who are dearest to us. Thus the simple prayer of the Rosary marks the rhythm of human life".[5]

With these words, dear brothers and sisters, I set the first year of my Pontificate within the daily rhythm of the Rosary. Today, as I begin the twenty-fifth year of my service as the Successor of Peter, I wish to do the same. How many graces have I received in these years from the Blessed Virgin through the Rosary: *Magnificat anima mea Dominum*! I wish to lift up my thanks to the Lord in the words of his Most Holy Mother, under whose protection I have placed my Petrine ministry: *Totus Tuus*!

October 2002 – October 2003: The Year of the Rosary

3. Therefore, in continuity with my reflection in the Apostolic Letter *Novo Millennio Ineunte*, in which, after the experience of the Jubilee, I invited the people of God to "start afresh from Christ",[6] I have felt drawn to offer a reflection on the Rosary, as a kind of Marian complement to that Letter and an exhortation to contemplate the face of Christ in union with, and at the school of, his Most Holy Mother. To recite the Rosary is nothing other than to contemplate with Mary the face of Christ. As a way of highlighting this invitation, prompted by the forthcoming 120th anniversary of the aforementioned Encyclical of Leo XIII, I desire that during the course of this year the Rosary should be especially emphasized and promoted in the various Christian communities. I therefore proclaim the year from October 2002 to October 2003 the Year of the Rosary.

I leave this pastoral proposal to the initiative of each ecclesial community. It is not my intention to encumber but rather to complete and consolidate pastoral programs of the Particular Churches. I am confident that the proposal will find a ready and generous reception. The Rosary, reclaimed in its full meaning, goes to the very heart of Christian life; it offers a familiar yet fruitful spiritual and educational opportunity for personal contemplation, the formation of the People of God, and the new evangelization. I am pleased to reaffirm this also in the joyful remembrance of another anniversary: the fortieth anniversary of the opening of the Second Vatican Ecumenical Council on October 11, 1962, the "great grace" disposed by the Spirit of God for the Church in our time.[7]

Objections to the Rosary

4. The timeliness of this proposal is evident from a number of considerations. First, the urgent need to counter a certain crisis of the Rosary, which in the present historical and theological context can risk being wrongly devalued, and therefore no longer taught to the younger generation. There are some who think that the centrality of the Liturgy, rightly stressed by the Second Vatican Ecumenical Council, necessarily entails giving lesser importance to the Rosary. Yet, as Pope Paul VI made clear, not only does this prayer not conflict with the Liturgy, it sustains it, since it serves as an excellent introduction and a faithful echo of the Liturgy, enabling people to participate fully and interiorly in it and to reap its fruits in their daily lives.

Perhaps too, there are some who fear that the Rosary is somehow unecumenical because of its distinctly Marian character. Yet the Rosary clearly belongs to the kind of veneration of the Mother of God described by the Council: a devotion directed to the Christological center of the Christian faith, in such a way that "when the Mother is honored, the Son ... is duly known, loved and glorified".[8] If properly revitalized, the Rosary is an aid and certainly not a hindrance to ecumenism!

A Path of Contemplation

5. But the most important reason for strongly encouraging the practice of the Rosary is that it represents a most effective means of fostering among the faithful that commitment to the contemplation of the Christian mystery which I have proposed in the Apostolic Letter *Novo Millennio Ineunte* as a genuine "training in holiness": "What is needed is a Christian life distinguished above all in the art of prayer".[9] Inasmuch as contemporary culture, even amid so many indications to the contrary, has witnessed the flowering of a new call for spirituality, due also to the influence of other religions, it is more urgent than ever that our Christian

communities should become "genuine schools of prayer".[10]

The Rosary belongs among the finest and most praiseworthy traditions of Christian contemplation. Developed in the West, it is a typically meditative prayer, corresponding in some way to the "prayer of the heart" or "Jesus prayer" which took root in the soil of the Christian East.

Prayer for Peace and for the Family

6. A number of historical circumstances also make a revival of the Rosary quite timely. First of all, the need to implore from God the gift of peace. The Rosary has many times been proposed by my predecessors and myself as a prayer for peace. At the start of a millennium which began with the terrifying attacks of 11 September 2001, a millennium which witnesses every day in numerous parts of the world fresh scenes of bloodshed and violence, to rediscover the Rosary means to immerse oneself in contemplation of the mystery of Christ who "is our peace", since He made "the two of us one, and broke down the dividing wall of hostility" (*Eph* 2:14). Consequently, one cannot recite the Rosary without feeling caught up in a clear commitment to advancing peace, especially in the land of Jesus, still so sorely afflicted and so close to the heart of every Christian.

A similar need for commitment and prayer arises in relation to another critical contemporary issue: the family, the primary cell of society, increasingly menaced by forces of disintegration on both the ideological and practical planes, so as to make us fear for the future of this fundamental and indispensable institution and, with it, for the future of society as a whole. The revival of the Rosary in Christian families, within the context of a broader pastoral ministry to the family, will be an effective aid to countering the devastating effects of this crisis typical of our age.

"Behold, Your Mother!" (*Jn* 19:27)

7. Many signs indicate that still today the Blessed Virgin desires to exercise through this same prayer that maternal concern to which the dying Redeemer entrusted, in the person of the beloved disciple, all the sons and daughters of the Church: "Woman, behold

your son!" (*Jn*19:26). Well-known are the occasions in the nineteenth and the twentieth centuries on which the Mother of Christ made her presence felt and her voice heard, in order to exhort the People of God to this form of contemplative prayer. I would mention in particular, on account of their great influence on the lives of Christians and the authoritative recognition they have received from the Church, the apparitions of Lourdes and of Fatima;[11] these shrines continue to be visited by great numbers of pilgrims seeking comfort and hope.

Following the Witnesses
8. It would be impossible to name all the many Saints who discovered in the Rosary a genuine path to growth in holiness. We need but mention Saint Louis Marie Grignion de Montfort, the author of an excellent work on the Rosary,[12] and, closer to ourselves, Padre Pio of Pietrelcina, whom I recently had the joy of canonizing. As a true apostle of the Rosary, Blessed Bartolo Longo had a special charism. His path to holiness rested on an inspiration heard in the depths of his heart: "Whoever spreads the Rosary is saved!"[13] As a result, he felt called to build a Church dedicated to Our Lady of the Holy Rosary in Pompei, against the background of the ruins of the ancient city, which scarcely heard the proclamation of Christ before being buried in 79 A.D. during an eruption of Mount Vesuvius, only to emerge centuries later from its ashes as a witness to the lights and shadows of classical civilization. By his whole life's work and especially by the practice of the "Fifteen Saturdays", Bartolo Longo promoted the Christocentric and contemplative heart of the Rosary, and received great encouragement and support from Leo XIII, the "Pope of the Rosary".

CHAPTER I

CONTEMPLATING CHRIST WITH MARY

A Face Radiant as the Sun

9. "And He was transfigured before them, and His face shone like the sun" (*Mt* 17:2). The Gospel scene of Christ's transfiguration, in which the three Apostles Peter, James and John appear entranced by the beauty of the Redeemer, can be seen as an icon of Christian contemplation. To look upon the face of Christ, to recognize its mystery amid the daily events and the sufferings of His human life, and then to grasp the divine splendor definitively revealed in the Risen Lord, seated in glory at the right hand of the Father: this is the task of every follower of Christ and therefore the task of each one of us. In contemplating Christ's face we become open to receiving the mystery of Trinitarian life, experiencing ever anew the love of the Father and delighting in the joy of the Holy Spirit. Saint Paul's words can then be applied to us: "Beholding the glory of the Lord, we are being changed into His likeness, from one degree of glory to another; for this comes from the Lord who is the Spirit" (*2 Cor* 3:18).

Mary, Model of Contemplation

10. The contemplation of Christ has an incomparable model in Mary. In a unique way the face of the Son belongs to Mary. It was in her womb that Christ was formed, receiving from her a human resemblance which points to an even greater spiritual closeness. No one has ever devoted himself to the contemplation of the face of Christ as faithfully as Mary. The eyes of her heart already turned to Him at the Annunciation, when she conceived Him by the power of the Holy Spirit. In the months that followed she began to sense His presence and to picture His features. When at last she gave birth to Him in Bethlehem, her eyes were able to gaze tenderly on the face of her Son, as she "wrapped Him in swaddling cloths, and laid Him in a manger" (*Lk* 2:7).

Thereafter Mary's gaze, ever filled with adoration and wonder, would never leave Him. At times it would be a questioning look, as in the episode of the finding in the Temple: "Son, why have you treated us so?" (*Lk* 2:48); it would always be a penetrating gaze, one capable of deeply understanding Jesus, even to the point of perceiving His hidden feelings and anticipating His decisions, as at Cana (cf. *Jn* 2:5). At other times it would be a look of sorrow, especially beneath the Cross, where her vision would still be that of a mother giving birth, for Mary not only shared the passion and death of her Son, she also received the new son given to her in the beloved disciple (cf. Jn 19:26-27). On the morning of Easter hers would be a gaze radiant with the joy of the Resurrection, and finally, on the day of Pentecost, a gaze afire with the outpouring of the Spirit (cf. *Acts* 1:14).

Mary's Memories

11. Mary lived with her eyes fixed on Christ, treasuring His every word: "She kept all these things, pondering them in her heart" (*Lk* 2:19; cf. 2:51). The memories of Jesus, impressed upon her heart, were always with her, leading her to reflect on the various moments of her life at her Son's side. In a way those memories were to be the "rosary" which she recited uninterruptedly throughout her earthly life.

Even now, amid the joyful songs of the heavenly Jerusalem, the reasons for her thanksgiving and praise remain unchanged. They inspire her maternal concern for the pilgrim Church, in which she continues to relate her personal account of the Gospel. Mary constantly sets before the faithful the "mysteries" of her Son, with the desire that the contemplation of those mysteries will release all their saving power. In the recitation of the Rosary, the Christian community enters into contact with the memories and the contemplative gaze of Mary.

The Rosary, a Contemplative Prayer

12. The Rosary, precisely because it starts with Mary's own experience, is an exquisitely contemplative prayer. Without this contemplative dimension, it would lose its meaning, as Pope Paul VI clearly pointed out: "Without contemplation, the Rosary is a body without a soul, and its recitation runs the risk of becoming a

mechanical repetition of formulas, in violation of the admonition of Christ: 'In praying do not heap up empty phrases as the Gentiles do; for they think they will be heard for their many words' (*Mt* 6:7). By its nature the recitation of the Rosary calls for a quiet rhythm and a lingering pace, helping the individual to meditate on the mysteries of the Lord's life as seen through the eyes of her who was closest to the Lord. In this way the unfathomable riches of these mysteries are disclosed".[14]

It is worth pausing to consider this profound insight of Paul VI, in order to bring out certain aspects of the Rosary which show that it is really a form of Christocentric contemplation.

Remembering Christ with Mary

13. Mary's contemplation is above all a remembering. We need to understand this word in the biblical sense of remembrance (*zakar*) as a making present of the works brought about by God in the history of salvation. The Bible is an account of saving events culminating in Christ Himself. These events not only belong to "yesterday"; they are also part of the "today" of salvation. This making present comes about above all in the Liturgy: what God accomplished centuries ago did not only affect the direct witnesses of those events; it continues to affect people in every age with its gift of grace. To some extent this is also true of every other devout approach to those events: to "remember" them in a spirit of faith and love is to be open to the grace which Christ won for us by the mysteries of His life, death and resurrection.

Consequently, while it must be reaffirmed with the Second Vatican Council that the Liturgy, as the exercise of the priestly office of Christ and an act of public worship, is "the summit to which the activity of the Church is directed and the font from which all its power flows",[15] it is also necessary to recall that the spiritual life "is not limited solely to participation in the liturgy. Christians, while they are called to prayer in common, must also go to their own rooms to pray to their Father in secret (cf. *Mt* 6:6); indeed, according to the teaching of the Apostle, they must pray without ceasing (cf.*1 Thes* 5:17)".[16] The Rosary, in its own particular way, is part of this varied panorama of "ceaseless" prayer. If the Liturgy, as the activity of Christ and the Church, is a saving action par excellence, the Rosary too, as a "meditation" with Mary on Christ, is a salutary contemplation. By immersing us in the mysteries of the Redeemer's life, it ensures that what He has done and what the liturgy makes present is profoundly assimilated and shapes our existence.

Learning Christ from Mary

14. Christ is the supreme Teacher, the revealer and the one revealed. It is not just a question of learning what He taught but of "learning Him". In this regard could we have any better teacher than Mary? From the divine standpoint, the Spirit is the interior teacher who leads us to the full truth of Christ (cf. *Jn* 14:26;15:26;16:13). But among creatures no one knows Christ better than Mary; no one can introduce us to a profound knowledge of His mystery better than His Mother.

The first of the "signs" worked by Jesus – the changing of water into wine at the marriage in Cana – clearly presents Mary in the guise of a teacher, as she urges the servants to do what Jesus commands (cf. Jn 2:5). We can imagine that she would have done likewise for the disciples after Jesus' Ascension, when she joined them in awaiting the Holy Spirit and supported them in their first mission. Contemplating the scenes of the Rosary in union with Mary is a means of learning from her to "read" Christ, to discover His secrets and to understand His message.

This school of Mary is all the more effective if we consider that she teaches by obtaining for us in abundance the gifts of the Holy Spirit, even as she offers us the incomparable example of her own "pilgrimage of faith".[17] As we contemplate each mystery of her Son's life, she invites us to do as she did at the Annunciation: to ask humbly the questions which open us to the light, in order to end with the obedience of faith: "Behold I am the handmaid of the Lord; be it done to me according to your word" (*Lk* 1:38).

Being Conformed to Christ with Mary

15. Christian spirituality is distinguished by the disciple's commitment to become conformed ever more fully to His Master (cf. *Rom*

8:29; *Phil* 3:10,12). The outpouring of the Holy Spirit in Baptism grafts the believer like a branch onto the vine which is Christ (cf. *Jn* 15:5) and makes him a member of Christ's mystical Body (cf. *1 Cor* 12:12; Rom 12:5). This initial unity, however, calls for a growing assimilation which will increasingly shape the conduct of the disciple in accordance with the "mind" of Christ: "Have this mind among yourselves, which was in Christ Jesus" (*Phil* 2:5). In the words of the Apostle, we are called "to put on the Lord Jesus Christ" (cf. *Rom* 13:14; *Gal* 3:27).

In the spiritual journey of the Rosary, based on the constant contemplation – in Mary's company – of the face of Christ, this demanding ideal of being conformed to Him is pursued through an association which could be described in terms of friendship. We are thereby enabled to enter naturally into Christ's life and as it were to share His deepest feelings. In this regard Blessed Bartolo Longo has written: "Just as two friends, frequently in each other's company, tend to develop similar habits, so too, by holding familiar converse with Jesus and the Blessed Virgin, by meditating on the mysteries of the Rosary and by living the same life in Holy Communion, we can become, to the extent of our lowliness, similar to them and can learn from these supreme models a life of humility, poverty, hiddenness, patience and perfection".[18]

In this process of being conformed to Christ in the Rosary, we entrust ourselves in a special way to the maternal care of the Blessed Virgin. She who is both the Mother of Christ and a member of the Church, indeed her "pre-eminent and altogether singular member",[19] is at the same time the "Mother of the Church". As such, she continually brings to birth children for the mystical Body of her Son. She does so through her intercession, imploring upon them the inexhaustible outpouring of the Spirit. Mary is the perfect icon of the motherhood of the Church.

The Rosary mystically transports us to Mary's side as she is busy watching over the human growth of Christ in the home of Nazareth. This enables her to train us and to mold us with the same care, until Christ is "fully formed" in us (cf. Gal 4:19). This role of Mary, totally grounded in that of Christ and radically subordinated to it, "in no way obscures or diminishes the unique mediation of

Christ, but rather shows its power".[20] This is the luminous principle expressed by the Second Vatican Council which I have so powerfully experienced in my own life and have made the basis of my episcopal motto: *Totus Tuus.*[21] The motto is of course inspired by the teaching of Saint Louis Marie Grignion de Montfort, who explained in the following words Mary's role in the process of our configuration to Christ: "Our entire perfection consists in being conformed, united and consecrated to Jesus Christ. Hence the most perfect of all devotions is undoubtedly that which conforms, unites and consecrates us most perfectly to Jesus Christ. Now, since Mary is of all creatures the one most conformed to Jesus Christ, it follows that among all devotions that which most consecrates and conforms a soul to our Lord is devotion to Mary, His Holy Mother, and that the more a soul is consecrated to her the more will it be consecrated to Jesus Christ".[22] Never as in the Rosary do the life of Jesus and that of Mary appear so deeply joined. Mary lives only in Christ and for Christ!

Praying to Christ with Mary

16. Jesus invited us to turn to God with insistence and the confidence that we will be heard: "Ask, and it will be given to you; seek, and you will find; knock, and it will be opened to you" (*Mt* 7:7). The basis for this power of prayer is the goodness of the Father, but also the mediation of Christ Himself (cf. *1 Jn* 2:1) and the working of the Holy Spirit who "intercedes for us" according to the will of God (cf. *Rom* 8:26-27). For "we do not know how to pray as we ought" (*Rom* 8:26), and at times we are not heard "because we ask wrongly" (cf. *Jas* 4:2-3).

In support of the prayer which Christ and the Spirit cause to rise in our hearts, Mary intervenes with her maternal intercession. "The prayer of the Church is sustained by the prayer of Mary".[23] If Jesus, the one Mediator, is the Way of our prayer, then Mary, his purest and most transparent reflection, shows us the Way. "Beginning with Mary's unique cooperation with the working of the Holy Spirit, the Churches developed their prayer to the Holy Mother of God, centering it on the person of Christ manifested in His mysteries".[24] At the wedding of Cana the Gospel clearly shows the power of Mary's intercession as she makes known to Jesus the needs of others: "They have no wine" (*Jn* 2:3).

The Rosary is both meditation and supplication. Insistent prayer to the Mother of God is based on confidence that her maternal intercession can obtain all things from the heart of her Son. She is "all-powerful by grace", to use the bold expression, which needs to be properly understood, of Blessed Bartolo Longo in his Supplication to Our Lady.[25] This is a conviction which, beginning with the Gospel, has grown ever more firm in the experience of the Christian people. The supreme poet Dante expresses it marvelously in the lines sung by Saint Bernard: "Lady, thou art so great and so powerful, that whoever desires grace yet does not turn to thee, would have his desire fly without wings".[26] When in the Rosary we plead with Mary, the sanctuary of the Holy Spirit (cf. *Lk* 1:35), she intercedes for us before the Father who filled her with grace and before the Son born of her womb, praying with us and for us.

Proclaiming Christ with Mary

17. The Rosary is also a path of proclamation and increasing knowledge, in which the mystery of Christ is presented again and again at different levels of the Christian experience. Its form is that of a prayerful and contemplative presentation, capable of forming Christians according to the heart of Christ. When the recitation of the Rosary combines all the elements needed for an effective meditation, especially in its communal celebration in parishes and shrines, it can present a significant catechetical opportunity which pastors should use to advantage. In this way too Our Lady of the Rosary continues her work of proclaiming Christ. The history of the Rosary shows how this prayer was used in particular by the Dominicans at a difficult time for the Church due to the spread of heresy. Today we are facing new challenges. Why should we not once more have recourse to the Rosary, with the same faith as those who have gone before us? The Rosary retains all its power and continues to be a valuable pastoral resource for every good evangelizer.

CHAPTER II

MYSTERIES OF CHRIST – MYSTERIES OF HIS MOTHER

The Rosary, "a Compendium of the Gospel"

18. The only way to approach the contemplation of Christ's face is by listening in the Spirit to the Father's voice, since "no one knows the Son except the Father" (*Mt* 11:27). In the region of Caesarea Philippi, Jesus responded to Peter's confession of faith by indicating the source of that clear intuition of His identity: "Flesh and blood has not revealed this to you, but My Father who is in heaven" (*Mt* 16:17). What is needed, then, is a revelation from above. In order to receive that revelation, attentive listening is indispensable: "Only the experience of silence and prayer offers the proper setting for the growth and development of a true, faithful and consistent knowledge of that mystery".[27]

The Rosary is one of the traditional paths of Christian prayer directed to the contemplation of Christ's face. Pope Paul VI described it in these words: "As a Gospel prayer, centered on the mystery of the redemptive Incarnation, the Rosary is a prayer with a clearly Christological orientation. Its most characteristic element, in fact, the litany-like succession of Hail Marys, becomes in itself an unceasing praise of Christ, who is the ultimate object both of the Angel's announcement and of the greeting of the Mother of John the Baptist: 'Blessed is the fruit of your womb' (*Lk* 1:42). We would go further and say that the succession of Hail Marys constitutes the warp on which is woven the contemplation of the mysteries. The Jesus that each Hail Mary recalls is the same Jesus whom the succession of mysteries proposes to us now as the Son of God, now as the Son of the Virgin".[28]

A Proposed Addition to the Traditional Pattern

19. Of the many mysteries of Christ's life, only a few are indicated by the Rosary in the form that has become generally established with the seal of the Church's approval. The selection was

determined by the origin of the prayer, which was based on the number 150, the number of the Psalms in the Psalter.

I believe, however, that to bring out fully the Christological depth of the Rosary it would be suitable to make an addition to the traditional pattern which, while left to the freedom of individuals and communities, could broaden it to include the mysteries of Christ's public ministry between His Baptism and His Passion. In the course of those mysteries we contemplate important aspects of the person of Christ as the definitive revelation of God. Declared the beloved Son of the Father at the Baptism in the Jordan, Christ is the one who announces the coming of the Kingdom, bears witness to it in His works and proclaims its demands. It is during the years of His public ministry that the mystery of Christ is most evidently a mystery of light: "While I am in the world, I am the light of the world" (*Jn* 9:5).

Consequently, for the Rosary to become more fully a "compendium of the Gospel", it is fitting to add, following reflection on the Incarnation and the hidden life of Christ (the joyful mysteries) and before focusing on the sufferings of his Passion (the sorrowful mysteries) and the triumph of his Resurrection (the glorious mysteries), a meditation on certain particularly significant moments in His public ministry (the mysteries of light). This addition of these new mysteries, without prejudice to any essential aspect of the prayer's traditional format, is meant to give it fresh life and to enkindle renewed interest in the Rosary's place within Christian spirituality as a true doorway to the depths of the Heart of Christ, ocean of joy and of light, of suffering and of glory.

The Joyful Mysteries

20. The first five decades, the "joyful mysteries", are marked by the joy radiating from the event of the Incarnation. This is clear from the very first mystery, the Annunciation, where Gabriel's greeting to the Virgin of Nazareth is linked to an invitation to messianic joy: "Rejoice, Mary". The whole of salvation history, in some sense the entire history of the world, has led up to this greeting. If it is the Father's plan to unite all things in Christ (cf. *Eph* 1:10), then the whole of the universe is in some way touched by the divine favor

with which the Father looks upon Mary and makes her the Mother of His Son. The whole of humanity, in turn, is embraced by the fiat with which she readily agrees to the will of God.

Exultation is the keynote of the encounter with Elizabeth, where the sound of Mary's voice and the presence of Christ in her womb cause John to "leap for joy" (cf. *Lk* 1:44). Gladness also fills the scene in Bethlehem, when the birth of the divine Child, the Savior of the World, is announced by the song of the angels and proclaimed to the shepherds as "news of great joy" (*Lk* 2:10).

The final two mysteries, while preserving this climate of joy, already point to the drama yet to come. The Presentation in the Temple not only expresses the joy of the Child's consecration and the ecstasy of the aged Simeon; it also records the prophecy that Christ will be a "sign of contradiction" for Israel and that a sword will pierce His mother's heart (cf *Lk* 2:34-35). Joy mixed with drama marks the fifth mystery, the finding of the twelve-year-old Jesus in the Temple. Here He appears in His divine wisdom as He listens and raises questions, already in effect one who "teaches". The revelation of His mystery as the Son wholly dedicated to His Father's affairs proclaims the radical nature of the Gospel, in which even the closest of human relationships are challenged by the absolute demands of the Kingdom. Mary and Joseph, fearful and anxious, "did not understand" His words (*Lk* 2:50).

To meditate upon the "joyful" mysteries, then, is to enter into the ultimate causes and the deepest meaning of Christian joy. It is to focus on the realism of the mystery of the Incarnation and on the obscure foreshadowing of the mystery of the saving Passion. Mary leads us to discover the secret of Christian joy, reminding us that Christianity is, first and foremost, *euangelion*, "good news", which has as its heart and its whole content the person of Jesus Christ, the Word made flesh, the one Savior of the world.

The Mysteries of Light

21. Moving on from the infancy and the hidden life in Nazareth to the public life of Jesus, our contemplation brings us to those mysteries which may be called in a special way "mysteries of light". Certainly the whole mystery of Christ is a mystery of light. He is

the "light of the world" (*Jn* 8:12). Yet this truth emerges in a special way during the years of His public life, when He proclaims the Gospel of the Kingdom. In proposing to the Christian community five significant moments – "luminous" mysteries – during this phase of Christ's life, I think that the following can be fittingly singled out: 1. His Baptism in the Jordan, 2. His self-manifestation at the wedding of Cana, 3. His proclamation of the Kingdom of God, with His call to conversion, 4. His Transfiguration, and finally, 5. His institution of the Eucharist, as the sacramental expression of the Paschal Mystery.

Each of these mysteries is a revelation of the Kingdom now present in the very person of Jesus. The Baptism in the Jordan is first of all a mystery of light. Here, as Christ descends into the waters, the innocent one who became "sin" for our sake (cf. *2 Cor* 5:21), the heavens open wide and the voice of the Father declares Him the beloved Son (cf. *Mt* 3:17 and parallels), while the Spirit descends on Him to invest Him with the mission which He is to carry out. Another mystery of light is the first of the signs, given at Cana (cf. *Jn* 2:1-12), when Christ changes water into wine and opens the hearts of the disciples to faith, thanks to the intervention of Mary, the first among believers.

Another mystery of light is the preaching by which Jesus proclaims the coming of the Kingdom of God, calls to conversion (cf. *Mk* 1:15) and forgives the sins of all who draw near to Him in humble trust (cf. *Mk* 2:3-13; *Lk* 7:47- 48): the inauguration of that ministry of mercy which He continues to exercise until the end of the world, particularly through the Sacrament of Reconciliation which He has entrusted to His Church (cf. *Jn* 20:22-23). The mystery of light par excellence is the Transfiguration, traditionally believed to have taken place on Mount Tabor. The glory of the Godhead shines forth from the face of Christ as the Father commands the astonished Apostles to "listen to Him" (cf. *Lk* 9:35 and parallels) and to prepare to experience with Him the agony of the Passion, so as to come with Him to the joy of the Resurrection and a life transfigured by the Holy Spirit. A final mystery of light is the institution of the Eucharist, in which Christ offers His Body and Blood as food under the signs of bread and wine, and testifies "to the end"

His love for humanity (*Jn* 13:1), for whose salvation He will offer Himself in sacrifice.

In these mysteries, apart from the miracle at Cana, the presence of Mary remains in the background. The Gospels make only the briefest reference to her occasional presence at one moment or other during the preaching of Jesus (cf. *Mk* 3:31-35; *Jn* 2:12), and they give no indication that she was present at the Last Supper and the institution of the Eucharist. Yet the role she assumed at Cana in some way accompanies Christ throughout His ministry. The revelation made directly by the Father at the Baptism in the Jordan and echoed by John the Baptist is placed upon Mary's lips at Cana, and it becomes the great maternal counsel which Mary addresses to the Church of every age: "Do whatever He tells you" (*Jn* 2:5). This counsel is a fitting introduction to the words and signs of Christ's public ministry and it forms the Marian foundation of all the "mysteries of light".

The Sorrowful Mysteries
22. The Gospels give great prominence to the sorrowful mysteries of Christ. From the beginning Christian piety, especially during the Lenten devotion of the Way of the Cross, has focused on the individual moments of the Passion, realizing that here is found the culmination of the revelation of God's love and the source of our salvation. The Rosary selects certain moments from the Passion, inviting the faithful to contemplate them in their hearts and to relive them. The sequence of meditations begins with Gethsemane, where Christ experiences a moment of great anguish before the will of the Father, against which the weakness of the flesh would be tempted to rebel. There Jesus encounters all the temptations and confronts all the sins of humanity, in order to say to the Father: "Not My will but Yours be done" (*Lk* 22:42 and parallels). This "Yes" of Christ reverses the "No" of our first parents in the Garden of Eden. And the cost of this faithfulness to the Father's will is made clear in the following mysteries; by His scourging, His crowning with thorns, His carrying the Cross and His death on the Cross, the Lord is cast into the most abject suffering: *Ecce homo!*

This abject suffering reveals not only the love of God but also the meaning of man Himself.

Ecce homo: the meaning, origin and fulfillment of man is to be found in Christ, the God who humbles Himself out of love "even unto death, death on a cross" (*Phil* 2:8). The sorrowful mysteries help the believer to relive the death of Jesus, to stand at the foot of the Cross beside Mary, to enter with her into the depths of God's love for man and to experience all its life-giving power.

The Glorious Mysteries

23. "The contemplation of Christ's face cannot stop at the image of the Crucified One. He is the Risen One!"[(29)] The Rosary has always expressed this knowledge born of faith and invited the believer to pass beyond the darkness of the Passion in order to gaze upon Christ's glory in the Resurrection and Ascension. Contemplating the Risen One, Christians rediscover the reasons for their own faith (cf. *1 Cor* 15:14) and relive the joy not only of those to whom Christ appeared – the Apostles, Mary Magdalene and the disciples on the road to Emmaus – but also the joy of Mary, who must have had an equally intense experience of the new life of her glorified Son. In the Ascension, Christ was raised in glory to the right hand of the Father, while Mary herself would be raised to that same glory in the Assumption, enjoying beforehand, by a unique privilege, the destiny reserved for all the just at the resurrection of the dead. Crowned in glory – as she appears in the last glorious mystery – Mary shines forth as Queen of the Angels and Saints, the anticipation and the supreme realization of the eschatological state of the Church.

At the center of this unfolding sequence of the glory of the Son and the Mother, the Rosary sets before us the third glorious mystery, Pentecost, which reveals the face of the Church as a family gathered together with Mary, enlivened by the powerful outpouring of the Spirit and ready for the mission of evangelization. The contemplation of this scene, like that of the other glorious mysteries, ought to lead the faithful to an ever greater appreciation of their new life in Christ, lived in the heart of the Church, a life of which the scene of Pentecost itself is the great "icon". The glorious mysteries thus lead the faithful to greater hope for the eschatological goal towards which they journey as members of the pilgrim People of God in history. This can only impel them to bear courageous witness to that "good news" which gives meaning to their entire existence.

From "Mysteries" to the "Mystery": Mary's Way

24. The cycles of meditation proposed by the Holy Rosary are by no means exhaustive, but they do bring to mind what is essential and they awaken in the soul a thirst for a knowledge of Christ continually nourished by the pure source of the Gospel. Every individual event in the life of Christ, as narrated by the Evangelists, is resplendent with the Mystery that surpasses all understanding (cf. *Eph* 3:19): the Mystery of the Word made flesh, in whom "all the fullness of God dwells bodily" (*Col* 2:9). For this reason the Catechism of the Catholic Church places great emphasis on the mysteries of Christ, pointing out that "everything in the life of Jesus is a sign of His Mystery".[30] The "*duc in altum*" of the Church of the third millennium will be determined by the ability of Christians to enter into the "perfect knowledge of God's mystery, of Christ, in whom are hidden all the treasures of wisdom and knowledge" (*Col* 2:2-3). The Letter to the Ephesians makes this heartfelt prayer for all the baptized: "May Christ dwell in your hearts through faith, so that you, being rooted and grounded in love, may have power... to know the love of Christ which surpasses knowledge, that you may be filled with all the fullness of God" (3:17-19).

The Rosary is at the service of this ideal; it offers the "secret" which leads easily to a profound and inward knowledge of Christ. We might call it Mary's way. It is the way of the example of the Virgin of Nazareth, a woman of faith, of silence, of attentive listening. It is also the way of a Marian devotion inspired by knowledge of the inseparable bond between Christ and His Blessed Mother: the mysteries of Christ are also in some sense the mysteries of His Mother, even when they do not involve her directly, for she lives from Him and through Him. By making our own the words of the Angel Gabriel and Saint Elizabeth contained in the Hail Mary, we find ourselves constantly drawn to seek out afresh in Mary, in her arms and in her heart, the "blessed fruit of her womb" (cf *Lk* 1:42).

Mystery of Christ, Mystery of Man

25. In my testimony of 1978 mentioned above, where I described the Rosary as my favorite prayer, I used an idea to which I would like to return. I said then that "the simple prayer of the Rosary marks the rhythm of human life".[31]

In the light of what has been said so far on the mysteries of Christ, it is not difficult to go deeper into this anthropological significance of the Rosary, which is far deeper than may appear at first sight. Anyone who contemplates Christ through the various stages of His life cannot fail to perceive in Him the truth about man. This is the great affirmation of the Second Vatican Council which I have so often discussed in my own teaching since the Encyclical Letter *Redemptor Hominis*: "it is only in the mystery of the Word made flesh that the mystery of man is seen in its true light".[32] The Rosary helps to open up the way to this light.

Following in the path of Christ, in whom man's path is "recapitulated",[33] revealed and redeemed, believers come face to face with the image of the true man. Contemplating Christ's birth, they learn of the sanctity of life; seeing the household of Nazareth, they learn the original truth of the family according to God's plan; listening to the Master in the mysteries of His public ministry, they find the light which leads them to enter the Kingdom of God; and following Him on the way to Calvary, they learn the meaning of salvific suffering. Finally, contemplating Christ and His Blessed Mother in glory, they see the goal towards which each of us is called, if we allow ourselves to be healed and transformed by the Holy Spirit. It could be said that each mystery of the Rosary, carefully meditated, sheds light on the mystery of man.

At the same time, it becomes natural to bring to this encounter with the sacred humanity of the Redeemer all the problems, anxieties, labors and endeavors which go to make up our lives. "Cast your burden on the Lord and He will sustain you" (Ps 55:23). To pray the Rosary is to hand over our burdens to the merciful hearts of Christ and His Mother. Twenty-five years later, thinking back over the difficulties which have also been part of my exercise of the Petrine ministry, I feel the need to say once more, as a warm invitation to everyone to experience it personally: the Rosary does indeed "mark the rhythm of human life", bringing it into harmony with the "rhythm" of God's own life, in the joyful communion of the Holy Trinity, our life's destiny and deepest longing.

CHAPTER III

"FOR ME, TO LIVE IS CHRIST"

The Rosary, a Way of Assimilating the Mystery

26. Meditation on the mysteries of Christ is proposed in the Rosary by means of a method designed to assist in their assimilation. It is a method based on repetition. This applies above all to the Hail Mary, repeated ten times in each mystery. If this repetition is considered superficially, there could be a temptation to see the Rosary as a dry and boring exercise. It is quite another thing, however, when the Rosary is thought of as an outpouring of that love which tirelessly returns to the person loved with expressions similar in their content but ever fresh in terms of the feeling pervading them.

In Christ, God has truly assumed a "heart of flesh". Not only does God have a divine heart, rich in mercy and in forgiveness, but also a human heart, capable of all the stirrings of affection. If we needed evidence for this from the Gospel, we could easily find it in the touching dialogue between Christ and Peter after the Resurrection: "Simon, son of John, do you love Me?" Three times this question is put to Peter, and three times he gives the reply: "Lord, You know that I love You" (cf. *Jn* 21:15-17). Over and above the specific meaning of this passage, so important for Peter's mission, none can fail to recognize the beauty of this triple repetition, in which the insistent request and the corresponding reply are expressed in terms familiar from the universal experience of human love. To understand the Rosary, one has to enter into the psychological dynamic proper to love.

One thing is clear: although the repeated Hail Mary is addressed directly to Mary, it is to Jesus that the act of love is ultimately directed, with her and through her. The repetition is nourished by the desire to be conformed ever more completely to Christ, the true program of the Christian life. Saint Paul expressed this project with words of fire: "For me to live is Christ and to die is gain" (*Phil* 1:21). And again: "It is no longer I that live, but Christ lives in me"

(*Gal* 2:20). The Rosary helps us to be conformed ever more closely to Christ until we attain true holiness.

A Valid Method...

27. We should not be surprised that our relationship with Christ makes use of a method. God communicates himself to us respecting our human nature and its vital rhythms. Hence, while Christian spirituality is familiar with the most sublime forms of mystical silence in which images, words and gestures are all, so to speak, superseded by an intense and ineffable union with God, it normally engages the whole person in all his complex psychological, physical and relational reality.

This becomes apparent in the Liturgy. Sacraments and sacramentals are structured as a series of rites which bring into play all the dimensions of the person. The same applies to non-liturgical prayer. This is confirmed by the fact that, in the East, the most characteristic prayer of Christological meditation, centered on the words "Lord Jesus Christ, Son of God, have mercy on me, a sinner"(34) is traditionally linked to the rhythm of breathing; while this practice favors perseverance in the prayer, it also in some way embodies the desire for Christ to become the breath, the soul and the "all" of one's life.

... which can nevertheless be improved

28. I mentioned in my Apostolic Letter *Novo Millennio Ineunte* that the West is now experiencing a renewed demand for meditation, which at times leads to a keen interest in aspects of other religions.(35) Some Christians, limited in their knowledge of the Christian contemplative tradition, are attracted by those forms of prayer. While the latter contain many elements which are positive and at times compatible with Christian experience, they are often based on ultimately unacceptable premises. Much in vogue among these approaches are methods aimed at attaining a high level of spiritual concentration by using techniques of a psychophysical, repetitive and symbolic nature. The Rosary is situated within this broad gamut of religious phenomena, but it is distinguished by characteristics of its own which correspond to specifically

Christian requirements.

In effect, the Rosary is simply a method of contemplation. As a method, it serves as a means to an end and cannot become an end in itself. All the same, as the fruit of centuries of experience, this method should not be undervalued. In its favor one could cite the experience of countless Saints. This is not to say, however, that the method cannot be improved. Such is the intent of the addition of the new series of *mysteria lucis* to the overall cycle of mysteries and of the few suggestions which I am proposing in this Letter regarding its manner of recitation. These suggestions, while respecting the well-established structure of this prayer, are intended to help the faithful to understand it in the richness of its symbolism and in harmony with the demands of daily life. Otherwise there is a risk that the Rosary would not only fail to produce the intended spiritual effects, but even that the beads, with which it is usually said, could come to be regarded as some kind of amulet or magic object, thereby radically distorting their meaning and function.

Announcing Each Mystery

29. Announcing each mystery, and perhaps even using a suitable icon to portray it, is as it were to open up a scenario on which to focus our attention. The words direct the imagination and the mind towards a particular episode or moment in the life of Christ. In the Church's traditional spirituality, the veneration of icons and the many devotions appealing to the senses, as well as the method of prayer proposed by Saint Ignatius of Loyola in the Spiritual Exercises, make use of visual and imaginative elements (the *compositio loci*), judged to be of great help in concentrating the mind on the particular mystery. This is a methodology, moreover, which corresponds to the inner logic of the Incarnation: in Jesus, God wanted to take on human features. It is through His bodily reality that we are led into contact with the mystery of His divinity.

This need for concreteness finds further expression in the announcement of the various mysteries of the Rosary. Obviously these mysteries neither replace the Gospel nor exhaust its content. The Rosary, therefore, is no substitute for *lectio divina*; on the contrary, it presupposes and promotes it. Yet, even though the mysteries contemplated in the Rosary, even with the addition of the *mysteria lucis*, do no more than outline the fundamental elements of the life of Christ, they easily draw the mind to a more expansive reflection on the rest of the Gospel, especially when the Rosary is prayed in a setting of prolonged recollection.

Listening to the Word of God

30. In order to supply a Biblical foundation and greater depth to our meditation, it is helpful to follow the announcement of the mystery with the proclamation of a related Biblical passage, long or short, depending on the circumstances. No other words can ever match the efficacy of the inspired word. As we listen, we are certain that this is the word of God, spoken for today and spoken "for me".

If received in this way, the word of God can become part of the Rosary's methodology of repetition without giving rise to the ennui derived from the simple recollection of something already well known. It is not a matter of recalling information but of allowing God to speak. In certain solemn communal celebrations, this word can be appropriately illustrated by a brief commentary.

Silence

31. Listening and meditation are nourished by silence. After the announcement of the mystery and the proclamation of the word, it is fitting to pause and focus one's attention for a suitable period of time on the mystery concerned, before moving into vocal prayer. A discovery of the importance of silence is one of the secrets of practicing contemplation and meditation. One drawback of a society dominated by technology and the mass media is the fact that silence becomes increasingly difficult to achieve. Just as moments of silence are recommended in the Liturgy, so too in the recitation of the Rosary it is fitting to pause briefly after listening to the word of God, while the mind focuses on the content of a particular mystery.

The "Our Father"

32. After listening to the word and focusing on the mystery, it is

natural for the mind to be lifted up towards the Father. In each of his mysteries, Jesus always leads us to the Father, for as He rests in the Father's bosom (cf. *Jn* 1:18) He is continually turned towards Him. He wants us to share in His intimacy with the Father, so that we can say with Him: "Abba, Father" (*Rom* 8:15; *Gal* 4:6). By virtue of His relationship to the Father He makes us brothers and sisters of Himself and of one another, communicating to us the Spirit which is both His and the Father's. Acting as a kind of foundation for the Christological and Marian meditation which unfolds in the repetition of the Hail Mary, the Our Father makes meditation upon the mystery, even when carried out in solitude, an ecclesial experience.

The Ten "Hail Marys"

33. This is the most substantial element in the Rosary and also the one which makes it a Marian prayer *par excellence*. Yet when the Hail Mary is properly understood, we come to see clearly that its Marian character is not opposed to its Christological character, but that it actually emphasizes and increases it. The first part of the Hail Mary, drawn from the words spoken to Mary by the Angel Gabriel and by Saint Elizabeth, is a contemplation in adoration of the mystery accomplished in the Virgin of Nazareth. These words express, so to speak, the wonder of heaven and earth; they could be said to give us a glimpse of God's own wonderment as He contemplates His "masterpiece" – the Incarnation of the Son in the womb of the Virgin Mary. If we recall how, in the Book of Genesis, God "saw all that He had made" (*Gen* 1:31), we can find here an echo of that "pathos with which God, at the dawn of creation, looked upon the work of His hands".[(36)] The repetition of the Hail Mary in the Rosary gives us a share in God's own wonder and pleasure: in jubilant amazement we acknowledge the greatest miracle of history. Mary's prophecy here finds its fulfillment: "Henceforth all generations will call me blessed" (*Lk* 1:48).

The center of gravity in the Hail Mary, the hinge as it were which joins its two parts, is the name of Jesus. Sometimes, in hurried recitation, this center of gravity can be overlooked, and with it the connection to the mystery of Christ being contemplated. Yet it is precisely the emphasis given to the name of Jesus and to His mystery that is the sign of a meaningful and fruitful recitation of the Rosary. Pope Paul VI drew attention, in his Apostolic Exhortation *Marialis Cultus*, to the custom in certain regions of highlighting the name of Christ by the addition of a clause referring to the mystery being contemplated.(37) This is a praiseworthy custom, especially during public recitation. It gives forceful expression to our faith in Christ, directed to the different moments of the Redeemer's life. It is at once a profession of faith and an aid in concentrating our meditation, since it facilitates the process of assimilation to the mystery of Christ inherent in the repetition of the Hail Mary. When we repeat the name of Jesus – the only name given to us by which we may hope for salvation (cf. *Acts* 4:12) – in close association with the name of His Blessed Mother, almost as if it were done at her suggestion, we set out on a path of assimilation meant to help us enter more deeply into the life of Christ.

From Mary's uniquely privileged relationship with Christ, which makes her the Mother of God, *Theotókos,* derives the forcefulness of the appeal we make to her in the second half of the prayer, as we entrust to her maternal intercession our lives and the hour of our death.

The "Gloria"

34. Trinitarian doxology is the goal of all Christian contemplation. For Christ is the way that leads us to the Father in the Spirit. If we travel this way to the end, we repeatedly encounter the mystery of the three divine Persons, to whom all praise, worship and thanksgiving are due. It is important that the Gloria, the high-point of contemplation, be given due prominence in the Rosary. In public recitation it could be sung, as a way of giving proper emphasis to the essentially Trinitarian structure of all Christian prayer. To the extent that meditation on the mystery is attentive and profound, and to the extent that it is enlivened – from one Hail Mary to another – by love for Christ and for Mary, the glorification of the Trinity at the end of each decade, far from being a perfunctory conclusion, takes on its proper contemplative tone, raising the mind as it were to the heights of heaven and enabling us in some way to

relive the experience of Tabor, a foretaste of the contemplation yet to come: "It is good for us to be here!" (*Lk* 9:33).

The concluding short prayer

35. In current practice, the Trinitarian doxology is followed by a brief concluding prayer which varies according to local custom. Without in any way diminishing the value of such invocations, it is worthwhile to note that the contemplation of the mysteries could better express their full spiritual fruitfulness if an effort were made to conclude each mystery with a prayer for the fruits specific to that particular mystery. In this way the Rosary would better express its connection with the Christian life. One fine liturgical prayer suggests as much, inviting us to pray that, by meditation on the mysteries of the Rosary, we may come to "imitate what they contain and obtain what they promise".[38] Such a final prayer could take on a legitimate variety of forms, as indeed it already does. In this way the Rosary can be better adapted to different spiritual traditions and different Christian communities. It is to be hoped, then, that appropriate formulas will be widely circulated, after due pastoral discernment and possibly after experimental use in centers and shrines particularly devoted to the Rosary, so that the People of God may benefit from an abundance of authentic spiritual riches and find nourishment for their personal contemplation.

The Rosary Beads

36. The traditional aid used for the recitation of the Rosary is the set of beads. At the most superficial level, the beads often become a simple counting mechanism to mark the succession of Hail Marys. Yet they can also take on a symbolism which can give added depth to contemplation.

Here the first thing to note is the way the beads converge upon the Crucifix, which both opens and closes the unfolding sequence of prayer. The life and prayer of believers is centered upon Christ. Everything begins from Him, everything leads towards Him, everything, through Him, in the Holy Spirit, attains to the Father.

As a counting mechanism, marking the progress of the prayer, the beads evoke the unending path of contemplation and of

Christian perfection. Blessed Bartolo Longo saw them also as a "chain" which links us to God. A chain, yes, but a sweet chain; for sweet indeed is the bond to God who is also our Father. A *"filial"* chain which puts us in tune with Mary, the "handmaid of the Lord" (Lk 1:38) and, most of all, with Christ Himself, who, though He was in the form of God, made Himself a "servant" out of love for us (*Phil* 2:7).

A fine way to expand the symbolism of the beads is to let them remind us of our many relationships, of the bond of communion and fraternity which unites us all in Christ.

The Opening and Closing

37.At present, in different parts of the Church, there are many ways to introduce the Rosary. In some places, it is customary to begin with the opening words of Psalm 70: "O God, come to my aid; O Lord, make haste to help me", as if to nourish in those who are praying a humble awareness of their own insufficiency. In other places, the Rosary begins with the recitation of the Creed, as if to make the profession of faith the basis of the contemplative journey about to be undertaken. These and similar customs, to the extent that they prepare the mind for contemplation, are all equally legitimate. The Rosary is then ended with a prayer for the intentions of the Pope, as if to expand the vision of the one praying to embrace all the needs of the Church. It is precisely in order to encourage this ecclesial dimension of the Rosary that the Church has seen fit to grant indulgences to those who recite it with the required dispositions.

If prayed in this way, the Rosary truly becomes a spiritual itinerary in which Mary acts as Mother, Teacher and Guide, sustaining the faithful by her powerful intercession. Is it any wonder, then, that the soul feels the need, after saying this prayer and experiencing so profoundly the motherhood of Mary, to burst forth in praise of the Blessed Virgin, either in that splendid prayer the Salve Regina or in the Litany of Loreto? This is the crowning moment of an inner journey which has brought the faithful into living contact with the mystery of Christ and His Blessed Mother.

Distribution Over Time
38. The Rosary can be recited in full every day, and there are those who most laudably do so. In this way it fills with prayer the days of many a contemplative, or keeps company with the sick and the elderly who have abundant time at their disposal. Yet it is clear – and this applies all the more if the new series of *mysteria lucis* is included – that many people will not be able to recite more than a part of the Rosary, according to a certain weekly pattern. This weekly distribution has the effect of giving the different days of the week a certain spiritual "color", by analogy with the way in which the Liturgy colors the different seasons of the liturgical year.

According to current practice, Monday and Thursday are dedicated to the "joyful mysteries", Tuesday and Friday to the "sorrowful mysteries", and Wednesday, Saturday and Sunday to the "glorious mysteries". Where might the "mysteries of light" be inserted? If we consider that the "glorious mysteries" are said on both Saturday and Sunday, and that Saturday has always had a special Marian flavor, the second weekly meditation on the "joyful mysteries", mysteries in which Mary's presence is especially pronounced, could be moved to Saturday. Thursday would then be free for meditating on the "mysteries of light".

This indication is not intended to limit a rightful freedom in personal and community prayer, where account needs to be taken of spiritual and pastoral needs and of the occurrence of particular liturgical celebrations which might call for suitable adaptations. What is really important is that the Rosary should always be seen and experienced as a path of contemplation. In the Rosary, in a way similar to what takes place in the Liturgy, the Christian week, centered on Sunday, the day of Resurrection, becomes a journey through the mysteries of the life of Christ, and He is revealed in the lives of His disciples as the Lord of time and of history.

CONCLUSION

"Blessed Rosary of Mary, Sweet Chain Linking Us to God"
39. What has been said so far makes abundantly clear the richness of this traditional prayer, which has the simplicity of a popular

devotion but also the theological depth of a prayer suited to those who feel the need for deeper contemplation. The Church has always attributed particular efficacy to this prayer, entrusting to the Rosary, to its choral recitation and to its constant practice, the most difficult problems. At times when Christianity itself seemed under threat, its deliverance was attributed to the power of this prayer, and Our Lady of the Rosary was acclaimed as the one whose intercession brought salvation.

Today I willingly entrust to the power of this prayer – as I mentioned at the beginning – the cause of peace in the world and the cause of the family.

Peace

40. The grave challenges confronting the world at the start of this new Millennium lead us to think that only an intervention from on high, capable of guiding the hearts of those living in situations of conflict and those governing the destinies of nations, can give reason to hope for a brighter future.

The Rosary is by its nature a prayer for peace, since it consists in the contemplation of Christ, the Prince of Peace, the one who is "our peace" (*Eph* 2:14). Anyone who assimilates the mystery of Christ – and this is clearly the goal of the Rosary – learns the secret of peace and makes it his life's project. Moreover, by virtue of its meditative character, with the tranquil succession of Hail Marys, the Rosary has a peaceful effect on those who pray it, disposing them to receive and experience in their innermost depths, and to spread around them, that true peace which is the special gift of the Risen Lord (cf. *Jn* 14:27;20.21).

The Rosary is also a prayer for peace because of the fruits of charity which it produces. When prayed well in a truly meditative way, the Rosary leads to an encounter with Christ in His mysteries and so cannot fail to draw attention to the face of Christ in others, especially in the most afflicted. How could one possibly contemplate the mystery of the Child of Bethlehem, in the joyful mysteries, without experiencing the desire to welcome, defend and promote life, and to shoulder the burdens of suffering children all over the world? How could one possibly follow in the footsteps of Christ the Revealer, in the mysteries of light, without resolving to bear witness to His "Beatitudes" in daily life? And how could one contemplate Christ carrying the Cross and Christ Crucified, without feeling the need to act as a "Simon of Cyrene" for our brothers and sisters weighed down by grief or crushed by despair? Finally, how could one possibly gaze upon the glory of the Risen Christ or of Mary Queen of Heaven, without yearning to make this world more beautiful, more just, more closely conformed to God's plan?

In a word, by focusing our eyes on Christ, the Rosary also makes us peacemakers in the world. By its nature as an insistent choral petition in harmony with Christ's invitation to "pray ceaselessly" (*Lk* 18:1), the Rosary allows us to hope that, even today, the difficult "battle" for peace can be won. Far from offering an escape from the problems of the world, the Rosary obliges us to see them with responsible and generous eyes, and obtains for us the strength to face them with the certainty of God's help and the firm intention of bearing witness in every situation to "love, which binds everything together in perfect harmony" (*Col* 3:14).

The Family: Parents...

41. As a prayer for peace, the Rosary is also, and always has been, a prayer of and for the family. At one time this prayer was particularly dear to Christian families, and it certainly brought them closer together. It is important not to lose this precious inheritance. We need to return to the practice of family prayer and prayer for families, continuing to use the Rosary.

In my Apostolic Letter *Novo Millennio Ineunte* I encouraged the celebration of the Liturgy of the Hours by the lay faithful in the ordinary life of parish communities and Christian groups;[(39)] I now wish to do the same for the Rosary. These two paths of Christian contemplation are not mutually exclusive; they complement one another. I would therefore ask those who devote themselves to the pastoral care of families to recommend heartily the recitation of the Rosary.

The family that prays together stays together. The Holy Rosary, by age-old tradition, has shown itself particularly effective as a prayer which brings the family together. Individual family members, in turning their eyes towards Jesus, also regain the ability to look one another in the eye, to communicate, to show solidarity, to forgive one another and to see their covenant of love renewed in the Spirit of God.

Many of the problems facing contemporary families, especially in economically developed societies, result from their increasing difficulty in communicating. Families seldom manage to come together, and the rare occasions when they do are often taken up with watching television. To return to the recitation of the family Rosary means filling daily life with very different images, images of the mystery of salvation: the image of the Redeemer, the image of His most Blessed Mother. The family that recites the Rosary together reproduces something of the atmosphere of the household of Nazareth: its members place Jesus at the center, they share His joys and sorrows, they place their needs and their plans in His hands, they draw from Him the hope and the strength to go on.

... and Children

42. It is also beautiful and fruitful to entrust to this prayer the growth and development of children. Does the Rosary not follow the life of Christ, from His conception to His death, and then to His Resurrection and His glory? Parents are finding it ever more difficult to follow the lives of their children as they grow to maturity. In a society of advanced technology, of mass communications and globalization, everything has become hurried, and the cultural distance between generations is growing ever greater. The most diverse messages and the most unpredictable experiences rapidly make their way into the lives of children and adolescents, and parents can become quite anxious about the dangers their children face. At times parents suffer acute disappointment at the failure of their children to resist the seductions of the drug culture, the lure of an unbridled hedonism, the temptation to violence, and the manifold expressions of meaninglessness and despair.

To pray the Rosary for children, and even more, with children, training them from their earliest years to experience this daily "pause for prayer" with the family, is admittedly not the solution to every problem, but it is a spiritual aid which should not be underestimated.

It could be objected that the Rosary seems hardly suited to the taste of children and young people of today. But perhaps the objection is directed to an impoverished method of praying it. Furthermore, without prejudice to the Rosary's basic structure, there is nothing to stop children and young people from praying it – either within the family or in groups – with appropriate symbolic and practical aids to understanding and appreciation. Why not try it? With God's help, a pastoral approach to youth which is positive, impassioned and creative – as shown by the World Youth Days! – is capable of achieving quite remarkable results. If the Rosary is well presented, I am sure that young people will once more surprise adults by the way they make this prayer their own and recite it with the enthusiasm typical of their age group.

The Rosary, a treasure to be rediscovered

43. Dear brothers and sisters! A prayer so easy and yet so rich truly deserves to be rediscovered by the Christian community. Let us do so, especially this year, as a means of confirming the direction outlined in my Apostolic Letter *Novo Millennio Ineunte*, from which the pastoral plans of so many particular Churches have drawn inspiration as they look to the immediate future.

I turn particularly to you, my dear Brother Bishops, priests and deacons, and to you, pastoral agents in your different ministries: through your own personal experience of the beauty of the Rosary, may you come to promote it with conviction.

I also place my trust in you, theologians: by your sage and rigorous reflection, rooted in the word of God and sensitive to the lived experience of the Christian people, may you help them to discover the Biblical foundations, the spiritual riches and the pastoral value of this traditional prayer.

I count on you, consecrated men and women, called in a particular way to contemplate the face of Christ at the school of Mary.

I look to all of you, brothers and sisters of every state of life, to you, Christian families, to you, the sick and elderly, and to you, young people: confidently take up the Rosary once again. Rediscover the Rosary in the light of Scripture, in harmony with the Liturgy, and in the context of your daily lives.

May this appeal of mine not go unheard! At the start of the twenty-fifth year of my Pontificate, I entrust this Apostolic Letter to the loving hands of the Virgin Mary, prostrating myself in spirit before her image in the splendid Shrine built for her by Blessed Bartolo Longo, the apostle of the Rosary. I willingly make my own the touching words with which he concluded his well-known Supplication to the Queen of the Holy Rosary: "O Blessed Rosary of Mary, sweet chain which unites us to God, bond of love which unites us to the angels, tower of salvation against the assaults of Hell, safe port in our universal shipwreck, we will never abandon you. You will be our comfort in the hour of death: yours our final kiss as life ebbs away. And the last word from our lips will be your sweet name, O Queen of the Rosary of Pompei, O dearest Mother, O Refuge of Sinners, O Sovereign Consoler of the Afflicted. May you be everywhere blessed, today and always, on earth and in heaven".

From the Vatican, on the 16th day of October in the year 2002, the beginning of the twenty- fifth year of my Pontificate.

JOHN PAUL II

Notes

(1)   Pastoral Constitution on the Church in the Modern World *Gaudium et Spes*, 45.

(2)   Pope Paul VI, Apostolic Exhortation *Marialis Cultus* (2 February 1974), 42: AAS 66 (1974), 153.

(3)   Cf. Acta Leonis XIII, 3 (1884), 280-289.

(4)   Particularly worthy of note is his Apostolic *Epistle on the Rosary Il religioso convegno* (29 September 1961): AAS 53 (1961), 641-647.

(5)   Angelus: *Insegnamenti di Giovanni Paolo II*, I (1978): 75-76.

(6)   AAS 93 (2001), 285.

(7)   During the years of preparation for the Council, Pope John XXIII did not fail to encourage the Christian community to recite the Rosary for the success of this ecclesial event: cf. Letter to the Cardinal Vicar (28 September 1960): AAS 52 (1960), 814-816.

(8)   Dogmatic Constitution on the Church *Lumen Gentium*, 66.

(9)   No. 32: AAS 93 (2001), 288.

(10)   Ibid., 33: loc. cit., 289.

(11)   It is well-known and bears repeating that private revelations are not the same as public revelation, which is binding on the whole Church. It is the

task of the Magisterium to discern and recognize the authenticity and value of private revelations for the piety of the faithful.

(12) The Secret of the Rosary.

(13) Blessed Bartolo Longo, *Storia del Santuario di Pompei*, Pompei, 1990, 59.

(14) Apostolic Exhortation Marialis Cultus (2 February 1974), 47: AAS (1974), 156.

(15) Constitution on the Sacred Liturgy *Sacrosanctum Concilium*, 10.

(16) Ibid., 12.

(17) Second Vatican Ecumenical Council, Dogmatic Constitution on the Church *Lumen Gentium*, 58.

(18) *I Quindici Sabati del Santissimo Rosario*, 27th ed., Pompei, 1916, 27.

(19) Second Vatican Ecumenical Council, Dogmatic Constitution on the Church *Lumen Gentium,* 53.

(20) Ibid., 60.

(21) Cf. First Radio Address *Urbi et Orbi* (17 October 1978): AAS 70 (1978), 927.

(22) Treatise on True Devotion to the Blessed Virgin Mary.

(23) Catechism of the Catholic Church, 2679.

(24) Ibid., 2675.

(25) The Supplication to the Queen of the Holy Rosary was composed by Blessed Bartolo Longo in 1883 in response to the appeal of Pope Leo XIII, made in his first Encyclical on the Rosary, for the spiritual commitment of all Catholics in combating social ills. It is solemnly recited twice yearly, in May and October.

(26) *Divina Commedia*, Paradiso XXXIII, 13-15.

(27) John Paul II, Apostolic Letter *Novo Millennio I*neunte (6 January 2001), 20: AAS 93 (2001), 279.

(28) Apostolic Exhortation Marialis Cultus (2 February 1974), 46: AAS 6 (1974), 155.

(29) John Paul II, Apostolic Letter *Novo Millennio Ineunte* (6 January 2001), 28: AAS 93 (2001), 284.

(30) No. 515.

(31) Angelus Message of 29 October 1978 : *Insegnamenti,* I (1978), 76.

(32) Second Vatican Ecumenical Council, Pastoral Constitution on the Church in the Modern World *Gaudium et Spes*, 22.

(33) Cf. Saint Irenaeus of Lyons, *Adversus Haereses*, III, 18, 1: PG 7, 932.

(34) Catechism of the Catholic Church, 2616.

(35) Cf. No. 33: AAS 93 (2001), 289.

(36) John Paul II, Letter to Artists (4 April 1999), 1: AAS 91 (1999), 1155.

(37) Cf. No. 46: AAS 66 (1974), 155. This custom has also been recently praised by the Congregation for Divine Worship and for the Discipline of the Sacraments in its *Direttorio su pietà popolare e liturgia. Principi e orientamenti* (17 December 2001), 201, Vatican City, 2002, 165.

(38) "*...concede, quaesumus, ut haec mysteria sacratissimo beatae Mariae*

Virginis Rosario recolentes, et imitemur quod continent, et quod promittunt assequamur". Missale Romanum 1960, in festo B.M. Virginis a Rosario.

(39)   Cf. No. 34: AAS 93 (2001), 290.

Living Under the Glory of God
Experiencing the Atmosphere of Heaven

Praise Until the Worship Comes
There are certain people on this planet earth who live under a powerful anointing of the Holy Spirit. They live at the very center of God's Will. Miracles, healings, deliverances, supernatural happenings are commonplace in their lives. How does one get into that inner sanctum, that manifest presence of God? I have written about this in my booklet, *Twelve Keys to the Anointing*, which is based upon the tabernacle experience.

Moses, in the desert, was asked by God to build a tabernacle with an outer court, a holy place and a holy of holies. In the outer court, there was the brazen altar and the laver. In the holy place was the golden lampstand, the daily showbread and the daily incense altar. In the holy of holies, was the ark of the covenant, containing the tablets of the covenant, Aaron's rod that miraculously budded and a pot of manna. Over the ark of the covenant were two cherubim and the mercy seat. The door to the outer court was called The Way door. The veil into the holy place was called The Truth veil. The veil into the holy of holies was called The Life veil.

Each one of these keys was a foreshadowing of a spiritual principle that leads us into the manifest presence of God. The Way door pointed to a personal relationship with Jesus, who *is* The Way. The brazen altar symbolized total consecration of our lives to God. The laver pointed to confession and the cleansing of our souls from sin through the Blood of the Lamb. The truth door leads one into the deeper things of God, beginning with an ability to be open to God's ongoing revelation as symbolized in the golden lampstand and to deep daily communion with Jesus as symbolized in the table of showbread.

Praise and Worship are the Keys

Just before entering through the life veil into the holy of holies, one had to begin a life of praise foreshadowed in the altar of incense. Praise would enable one to pass through the veil into the manifest glory of God, which is the heart of the holy of holies. For it is in the holy of holies that we stand in the glory called the *shekinah*. There, we live under the glory spout and experience the atmosphere of heaven. There we experience the fullness of Jesus' promise, "If you abide in Me and My word abides in you then you shall ask anything of Me you want and you shall have it." There we enter into the inner circle of wisdom, power, love and heavenly blessings.

As the poem goes

> "God saves His very best things for the few,
> Who dare to stand the test.
> He has to give His second choice
> To those who really do not want His best.
>
> It is not always open ill
> that risk the promise rest,
> Our better often is the foe,
> that keeps us from God's best.
>
> Sometimes I take the highest choice
> Then by trials pressed
> I shrink, I yield, I shun the cross
> And thus, I lose God's best.
>
> But give us today, O Lord
> Your highest choice
> Let others take the rest
> Their good things have no charm for us
> We want Your very best
> And to Your best, we now say "yes".

Getting Into God's Best Through Praise and Worship

Praise is a powerful principle of entering into the perfect will of God. We are here to give honor and glory, worship and praise to our God. Merlin Carothers, in his marvelous books, *From Prison to Praise*, and *Power to Praise*, has stressed this. The Psalms are primarily psalms of praise. Our whole lives are supposed to be geared for honor and praise. Paul exhorts us, "Whatever you do in word or work, do all for the honor and glory of God."

Jesus taught us the first and fundamental principle of prayer is worship and praise when He said, "After this manner pray, Our Father who art in heaven, hallowed be Thy name." We must learn to do everything out of God because all life and all holiness, all wisdom and power is given to us from above. God tells us to praise Him with the voice of thanksgiving (Ps. 26), with the voice of triumph (*Ps* 47:1), with the voice of a Psalm (*Ps* 98:5), and with the voice of rejoicing (*Ps* 118:15). The voice that John the Beloved heard in the book of Revelation was "the voice of a great multitude", the voice of many waters, and the "voice of mighty thunderings." Our praise should rise until it thunders like Niagara Falls. So great should be the rushing of sounds joining voice to voice that they become like mighty thunderings. The voices that John heard were saying, "Alleluia!" for the Lord God Almighty reigns. The voice of praise is always the voice of victory.

In order to get the Spirit of God to flow in us and through us with ease, we have to get into God. We have to work out of God, we have to experience the presence of God. Most Christians try to do God's work with human wisdom, human plans and human power. Therefore, they fail. God's work must be done with God's wisdom, God's plans, God's power and God's spirit.

Getting Into God

In order to get into God we have to get into worship and praise. As Psalm 84:4 states, "Blessed are they that dwell in Your house; they will be still praising Thee." So often we try to bring the Kingdom of God to earth through our vision and our power, but God is saying, "if you would only sow to the heavens, I will sow to the earth." And I will bring you into the promised land.

Three Mountain Movers

In Psalm 37:3-6, God says, "Trust in the Lord and He will bring you into the promised land. Delight in Him and He will give you the deepest desires of your heart. Commit all your ways unto Him and He will make your holiness shine as the noonday sun." Our responsibility is to trust, delight and commit. God's responsibility is to bring us into the holy land, to give us the deepest desires of our heart, and to make our holiness shine as the noonday sun. This is not a quietism. It is a response to the holiness of the Holy Spirit, who we allow to take the initiative. If we listen to the Lord, He will speak. And if we do what He tells us, God's results shall flow. For all life, all holiness comes from the "Father, through the Son, by the working of the Holy Spirit," as we say in the Mass.

Enter His Courts With Praise

In order to enter into this holy realm, we must praise. Praise is entering in. "Enter into His gates with thanksgiving and into His courts with praise" (*Ps* 104). As we enter into that realm by praise, God will teach us His ways and how to walk in His paths. In Hosea 2:21-23, God says, "And it shall come to pass on that day I will hear, says the Lord, I will hear the heavens and they shall hear the earth." Because we have sowed heavenward with worship and praise, God sows in the earth with His wisdom, love and power. God is not only the harvester, He is also the sower. Too many people think that they are to sow and ask God to bless it, that they are to make plans and ask God to bring them about. But the Psalmist tells us, "the Lord brings to naught the plans of the nations" (*Ps* 33).

When we begin to praise God, we are sowing heavenward. In return, God is making sure that we receive His anointing, His wisdom, love and power. *If you wish to progress into God, you must do it through worship and praise*. And as you praise and worship God, God leads you into deeper realms, greater capacities, more powerful abilities, and more fruitful skills. He teaches us how to surrender more, how to listen more. We never outgrow praise.

Lifted Hands

As we progress in praise, the Lord tells us to lift our hands. Lifted hands are a symbol of lifted hearts in total surrender. Lifted hands gives us the freedom and praise like little children. Not only does the Lord ask that we lift our hands, but we must move our feet. Dancing brings us still deeper anointing, as David discovered when he danced before the ark (2 *Sam* 6:16). The Lord promises us, "if you want to feed a nation, if you want to feed a triple portion, you must dance," as David did. Dancing is a very effective way to praise the Lord. There is power in lifted hands, there is power in songs of praise, there's power in feet dancing.

Worship the Natural Progression of Praise

We praise God for all that He has done for us, for His goodness and kindness and His mercy toward us. We worship Him for who He is in Himself. Jesus told us that God is spirit, and they that worship Him must worship in spirit and truth. He is seeking such worshipers. If you want to live in the glory realm, you must worship the Father through Jesus in spirit and truth.

The difference between praising and worship is as picturing myself as part of a Palm Sunday procession. I join others as we take off our coats and throw them down, exuberantly, so the lord can ride over them. I pluck palm branches and wave them. I sing Hosanna, Blessed is He who has come. All that is praise, but I suddenly stop. Jesus the King of kings and Lord of lords is looking at me and saying , "I love you." Tears stream down my cheeks as I say, "I love You, Lord."

I am no longer waving palms and shouting, Hosanna. I am bowing and worshipping and saying, "My Lord and my God." It seems the crowd is no longer present. I'm totally oblivious to everything except Him. He is looking at me and all of His love is being poured into my soul. I'm slightly in ecstasy as the image of who He is fills me. Worship sets you alone with God. It can happen in a quiet chapel or in a busy street. There can be many such moments in a day.

The Glorious Presence of the Lord

As I enter into that place of intimacy and worship, I can experience the glorious presence of God. One of the first secrets of worship is how it differs from praise. When I praise the Lord I *will* to praise. When I come into the house of the Lord, I offer my lips and my will to praise. But you do not *will* to worship. The spirit of worship must be given from above. The spirit of worship must come upon you. It helps to sing worship songs that are not very complicated. If your mind is too involved with words, you'll be too busy thinking and your spirit will not ascend. When a song leader is conscious that the spirit of worship has come, he should slip quickly into songs of worship. The ministry of praise increases the anointing in the service. The ministry of worship brings the glory.

Praise brings the anointed to worship and worship brings the anointed to glory. *Just as we praise until the worship comes, we must worship until the glory comes.* With every move of God comes praise. But we praise God until He gives us the power to worship Him.

Here's an example from human relationships. Many husbands say of their wives, *"She's a good cook, keeps a clean house and cares for the children."* Yet it was not those things that made him love her. No, it was the way she smiled, the touch of her hands, her gentle words. That's what made him fall in love. Women, too, forget what made them fall in love with their husbands. It wasn't what he did, but it was his gentle smile, the way he stood that communicated his strength. It is the same in our relationship with the Lord. When we first meet Him, we say, "He saved me. He filled me with the Holy Spirit. He healed me. He answered my prayers. Therefore, I praise Him for what he does."

But what about Him as a person. We have to love Him as a person and be able to enter into communion with Him as a person. That's the function of worship. The angels in heaven worship the person of the Lord. They worship Him because they know Him, not because they have been saved or healed or filled with the Holy Spirit. I'm not minimizing praising God for what He does. We should not fail to do it. But I am stressing that God wants us to know Him, who He is in Himself so that we can feel His presence and to come into His presence in such a way that we will worship Him in the beauty of His holiness. Our primary aspiration should be to be a worshiper of the Lord and to impart the desire of worship into others. If the Father is seeking those who will worship Him in spirit and truth, then you and I will need to be those who listen to the heart of the Father and worship Him in spirit and in truth. We should not let an hour go by without worshipping Him.

Longing to See God's Face

Moses spent the first of 40 days and 40 nights seeking the face of the Lord and was so filled with the glory of the Lord that his face was aglow. Literally, they had to put a veil over it because he was too much for the Israelites to gaze upon. St. Paul uses this example of encouraging the early Church so that "we with unveiled faces will reflect like mirrors the brightness of the Son who is our glory. For it is the work of the Spirit to transform us from glory into glory into him whom we reflect (*2 Cor* 3:18).

St. John on the Isle of Patmos had a vision of the Lord. He related, "and immediately I was in the Spirit; and, behold, a throne was set in heaven, and one sat on the throne. And He that sat was to look upon like a jasper and a carnelian stone; and there was a rainbow around about the throne, in sight like unto an emerald. And round about the throne were four and 20 seats, and upon the seats I saw four and twenty elder sitting, clothed in white raiment; and they had on their heads crowns of gold. .... The four and twenty elders fell down before Him who sat on the throne and worshipped Him who lives forever and ever, and cast their crowns upon the throne saying, 'Thou art worthy oh Lord to receive glory and honor and power for You have created all things, and for Your pleasure they are and were created" (*Rev* 4:2-11).

The Mass:
A great way to worship the Father in spirit and in truth

Every liturgy needs both praise and worship. We should praise until the spirit of worship comes, then worship until the glory comes. Praise brings an increase of the anointing; but worship brings the majesty of God into the midst of His people. Praise is usually more exuberant, more wordy, worship has that holy hush. It is awesome, it is less wordy, sometimes even without words. Sometimes it produces total silence as heart speaks to heart. There should be time for total silence after each communion when each worshiper worships the Father in spirit and in truth in the quiet of their own hearts.

The Glory Realm
What is the glory realm? It is the revelation of the presence of God, the manifestation of His presence. God is glory. He is everywhere. The glory is the manifestation of that reality. Earth has the atmosphere of air, whereas the heavenly atmosphere is glory. When the glory comes down, it is heaven's atmosphere coming to earth, a taste of God's manifest presence. Just as we don't see air for in it we live and move and breathe, the same way we don't see the God in Him whom we live and move and have our being. Sometimes, as at Pentecost, the glory comes in balls of fire. Sometimes, as in the tabernacle. Sometimes, it comes as a mist. We are only beginning to see the glorious day of the Lord.

The Power that Flows from the Glory
Once we get into the glory realm, the power and wisdom and spirit of God is released. Healings happen, deliverances occur, insights flow. The glory brings an ease with the things of God. The glory brings further revelations. The glory brings on miracles. The glory brings healings.

Seeing the Face of the Lord
As we worship, we begin to look for the Lord. We begin to look and see the Lord. The glory brings an anointing to see. Many of us have never seen the glory of the Lord. But if you worship until the glory comes, you will begin to see Him. The knowledge of the glory of God comes from the face of Christ. Because we are not taught to see the glory of God, many of us go without seeing Him. If someone doesn't hear, we say he's deaf. If he hears a little, we say he is hard of hearing. The same thing can be said of those who

do not hear the Lord clearly. And if a person doesn't see, we say he is blind. Or if he only sees a little, we say he sees dimly.

The same can be true in the spiritual realm. God wants to take us in vision to His throne. He wants to show us the face of Jesus. In seeing Jesus, we are changed. Every time we stand in His glory, we are changed a little more. Every time we look into His face, we have a keener desire to be more like Him. It's in the glory that I see Him and really desire to be like Him. In the glory I know what it is to be like Him. I know what His compassion feels like. I know what His holiness is like. I know what His love is like, what His mercy is like. In the glory I know Him in a way that I can't know Him in any other way.

Lord, That I May See

The Lord wants us to be anointed To see anything that Ezekiel saw, you and I can see. Anything that John saw, we can see. God teaches us that it is easy to see the face of the Lord. When you look expecting to see, you begin to see. No matter what the experience you have in God, you'll never have anything more thrilling than looking at His face. The more you gradually learn how to come in and see His face more often, His face is not then so elusive. You do not see it in a glass darkly, you see Him face to face. And He will show Himself to you in so many wonderful ways.

In so many scriptures, God tells us, "seek my face." "And in the midst of the seven candlesticks, one like under the Son of man, clothed with a garment unto the foot, and girt about with a golden sash, His head and His hair were white like wool, as white as snow; and His eyes were as a flame of fire" (*Rev* 1:13-14).

Once you have looked into the flaming eyes of Jesus, you will feel His love burning in your heart. You will be given His passion for souls, You will be able to look into His eyes and see His heart cry. Knowledge and wisdom will flow from seeing the face of Jesus. He may take you into the music room of heaven and you may see angels pulling out manuscripts and dropping them into the minds of believers who want to sing new songs. He may take you into the command room of heaven and show you how he is ordering the movement of His angels at that moment. You may see the heavenly hosts being sent forth. You might see Him sending and commissioning special angels to help in particular areas. God wants all of us to be anointed to see. "Eye has not seen nor ear heard nor has it entered into the heart of man the things which God has prepared for those who love Him **but God has revealed them to us by His Spirit**" (*1 Cor* 2:9-10). God wants us to live in the realm of revelation. We can only live in the realm of revelation as we live in the glory of the Lord.

The Mass - the Greatest Locus of Worship and Praise

The greatest way to worship the Father in Spirit and in truth, of course, is within context of the sacred liturgy designed in heaven. This liturgy was foreshadowed in the tabernacle experience and is revealed fully in the book of Revelation where the whole angelic chorus, in union with all the saints, are saying, "Holy, Holy, Holy is the Lord God of Hosts." Therein, we see the throne room of God with the Father on the throne and Jesus, the Lamb who was slain, and the Holy Spirit surrounded by all the angels and saints including Mary giving worship, adoration and praise to our God — one in three.

It is into this eternal celestial liturgy of worship and praise that we enter whenever we worship and praise God especially within the context of the Mass. For there is Christ, the eternal High Priest, in union with the whole Church, offering through His Father, the one, eternal, life-giving sacrifice of praise. It is within the Mass that the offering of ourselves is in union with Christ and the whole Church. It is within the Mass that we are most fully transformed into the Body, Blood, Soul and Divinity of Jesus. It is within the Mass that we offer to God the praise and worship that is due to Him as Father, as Son and as Spirit. It is in the Mass that we say, "Holy, Holy, Holy to the Lord God of Hosts. Heaven and earth are full of your glory. Hosanna in the highest!"

Practical Steps to Worship and Praise

1. Ask the Holy Spirit to teach you how to praise and worship. Step out in faith and begin to praise God in all that you do. When you wake up in the morning, offer prayers of thanksgiving and

praise. On your way to Mass, continue to offer praises to God, such as, "*Heavenly Father, I worship You, I honor You, I adore You, I love You. Jesus, Holy God, I praise Your name. Spirit, Lord and Giver of life, I praise You for Your presence in my soul.*"

2. Try to attend daily Mass. This, as we have seen, is the best way to worship the Father in spirit and in truth. Be mindful, above all at Mass, that you are there to adore God. Listen attentively to the readings, offer yourself fully at the offertory, realize that the whole heavenly court of angels and saints surround you, encouraging you to praise. Receive communion with great devotion, and spend quiet minutes before and after Mass worshipping and praising.

3. Throughout the day, try to live a life of praise, constantly lifting up your mind and heart. Let everything you do be for God's honor and glory. Let the attitude of your soul be, "All for the honor and glory of God."

4. Try to attend frequently, a prayer meeting that really gets into worship and praise. Remember the principle — praise until the spirit of worship comes, worship until the glory comes, and stand in the glory.

5. Offer litanies that praise God, such as the litany of the Holy Name of Jesus, the Most Precious Blood of Jesus, the Most Sacred Heart of Jesus, the Holy Face of Jesus, Christ the King, the Blessed Sacrament, the Holy Cross, the Passion, the Holy Spirit. You will find these litanies in *A Prayer Book of Favorite Litanies*, 116 of them, published by Tan Publishers of Rockford, IL. Even better, write your own litany or song of praise.

6. Be willing to sing, to raise your arms, to clap your hands, and to dance as the Spirit moves you. David was able to praise the Lord with reckless abandon, and God called him a man after God's own heart. There are so many praise and worship tapes available that you can play both at home and in your car. Think about joining a choir or a praise group.

7. Be willing to read the breviary, the official prayer treasury of the Church. There you will especially find the Psalms, which are filled with praise, most especially Psalm 145.

8. Have your own Jesus chair where you can easily go for meditation, prayer and praise. As you meditate, certain insights will inspire you to worship and praise. Let meditation flow into praise. Let praise flow into worship, and let worship flow into the glory.

9. Remember that every bush is burning. Every sunset, every flower, every bit of natural beauty, every experience, every person, every happening of our lives can be an occasion of praise. Everything that is, is inscaped with Jesus, You can see Him in the flowers, you can see His cross in every tree, His Blood on every rose. For the mystic and the saint, all things bespeak the glory of the Lord.

10. Remember that the Spirit of the Lord will teach you all things, especially how to worship and praise. Ask Him and receive ongoing revelation. He will lead you into all worship.

Epilogue

We have just begun to set out into the deep, hand-in-hand with Christ, with His mother and with our beloved John Paul II, centering our lives upon the Eucharist and sincerely striving to be holy, to be more prayerful, to praise and worship God more, and to listen to the inspirations of the Spirit, to attend Mass more faithfully and devotedly, to spend more time in Eucharistic adoration, to go to Confession more frequently, to rely upon the Spirit as we meditation upon the word and the Catechism; to recite the rosary; and to bring the gospel of truth and life to a dark and broken world.

This is the call upon our lives. Christ is counting upon us. Mary is counting upon us. The Church is counting upon us. The Pope is counting upon us. We are the faithful remnant, Christ's mystical body, His light to a dark and broken world.

"We are called to take his light into that world where wrong seems right. What could be too great a cost for sharing life with one who's lost. Through their tears, our hearts can feel all the pain they bear. They must hear the words of life only we can share. People need the Lord. People need the Lord. We must help them realize, people need the Lord."

A dear friend, retired Archbishop Phillip Hannon of New Orleans, has endorsed this Pastoral Plan of the Pope and urges that Eucharistic congresses, Forty Hour devotions and Benedictions be fully restored to the Church. The more we lift up the Eucharist and sow to the heavenlies, the more God will sow to the earth. Bishop Thomas Dailey of Brooklyn is just one of many bishops and priests who, along with Pope John Paul II, has renewed a fervent call for Eucharist Adoration in parishes throughout the country.

Jesus said it all. "With all the earnestness I possess, I tell you this, 'Unless you feed upon the Flesh of the Son of Man and drink His Blood you have no life within you.'"